THE
CHAINBREAKER
BIKE BOOK

An Illustrated Manual of Radical Bicycle Maintenance, Culture, & History

UPDATED AND EXPANDED

10TH ANNIVERSARY EDITION

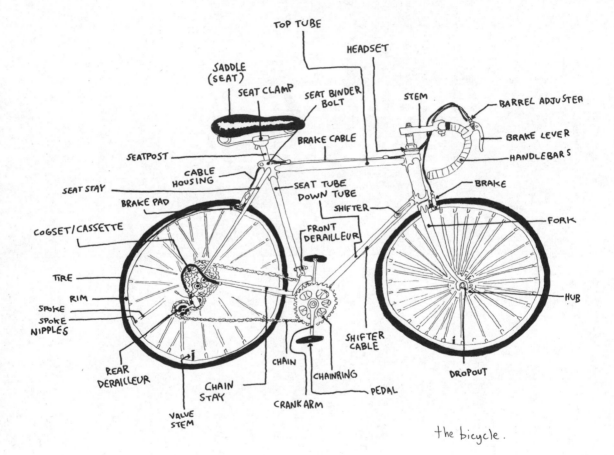

TOP TUBE

HEADSET

SADDLE (SEAT)

SEAT CLAMP

SEAT BINDER BOLT

STEM

BARREL ADJUSTER

BRAKE LEVER

BRAKE CABLE

HANDLEBARS

SEATPOST

CABLE HOUSING

SEAT STAY

SEAT TUBE
DOWN TUBE

BRAKE

BRAKE PAD

SHIFTER

FORK

COGSET/CASSETTE

FRONT DERAILLEUR

TIRE

RIM

HUB

SPOKE

SPOKE NIPPLES

SHIFTER CABLE

REAR DERAILLEUR

CHAIN

CHAINRING

DROPOUT

CHAIN STAY

CRANK ARM

PEDAL

VALVE STEM

the bicycle.

THE CHAINBREAKER BIKE BOOK

An Illustrated Manual of Radical Bicycle Maintenance, Culture, & History

UPDATED AND EXPANDED
10TH ANNIVERSARY EDITION

Ethan Clark and Shelley Lynn Jackson
illustrated by Ethan, Shelley, and Happy

Microcosm Publishing
Portland, Ore.

MICROCOSM · PUBLISHING

Microcosm Publishing is Portland's most diversified publishing house and distributor with a focus on the colorful, authentic, and empowering. Our books and zines have put your power in your hands since 1996, equipping readers to make positive changes in their lives and in the world around them. Microcosm emphasizes skill-building, showing hidden histories, and fostering creativity through challenging conventional publishing wisdom with books and bookettes about DIY skills, food, bicycling, gender, self-care, and social justice. What was once a distro and record label was started by Joe Biel in his bedroom and has become among the oldest independent publishing houses in Portland, OR. We are a politically moderate, centrist publisher in a world that has inched to the right for the past 80 years.

dedicated to Billy Moss

OWNER OF FRENCH QUARTER BICYCLES
IN NEW ORLEANS

I dedicate this book to Billy, not just for
teaching me everything I know about bike repair, but also for taking
a chance on hiring me, and for being the constant source of humor
& frustration that kept me loving the job for as long as I had it. Billy
was a great mechanic and generous shop owner. He was run over
on a beautiful spring day, by a too-big-truck while walking down the
street in front of the famous Vaughns Bar, just a block from his home.
He was given a jazz funeral fit for a king, attended by every mechanic
he ever hired who mattered. We hope this book serves as a token
of our gratitude, passing Billy's knowledge down to others. For our
enlightened teacher:

We all love and miss you, Billy Moss.

Chainbreaker Bike Book: **An Illustrated Manual of Radical Bicycle Maintenance, Culture, & History**

UPDATED AND EXPANDED 10TH ANNIVERSARY EDITION

© Shelley Jackson and Ethan Clark, 2008, 2010, 2018

© This edition Microcosm Publishing 2009, 2010, 2019

First published - 5,000 copies - 2/1/2009

Second edition - 5,000 copies - 9/1/2010

Third edition - 3,000 copies - 5/12/2019

ISBN 978-1-62106-126-7

This is Microcosm #33

Book design by Joe Biel

To join the ranks of high-class stores that feature Microcosm titles, talk to your local rep: In the U.S. **Como** (Atlantic), **Fujii** (Midwest), **Book Travelers West** (Pacific), **Turnaround** in Europe, **UTP/Manda** in Canada, **New South** in Australia, and **GPS** in Asia, Africa, India, South America, and other countries.

For a catalog, write or visit:

Microcosm Publishing

2752 N Williams Ave.

Portland, OR 97227

www.Microcosm.Pub

If you bought this on Amazon, I'm so sorry because you could have gotten it cheaper and supported a small, independent publisher at www.Microcosm.Pub

Global labor conditions are bad, and our roots in industrial Cleveland in the 70s and 80s made us appreciate the need to treat workers right. Therefore, our books are MADE IN THE USA.

TABLE OF CONTENTS

TABLE OF CONTENTS (cont.)

Foreword

"It's just like a bottle cap, to open you just gotta turn it to the left,"

"To the left?"

"Okay fine, technically speaking it's counter clockwise, but the point is that you will know how to loosen a bolt if you remember how to open a bottle cap."

That is one of the first bits of advice I used to give to people the first time they walked into Free Ride, our community bike shop in Pittsburgh, Pennsylvania. A founding mantra for those of us who tinker in the community bike world is that anyone can learn to fix a bike with some elbow grease, patience, and the right tools.

Opening up *Chainbreaker* is just like walking into a community bike workshop. Shelley and Ethan break down all the basic knowledge you will need to repair your bike, that is if it isn't carbon STI levers and a whole bunch of other fancy shit. They tell you what tools are helpful, like adjustable wrenches, and which aren't, like vice grips. They also share tidbits of knowledge acquired from years of chatting with fellow cyclists, like NEVER, repeat NEVER, leave your bike unlocked or it will most likely be stolen. And do a safety check before you ever get on a bike you haven't ridden before. You can even learn how to make a comic version of your resume to score the perfect bike mechanic job.

In an era where you can search for all kinds of bike repair manuals on YouTube, *Chainbreaker* is still worth reading and owning. It is more resistant to bike grease than your smart phone and no video tutorial can teach you how to clean your ball bearings, true your wheels, and build bucket panniers at the same time.

I contributed to the *Chainbreaker* zine 15 years ago, sending in stories that I published in my zine *Clitical Mass*, which I wrote on my Mom's ancient typewriter and pasted on top of cut-and-paste photocopied images of bike parts. At that time, there were few female bike mechanics. Myself and a few other women shared our testimonies in three different editions of *Chainbreaker*, where we critiqued the constant sexism that we found ourselves subject to. Fast forward to 2018 and the situation has barely changed.

I now live in Mexico City and recently participated in a lady powered bike ride, Clitoral Mass, inspired by the Ovarian Psychos, a women of color bike crew in L.A. The few dozen women who participated shared stories of not only being discriminated against for wanting to fix a bike, but merely riding one and being subject to constant cat-calls. The idea surged to create a new *Chainbreaker* or *Clitical Mass* style zine featuring all the female cyclists' stories.

Almost a decade has passed since this was first published; yet many of us still ride the same bikes, battle with the same cars in the road and the same dude-bros in the shop. Deep down we still hold the belief that bicycles are a tool for building autonomy and social change.

—*Andalusia Knoll* — *twitter & instagram @andalalucha*

Introduction
Shelley 2018

It is really exciting to see a ten year anniversary edition of the *Chainbreaker Bicycle Book*!

Chainbreaker may be ten years old but it's fresh as those newly rebuilt bikes! When we decided to write this rough guide to bike maintenance, it was never meant to be a modern, regularly updated guide from the point of view of up to the minute advances in bicycle technology. *Chainbreaker*, the bike repair manual and the zine that gave birth to it, was written to help you learn to repair any old or new bike you might come across and to be inspired to search out answers and learn about things in the world, from the things we didn't cover in this book and beyond. So, while I have gotten many suggestions on how to update the book, I don't really want to! The basics of the bike, the brakes, bearing systems, the nuts and bolts that make a bike recognizable from the inception of the world's first bicycle, to the most advanced technologies we see today never really changes! Like bikes themselves, no matter how cutting edge, most of the parts are recognizable shapes with the same basic components that make them run. What made bikes and working on bikes so fun to me was the simplicity of it all, so why complicate it now!? There's plenty of information here to get you going and keep you going, and it all starts with just having the guts to get in there and look and get our hands dirty.

As far as changes in the book, we have made a few… new introductions to the book and the zine section in the back of the book, and a few tweaks and edits here and there. If there was anything French Quarter Bikes taught me, it's if you're happy and good at what you do, it's ok to stay the same. So, if you ask, why not change the drawings or add digital photographs? It's because the drawings gave me and Ethan an excuse to sit in a cafe and drink coffee and draw for a week! Who wants to forget that?! One important change we made to this book was the new subtitle, "An Illustrated Manual of Radical Bicycle Maintenance, Culture and History." My first thought was, "What is radical about fixing a bike?" or "What is radical about a girl fixing a bike?" Well, in some ways, nothing. But, in terms of our modern throw-away culture, and in terms of a history that has limited how we define the roles and jobs of women or people of color, fixing a bike is radical! Especially when a girl does it! And we hope that we can inspire the reader to be a little radical and keep being radical until radical is not radical anymore! Radical means: favoring changes in existing views, habits, conditions, or institutions. If this book does anything, I hope it is that it can fundamentally change the way you relate to the objects in your world and how the eventual breakdown of those items can cause you to step up to the plate,

no limits, no boundaries, and ask yourself what you can do about it. And hopefully that engagement will eventually change how the world relates back to us. If that's radical, fine.

As for what I am doing these days… well, my life is not as completely wrapped around bikes as it once was. This book, as the zine was, is an ode to a short and beautiful time in my life, a time of a deep immersion in bicycle culture in New Orleans, from bike punks to bike repair, from bike parades to bike symposiums! That time may be over for me, but the lessons learned from that time have not left me. Quite the contrary! In the past ten years I have had the fortune to have the opportunity to apply the lessons of the bike shop to many other aspects of my life. In short, I bought a gutted and moldy house post Hurricane Katrina and applied the simple mechanics I knew to replace the plumbing and electrical, to rebuild and re-design the house wall by wall (in fact, most of this book was written during the evenings after long days of work making my home habitable, from one functional room plugged into the only functional outlet in the house.) A few years later began a whole new lifetime within this one when I bought a bit of land in the Ozark hills next to a budding Buddhist retreat center. I have had the privilege of helping turn a 100 year old barn into an extraordinary Tibetan Buddhist temple, building multiple homes and retreat cabins, making minor to major repairs to about everything imaginable, and turning my own 50-year-old single-wide mobile home into a palace of my dreams. I couldn't have done any of that had Bill Moss not hired me to turn wrenches at French Quarter Bikes, which opened me up to problem solving and fixing in a way that truly changed my life. That I know.

I hope you can enjoy what *Chainbreaker Bike Book* is here to offer: a simple and clear introduction to the bicycle, with anecdotes from a special time in the lives of me and Ethan and a New Orleans subculture, that may, just by chance, lead you to learning to dive into

a problem and fix some broken thingy! I hope it gives you a new perspective that inspires the courage and mental tools to notice, decipher and repair any issue in your life, from a squealing brake to a leaky gutter to new ways of connecting to the world and beings around you! May all bike riders benefit!

Shelley 2008

I haven't been a "professional" mechanic for a couple years now. The shop I worked at in the French Quarter in New Orleans for about 6 years closed a few months before Hurricane Katrina hit. Now, I have lost my wrench-turning calluses and a bit of memory for what it feels like to work on all different bikes in a shop, day after day. My bike fixing experiences were at a shop that worked on virtually no fancy bikes, and at Plan B, a volunteer-run space for bike recycling. At the shop it seemed like the tools we used most were hammers and drills, and at Plan B we struggled to keep functioning components stocked as we pieced together bikes with mismatched, used parts. But, at both places, we worked so hard to make things work well and to provide people with a solid form of transportation. We learned a lot more about bikes doing things the way we did. It was way more than just take off and replace, like most things in the modern world. We worked really hard to make even the jankiest of bikes run well. Because of this, I will never forget how to be a mechanic. It is like learning to ride a bike, I suppose. Once you got it, you got it for life. This is my attempt at sharing the little useful bits of bike repair that I learned over those years.

This repair manual is slightly limited and maybe even a little old school for the type of bikes that are on the road these days. At the very least, what this manual covers is the basics of mechanics and repair, a starting point for a person who wants to learn to work on their bicycle. At best, it is inspiration for learning to look at your surroundings in a whole new way, because what I want to express here is not simply how to make a broken bicycle work again, but how to make anything

broken work again. So that you feel like you can look at a problem and not just feel daunted by it, but to actually feel inspired by it, to see every problem as an opportunity to learn something new and useful. I mean, we live in a world full of impermanence. It is the law of nature that the things around us, tangible and intangible, change and sometimes fall apart. Embrace it! Learn to look at problem solving in a whole new way.

Honestly, I believe it was moving to New Orleans and getting myself on a bicycle that really made a huge positive change in my life. Riding around this beautiful city helped me slow down a little. Having a bike in a place that I loved led to being alone and independent for the first time in my life. That was a small act that completely reshaped my future. I escaped the car bubble culture I had grown up with in Southern California. I was suddenly able to experience and interact with the outside world in ways I hadn't. I smelled the plants around me and began to notice the houses and architecture that made up my surroundings. Life became more engaging as I interacted more. Slowly this inspired the way I prioritized my life, and I began questioning my needs versus my wants and simplified it so that I could spend more time doing things that felt fulfilling. The seed for all of this was a simple, little bicycle. Being a bicycle mechanic and actually learning about how they work and how to fix them took all of this a step further. Getting to work on my own bike gave me a chance to learn things, to become more capable.

Think about it, just a simple machine like a bicycle can help you find simplicity, capability, and the genuine desire to live life to the fullest. Hopefully that inspires others to live their lives this way as well.

Ethan 2018

I don't want to write about bikes. I want to write about something else.

It's been ten years since *Chainbreaker*, the book, came out, but it's been thirteen years since *Chainbreaker*, the zine was first created. And that's what I want to write about. Thirteen years ago, Shelley and I were working in possibly the weirdest bike shop in North America, French Quarter Bikes. We fixed bikes for folks who relied on them for day- to-day existence. We also dealt with drunk coworkers passed out upstairs with naked strangers, patching giant inflatable penises, a pyromaniacal manager stalking an ex, and a boss who smoked cigars in the shop and occasionally drank whole bottles of Robitussin for kicks. Shelley and I were both part of the then small but devoted DIY punk scene in New Orleans. This was 2003, and none of us had cell phones or computers or, for a few, electricity. Or, like, walls. It was a chaotic place and time. I'd been putting out my zine, *Chihuahua and Pitbull*, for a minute or two. There were lots of really beautiful zines from New Orleans, in an almost competitive scene. People would spray-paint, stencil, or screen print the covers, sew things into them. My first one was all about the ocean and came in a bottle you had to break to actually get the zine.

Shelley and I were both standing at the workbench in French Quarter Bikes one morning. She was looking for bearings or something and I think I was truing a wheel. She told me, "I've been thinking about putting out a zine about bikes for a while now but I can't think of a title." I said, not to toot my own (piggy-shaped bicycle) horn, "I always thought that if I put out a zine about bikes I'd call it Chainbreaker." And Shelley made the cute, drop-jawed, eyes-bugged-out, "I'm in shock" face that she sometimes makes, the same face she made when she found out that I was not a Libra, as she'd believed, but a Virgo on the cusp.

And we were off.

It was Shelley's zine, don't get me wrong. She sank her heart and teeth into that thing. Really earnest writing, some instruction, some social commentary, and on the first one, with its drawing of a heart made of a bike chain, an image that in my mind is almost as iconic as a Warhol soup can. I was always happy to help with writing and art and suggestions, but I had my own zine and stuff so being Shelley's R2D2 was a perfectly happy role for me.

Zines were important to us then. It was how we formed bonds, with mix tapes, punk shows, letters, stick and poke friend tattoos, and zines. I remember the first time I really saw any zines. I was seventeen and living in a chaotic punk house in Philly. My friend Brian brought them over to show me. A copy of *Cometbus*, one of *Dishwasher*, and one of *Doris*. I already wrote, but I had no idea that this underground scene for writing existed. I loved them. I really had no idea that it would consume so much of my life and that I would go on to form bonds with the authors of each of those little xeroxed magazines.

By the time I got to New Orleans, around the turn of the century, the zine scene was starting to roll. And a lot followed. *Nose Dive*, *Full Gallop*, *Crude Noise*, *Rocket Queen*, *Emergency*, *I Hate This Part of Texas*, and countless more from people who just dropped in from time to time. To quote the Minutemen, "This is Bob Dylan to me." I remember once, when Kinko's switched over to a system that we couldn't figure out how to scam, I loaded up my friend Casey's little hatchback with zine masters and we drove to his hometown of Columbia, Missouri, because I knew the manager's code to get free copies there. I made so many copies of other New Orleans folks' zines that when we put them in the car I was worried about the axles holding up. I remember our friend Dan Beckman, editor of *Full Gallop,* once asked me, "Aren't you worried that writing about how cool New Orleans is will make young kids want to move here and ruin it?" at the time, I thought, "I'll be amazed if anyone reads any of this at all." Years later, I walked into a bakery in my neighborhood and was served by a girl with the Microcosm Publishing logo tattooed, saucer-sized, on her chest. I was so embarrassed I could hardly look at her. Later her co-worker told me, "Yeah, she used to always read this zine *Chainbreaker*, and thought it was cool, so she got that tattoo and moved to New Orleans." When I moved to Asheville, North Carolina, I was wearing a hoody with a patch that I cut off a thrift store shirt of a seventies, Grateful Dead-esque picture of a bike. At a party, a woman named Cinder said, "I have a zine with that picture on the back of it." Shelley and I had just plopped the hoody on the copy machine one night for that. Cinder and I are still good friends.

We had late night potlucks so that people could help us spray paint covers. Drunken collating mishaps. Letters from prisoners asking for our zines. But, now that I'm in my late thirties and my life feels very far away from all of that, I pine for some parts of it, and the parts I've shared, that feeling of community and sharing and building-something-out-of-nothing attitude? That's what I think about when I think about *Chainbreaker*.

So yeah, bikes rule. Embrace them, learn how to take care of them and utilize them and see the world in a different way with them. But when I think of *Chainbreaker*, it's a lot more than just bikes.

Ethan 2008

Once there was a time when my world revolved around my bike, (a pink Tommassini that I found in a dumpster in Boulder, Colorado), my courier bag, my little pouch of tools, my leatherman, my pump, my Nalgene bottle. That was about all that I owned, and I thought of myself as a little rolling autonomous zone—ready for anything. This was in New Orleans, where the ground is flat and the roads are bad and biking just makes more sense. There, it seemed that after food, a bike was the most important thing you could have. I hurled myself into cycling; working with Shelley at French Quarter Bikes, and volunteering at Plan B, the New Orleans Community Bike Project, where we helped people fix up bikes out of recycled parts. Eventually, I decided to take it a bit further. I went to frame building school in Ashland, Oregon,

then moved to Asheville, North Carolina, with the intent of working at a fancy bike shop where I would learn about more high end gear. I made a resume in comic strip form, got a list of the bike shops in town from the yellow pages, and set out, in the snow, to get a job. The first place I walked into was a bike/ski shop, an REI-type outdoorsy outfitter place, the kind with happy families of mannequins in khaki shorts rappelling down the walls. "This place is not going to hire me," I thought as I handed my resume over to the mustachioed golden-boy manager. But they did. I finally got to work with super-fancy, high-end parts. And you know what? It sucked! I hated it. All day long I dealt with cyclists, mostly either mountain bikers or racers. I adjusted shocks and disc brakes; I upgraded forks and put together titanium road bikes. It felt like I was on a different planet than when I was helping people with bikes they needed for getting to work. I didn't care about some accountant's three thousand dollar mountain bike! I wanted to be straightening bent forks on forty year old Schwinns! I'd gotten into bikes because I thought that they were empowering. Bikes give people self-reliance, but the high-end bike shop tries to take that away. Funny thing about capitalism; how that works. Like I said, I'm not as into cycling as I used to be, but I still have the utmost respect for the bicycle. It is the most efficient machine on earth, and in a world that's so full of crappy things, finding something like a bicycle, which is about as close to purity as you can get, is a life-changing thing. So when Shelley asked me to help with this book, I jumped at the chance. I may not be who I used to be, the guy that actually planned, once upon a time, to have "Bike Ride" tattooed on my knuckles, but I still want to share what I know about bikes and maintenance before it leaves my increasingly sieve-like memory for good.

Ok, on to mechanics!

What kind of repair manual this is

This manual can serve many people, from the very beginner to a decent mechanic who just likes to geek out and hear people talk a lot about bikes and turning wrenches. If you know everything in here already, or this seems too simple for you—that's great! Find a more advanced manual! You can take bikes as far as you want to, and with some attention and logic, the bikes this manual will help you fix should take you as far as you want to go.

Also, this manual is not written in high tech or "cool dude" language. It is written in the language we would be speaking in if we were standing in front of you. It is meant to help you identify what you are looking at and make it easy to think logically about what each part does and how they work together. It will help you locate a part on your bike even if it looks a little different than the ones in our illustrations. For me, I can look at most car engines (old ones) and find a carburetor, distributor, alternator, etc., and though they sometimes look radically different from car to car, by understanding each part's form and function I can troubleshoot the reason it may be malfunctioning. Doing this with a bike is way easier than with a car, and you shouldn't have a problem if you open your mind to it.

For some, certain descriptions may be difficult to grasp. If mechanics are new to you, then start with simple things to get you familiar with tools, the way they work, and with the way your own hands work. Start with fixing a flat, or adjusting your seat height. Or do something with a friend who can show you a little first. Or wing it! That's how I learned. Eventually, after some time and a lot of mistakes, I think I got it. So please, be patient with yourself. Sadly, no repair is problem free and there always seems to be a catch. From rusted-on nuts and banged up threads, to wrong tools and wrong parts, or maybe we just don't cover how to fix the exact kind of part on your bike. Things will happen. Difficulties will arise. Just be patient

and logical, and with your own ingenuity and a little guidance from this book, I think you can work it out.

There are a few basic things that bikes should be— functional, practical, simple, and, if you're so inclined, pretty. For some people, these things are prioritized differently. That is fine. But with this book, we'll start at the top. You'll learn first how to make your bike functional. Making it pretty is up to you, but we'll give you a few tips on that, too. The book is based around a full maintenance tune–up. It is set up to help you keep everything on your bike functioning well to help prevent larger problems that could come up from basic neglect. Lack of maintenance and attention leads to problems whose solutions are too difficult to handle in a simple repair manual like this one, leaving you dependent on some stranger to fix things for you. That ain't cheap. The preventative maintenance required to avoid this is actually quite easy.

Who this manual is for

We want this book to be accessible to everyone! For women and men, for people with plenty of financial resources and for those who live life by simpler means; all races, ages, abilities and strengths. It may seem obvious that bikes would be accessible to all types of people, but, sadly, this is not always true.

In the US, at least, we are brought up in a competitive world, steeped in capitalism and consumerism. It makes it difficult to know what our needs are. From a young age most of us looked forward to getting our first car; our driver's license. Most of us are taught to look forward to success in our lives: getting married, acquiring things, buying things. Our whole world is shaped by the idea of supply and demand, to think that if we can get anything we want, that it is not wrong to get everything we can. But, we will assume that many of you interested in bicycles may be longing for a simpler life. Hopefully, we can create one by learning from the faults of the macrocosm and not making the same mistakes in our microcosms. There is no need to impose the competition, greed, and caste systems of the rest of the world into our lives and communities.

I know it is natural for humans to break themselves down into groups, recognizable by dress, mode of transport, musical tastes, hairstyles. We like to be around people who look like us because we assume they have similar belief systems. This is not always true. Try not to create barriers between you and the people around you. Maybe this seems a silly topic for a bike repair manual, but we have seen plenty of sexism, racism, and competitiveness between people over who has the coolest shit in the biking scene. This is just silliness. Maybe you have cooler stuff, but why? Cause you worked harder and spent more money, or because you don't work and have hours upon hours each day to go dumpstering and scavenging all over town? You think you've never seen a woman totally kick ass as a mechanic? Well, just so you know, there are a lot of ladies out there who could teach some boys a thing or two. The bottom line is: it's not a competition. Everyone and every bike is allowed in, ok?

So while this book was made by a couple punks, one under thirty and one who likes to say she's pushing 40, it was made with the intention that anyone should have access to it! Help us do all we can, with our limited abilities, to make sure lots of people from all over the place get a look at this so they may learn something that can help them make a repair or want to get and ride a bike. Spread the word with us about how great and simple bikes are and all the great things they do for our lives, and we can help make our little bike scene a big, colorful, eclectic bike scene. Thanks.

Diversity

There is one area where I do hope this book has grown since the previous editions, and that is in inclusiveness. My intention for *Chainbreaker* from the beginning was to inspire women to get into bikes and especially bike repair as a way of empowering

them to see that life has no limits and we are able in every way to accomplish and excel at anything a man can. But by no means did I mean to limit the ways bikes inspire, and I hope I did not! Here in 2018, times around us are changing quickly, both in the forward direction and in the backward direction, and it has caused conversations about diversity to become more important than ever before. So while I did gear the book specifically towards women, I don't want to fail in my dreams of making this simple book about bike repair inspiring and accessible to everyone, leaving nobody feeling left out.

So, we have added some other voices of the bike community. Because of my personal life experience, I am comfortable speaking to women, about feminism and feminist values, about what it feels like to be a woman in male dominated careers. But we can't leave out the experiences of people of color, queer and trans communities, of people that represent all areas of our economic hierarchy. I hope we can fill those gaps by some additions we have made, interspersed throughout the book, by people speaking for their own communities, in their own ways, like how I feel comfortable speaking to women about being a woman!

Bikes and biking and the world that grew around me in relation to bikes was like a light going on in my life. The whole of it all turned my brain and my heart on and that has stayed with me two decades later. I sure hope there is space for that to happen for every person on this planet, no matter what.

Safer spaces

Anonymous, October, 2017

I've talked about the need for safer spaces for years and years, but to understand what a safer space means to me, I had to really dig into my assumptions. A safer space means different things to different people. In my experience, it means a place where you can go and feel welcome. Some people feel more welcomed by the rest of the world; the focus of making a safer space feel welcoming is less about them. To me, upholding a safer space has to do with creating a place where people of all backgrounds and experiences feel comfortable learning how to work on their bikes—not just the people who experience privilege in the context of the bike collective.

So you're in a bike collective, and you look over to a wall, and you see a big ole' sign. It probably starts with something like "We welcome all races, religions, countries of origin, sexual orientations, genders, abilities...." There's usually also a list of rules, guidelines, expectations, or a code of conduct established to support that statement.

The policy on this sign is just part of a safer space; it establishes clear priorities and boundaries. The rest of what makes something a safer space is the procedures in place to uphold the boundaries. This combination of agreement, procedures, and the will of the collective to uphold it are what I think makes a safer space in a bike collective.

Although the final burden of upholding a safer space agreement ultimately lies with the core volunteers, everyone who enters the shop is responsible for participating in that safer space. The reason it's a "safer" space is because it acknowledges that there are always new ways to build on and improve what's already there. Thinking about and talking about and upholding a safer space takes work. It can take a lot of individual and group effort, and a lot of ongoing discussion outside of regular open hours.

Now here's what's really key with safer spaces:

1. There's this concept of "comfort in, dump out". Say your best friend is dying. You're not dying, so you comfort your best friend, and your best friend can process this whole "dying" business with you. Then you in turn go and process this whole "friend dying" business with someone else, whose friend is not dying and is in a position to comfort you.

2. I recently learned the sociology terms "target groups" and "agent groups". An agent group/dominant social group is a group of people who, as I understand it, are typically favored by society based on which categories they're in, rather than merit. A target group is the flip side of that. If your experience tends toward being in the target groups, you probably already know it. If you're more in the dominant social groups, you probably have to work to notice that the deck is stacked: that the little things are more likely to go your way, that people are more likely to say things like "you seem like a nice young woman," to believe you, and to listen to what you say.

I left my local bike collective when they made it explicitly and implicitly clear to me through both words and actions that they were unwilling to prioritize a safer space.

In the last couple years, I have been watching this still mostly white male bike collective learn and grow from the sidelines. It makes me feel hopeful for the future of the collective when I see them thinking and talking and working toward safer spaces. This is a slow process, but well worth the effort.

So then, how to do that? How do you make bike collectives more accessible to a wider variety of people? Think about who's not using the space, or not using the space fully, and work from there. Here are a few good starting points:

- access to basic food

- if music, multicultural music

- build bikes for all uses and people of all heights

- pedagogically-oriented learning environment

- value all work, including admin work

- daily log for communication between shifts

- update handbook with official decisions after meetings

- safer space trainings for all volunteers

- upholding clear shop guidelines and boundaries for appropriate behavior

- physical shop: safety, accessibility, well-labeled everything (including volunteers)

- having a functioning, physical land line telephone in the shop

- being predictably and punctually open

- days with appointment-based stand time

- have contact info for a mediator available

- informative, accessible website

- providing an option for clearly defined volunteer tasks

The more you do to make a space accessible to a wider variety of volunteers and patrons, the less it will be exclusively the default crowd that shows up and sticks around.

Further Reading: I'm using "comfort in, dump out" but there's the *Stanford Encyclopedia of Philosophy* on "positive and negative liberty," "affirmative action,"and "equality of opportunity."

Also, while writing this I spent a lot of time thinking about a chapter in *The Art of Effective Facilitation* (Stylus, 2013) called "From Safer Spaces to Braver Spaces" by Brian Arao and Kristi Clemens.

A special note for women

Ok ladies, this is a little pep talk for you. I know it can be difficult at first to pick up a new skill, especially one that is often thought to be a man's thing. My (Shelley's) first job ever was selling tools in a hardware store, and it was the first time I experienced the kind of blatant sexism that would just bring me to tears, the kind that would follow me through many jobs ever since. It was worse at the bike shop, where I was often spoken down to, called sweetie, and asked if I needed help lifting something. Sometimes it was out of kindness, cause in the south, everyone called everyone sweetie, even when they're calling the cops

on you. But there were times when I was assumed to be the wife of the owner, or spoken about to the owner as if I wasn't in the room. Things like, "She can fix stuff?" spoken to my boss as I was working a bike on the stand.

The same kind of shit comes up whether we are working in a shop, in a free bike project, or working with a guy friend in the garage. It is easy to get a little nervous, shy, or frustrated when the person trying to teach us to fix something, or the person whose bike we are trying to fix, keeps taking the tools from our hands and doing the work for us (I am guilty of doing this myself). It is your job to stand up and be heard. Know what you want to learn, get to know the tools, the language, and, by all means, do the wrenching yourself, even if it means making mistakes. Ask questions and look for guidance, but look to your own sense of logic as well. I often find women to be more attentive and careful of their work, unlike a lot of bolt-breaking dudes I have worked with. Trust yourself and your work. If things get out of hand and you are feeling left out or condescended to, speak up, and let the person know you are totally capable of doing what you are meant to be doing. Keep up the hard work, and don't back down. You'll be happy about it in the end. I know I am. Empower yourself, and, by all means, don't stop there. Learn to be patient to help empower others as well! Let's hear it for the girls!!!

DIY

The Do-It-Yourself culture started way before the punks. People have always loved learning how to be better in touch with their surroundings by problem solving life's inevitable breakdowns and becoming proactive in keeping their world functioning. It is great to learn how to fix a leak in your plumbing or not have to pay some stranger to do a simple oil change on a vehicle. Learning to do it yourself aids in a lifestyle where one does not have (or want) a forty-hour work week. You can learn to get by on less by having to pay fewer people to do things you can easily do yourself. It is a great thing. When we learn how to fix things, our relationship between time and money shifts and our appreciation for the great, well-functioning things in our lives grows.

I remember when I was working on fixing a friend's house for seven dollars an hour. When my truck broke down, I couldn't go pick up sheetrock for the walls. I had two choices: take the afternoon off and lose twenty-one dollars in pay and go to the auto parts store, pick up the part and change it out on the truck in fifteen minutes, or, take the afternoon off, drive down to the auto shop and pay some stranger sixty dollars an hour (minimum one hour!) to do it for me. Then wasting more time the next morning picking the darn thing up (if it was finished by then!). Duh! My time is money, but in this world, another person's time usually costs a whole lot more. The

reasons we work on our bikes extend far beyond saving a buck, just as they are for most folks who like to do things themselves. Yes, we do it because it makes good economic sense, but mostly we do it out of love and because we wouldn't have it any other way!

On the other hand, there are also times when we just don't want to do the work. Maybe you are busy or just don't like mechanical stuff. Like when I changed the clutch in that same truck. Three days of struggling to get my transmission in and, by the end of it, I wished I had shelled out the two hundred bucks to have someone else do it—though, secretly, I was proud and happy that I did. While bike repair is almost never THAT difficult, not doing it yourself is ok, too! It comes down to knowing your limits. Knowing how far you are willing to go and/or how much time you can or are willing to invest. Not everyone needs to know how to fix a bike, or hang sheetrock, or fix a toilet! Do what feels right to you, and never make fun of someone who just wants to take her or his bike to a shop. Instead, offer your time to do a repair for them, send them to a good shop, or steer them away from a crappy one. Best yet, offer to teach them how to fix their bike. But let the person go to a shop if they want, and allow yourself to do it too sometimes. Just understand the trade-offs. When you decide to pay someone else, do it with joy, pick a nice shop, and treat your mechanic well. Good shops need our support too.

Getting Started
Dealing with a shop

Even an experienced mechanic will sometimes have to rely on a shop for advice, parts or accessories, especially if you live in town without a bike co-op or other types of free service or recycled bike spaces. So the best thing you can do for yourself is find a shop close to you that you can trust. The best way to do this is first to choose a shop that fits your needs. Every bike shop is different, from the employees, to the main sales of the shop, to the goals of the shop, etc. It is good to look at all of these things and find one that is good for you. Find a shop where you can communicate with the people working there. If you love fancy bikes and riding long rides on the weekends, find a shop that caters to that type of bike and maintenance and see if they have group rides you can go on, or a team or something. If you are into single speeds, or beaters, find a smaller shop where the people might be more attentive to your bike type, and who can give you good advice that will save you money. Either way, try to find one shop you like and stick with it. Buy your tubes there, tools, accessories, everything.

Once you have found a good shop, try to get to know the mechanics and build a good rapport with them. When you take your bike in for a repair, ask what they did, what parts they used. If they seem really receptive, ask if they could show you what they did and see if they will give you any pointers on doing the repair yourself. Some shops are simply too busy for this, or don't like to do it out of fear of losing a customer. But some will, and a mechanic just might help out a fellow biker now and then. These kinds of mechanics are priceless, and should be given tons of love and respect. They usually like a little interaction with a dedicated and self-reliant biker and will give you time when they can. If they love questions, ask them, but be respectful of their time and be sure not to step on their boss's toes if they happen to be around, in which case, laying a little low might be the best thing to do. I know where I worked we had real regular customers. I got to know their bikes, as well as the type and quality of work they expected. If they were really sweet, a struggling musician, or tipped me regularly, I would do little things on the side to make them happy, like tightening up a janky basket or doing a quick brake tightening for free if I was fixing a flat; little things to make them happy and keep them coming back. Being grumpy to your mechanic, condescending, or low-balling them on prices will not make you a popular customer. You don't want to piss off the person fixing your bike any more than you want to piss off a waiter alone in the kitchen with your food. You know what I mean? The mechanic

might just do something crazy, like fill your seat tube full of bb's (just kidding)! I have never been so extreme as to be negligent of a bike, but I have sure been known to leave the pain in the ass for last if I had a list of stuff to get done. But treat your mechanic right, and they will hook you up!

If you do find a great mechanic who understands your needs, do NOT, for any reason, ask for hook-ups or special favors in front of their boss. You can't assume every worker is on the same page as the boss. Don't get anyone in trouble or cast any doubt on them in the eyes of their employer. That happened to me quite a bit and it did nothing but make my boss paranoid that I was trying to rip him off; which I never did. So take care of those who take care of you, keep it on the down-low.

UPDATE!: My last years working in a bike shop were at the great Gerken's Bike shop in New Orleans. When I started working there, it had been about five years since I mechanic'd professionally and a lot changed in that time. Two things that changed the most: cell phones and the internet. SO…… If you go into a shop to have a repair or buy a part, pleaseeeeeeee pay attention to the person who is taking time to help you. Shops are busy and mechanics are often multi-tasking between repairs and sales assistance. Please put the cell phone down. AND pleaaaasseeeee don't internet shop comparable prices right there in the shop and try to lowball the shop based on those prices. If you want to internet shop, do that in the privacy of your home and let the bike shop do what they do: sell you something based on the need you have and information you supply to get you the most correct, functional and appropriate part to make you and your bike happy. People talking to people, the old way, ok?

A note for ladies in shops

It is really difficult being a woman in a bike shop sometimes! Seriously! Sadly they are often very male spaces, and no matter how tough we feel, walking into a shop can make a woman feel 15 again. So ladies, be forward, be assertive. You don't have to spout off a bunch of stuff about components or high end shit to get the respect you deserve. If you ride a crappy little three speed and you want to know why the brakes aren't working, ask the mechanic to show you why and where they are broken. That's actually how I got my job at the bike shop! Don't be afraid. If the male mechanic calls you sweetie, or honey, counter him with a straight-forward "sir", which draws a nice boundary and can diffuse annoying flirtation. Let him be sure the interaction is about bikes and nothing more. You can do it! Find a shop where the mechanic treats you like a customer, not a female customer. Better yet, seek out a shop with a lady mechanic. By the same token, don't think you are getting ahead by using your femininity to get extra attention. It might make you feel like you are in control, but in reality, you are just selling yourself short by playing into stereotypes.

Bike types

Of course the type of bikes one sees in their own city varies from place to place because of the terrain and economics of the town. Here in New Orleans, we mostly used to see big clunky single speed cruisers with coasters (kick back). Recently, I think due to an influx of folks from single-speed towns like Minneapolis and Portland, we see many more racing bikes converted to single speeds; a perfect bike for our city. How do you choose? Think about what you want to do with your bike and get something appropriate. Don't just get the hippest thing for fashion's sake. Ask yourself:

What kind of riding do you do? Are there a lot of hills where you live? Do you bike a long distance every day? Do you carry a lot of stuff, or move heavy things frequently? Is your bike for recreation or transportation? These questions will help you choose an appropriate bike for your town and your lifestyle. This list will help you figure out what kind of bike is best for the riding you do.

CRUISER: this is the single-speed, heavy-duty sit-up-straight style bike. In California we called them beach cruisers; in New Orleans we call them truck bikes. Cruisers have wide tires, wide seats, and are often weighted down by fenders, chain guards, and wide or tall handle bars. Schwinn made great ones, Murray made decent ones, and Huffy made some pretty crappy ones. New retro cruisers are making a comeback and even come with "distressed" paint to get that old school look that folks love these days. These are great bikes for big baskets and lots of hauling. Not so good for uphill riding. I ride my dog around on mine!

THREE SPEED: these were most popular in the '70s and '80s and were put in the mainstream by way of department stores. They are lighter than cruisers, usually have internally geared hubs and dove bars. These are great bikes and it isn't hard to find a good old one in nearly mint condition. They tune up well and

CRUISER
(THIS ONE HAS
A GIRL'S FRAME)

THREE-SPEED
BIKE

ROAD BIKE

ONE-SPEED ROAD BIKE

TRACK BIKE

MOUNTAIN BIKE

COMFORT
BIKE

BMX BIKE

are surprisingly fast, and when the hub goes, it's easily converted to a nice, light, single speed with a coaster wheel. These are strong and generally faster than cruisers. They'll hold a fair amount of weight too.

ROAD BIKE: light bikes with multiple gears (10-27), drop bars and made, in most cases, with either steel or aluminum. Built for racing, but used by commuters and weekend distance riders. Road bikes can be the fastest, but with the thinner tires and drop bars, they're not for everyone. These are the bikes that are often very easily converted to single speeds for flatter terrain. You can mount a good rack on the back of them for transporting light stuff.

TRACK BIKE: These were built for riding on a, um, track. They are light, road style bikes with one gear cog in the front and one in the rear. Unlike single-speeds, which have a freewheel in the back, track bikes have a fixed cog which prevents the bike from coasting, so if the wheels are turning, so are the cranks—pedaling all the time. These are popular with bike messengers, and are most easily recognized by the lack of brake levers. They are meant to be light and simple with no derailleurs, no brakes, cables, or shifters and almost never having anything extra like racks or baskets— though it has been done.

MOUNTAIN BIKE: mostly straight-framed bikes with larger knobby tires and multiple gears (usually 18-27). They usually have straight handlebars with low stems for a more aggressive ride, often with front and/or rear suspension shocks. The knobby tires slow you down a bit in the city, but can be switched out for slicks, unless you ride in dirt or grass or off-road a lot. Suspension complicates baskets and racks.

CROSS BIKE/HYBRID: similar looking to mountain bikes, only suited more for commuters. Often with cushier seats, slicker street tires (on narrower 700c wheels), higher handlebars and stems for a more upright position. Some have shocks, or seat post shocks.

Hybrids were almost the perfect city commuter bike, until most companies switched to only comfort bikes.

COMFORT BIKE: These are pretty new school as far as I can tell. I think I was working at French Quarter Bikes when the big switch happened and most companies left out the hybrid and got these. They are similar also to mountain bikes, usually have wider but slicker tires. They often come with shocks on the front forks and seat posts, and wide seats. They usually have very high adjusting handlebars and stems and are actually very comfortable. However, they are slower than hybrids, as well as more complicated for basketing (due to the shocks), which I think is pretty important for a commuter.

BMX: short dirt/street/jump/trick bikes, usually with 20 inch wheels and tiny frames. Fun for tricks, but a little difficult for transportation riding, though Ethan used to know a maniac who couriered on one.

Purchasing a Bike
Fit

Mistakes in fitting can make even the best bike feel crappy to ride. So often I see people riding around on bikes that don't fit them, or are just not adjusted properly to their size. It is important, when buying a bike, to get one that fits you! This means buying a bike that can be adjusted to fit you as well as possible. You don't want to hit your knees on the handlebars when you ride, or struggle to reach the pedals. At a good bike shop, the salesperson should help with finding the best size for you. At a department store they won't, and when buying a used bike it will really be up to you. Test riding a bike helps. Be realistic when you do this. A few years back, I was given a great used road bike converted to a single speed that I absolutely loved. It wasn't until I switched to another bike that I realized I had been riding a bike way too big for me. I could reach the pedals while riding, but couldn't stand over the thing at a stop, which can be pretty dangerous in the wrong situation. The next thing you know you're goin' around showing everyone your bruised privates.

Bikes are built for different heights and also different lengths. Height can be adjusted within limits, by raising or lowering your seatpost. Length can be adjusted, within limits, by adjusting your seats rails on the seat post and by the length of the stem you use. Check that your seat post clamp is on correctly with the clamp behind the post, otherwise your seat could be in front of the bottom bracket, which is weird. There is lots of geometry and math involved, but for now we'll start out with this:

Height: (ground to seat) You should be able to fully straighten your leg (pic. 1) while pedaling, and also stand flat footed (with none of your parts touching, y'heard?) (pic. 2) over the bike's top bar when stopped. This can be complicated when trying on ladies frame bikes, or these new, slopey "unisex" frames and frames with compact geometry. Some difference can be made up by adjusting your seat height. By loosening one bolt, you should be able to slide the seat post up or down. It shouldn't bottom out or be raised past the little dashy lines on the post, which denotes the safe height level.

Length: (seat to handlebars) This one is a little trickier. I think it is up to how you feel on the bike knowing there are, in fact, different lengths to choose from.

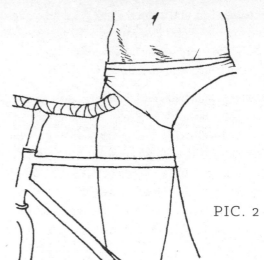

PIC. 2

One shouldn't feel cramped for space, or like you are really stretching and reaching for the bars. Try rides on different bikes to experience the contrasts, see what your preferences are. Mountain bikes and especially road bikes can feel really different when comparing lengths. And, again, you can change stem length and seat position to make up for minor problems. There are instructions on raising or lowering seat and stem height later in this book.

Materials (steel vs. aluminum)

Bike frames are made of all kinds of material. Aluminum, steel (chromoly, that is; a low alloy steel which is lighter than steel, but not as light as aluminum), carbon fiber, wood, bamboo, you name it. This is a good thing to think about when you are choosing a new bike, or building one up from a bike recycling shop. Lots of people ask about the differences between steel (chromoly) and aluminum, and the answer is pretty simple. Aluminum is light but stiff. It is more brittle and less forgiving. It is great if you have to carry a bike up four floors of steps, but it can be a little tough on the booty, meaning—it rides a lot bumpier. I love old steel frames. They ride softer and smoother and are welded strong, and if you build them right, you can keep them light. Using aluminum (often referred to as "alloy" when talking components and

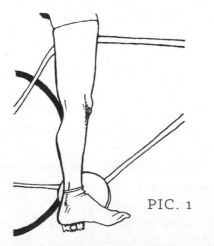

PIC. 1

wheels) components (rims, cranks, pedals, seatposts, handlebars, seats with aluminum parts) will keep them light and you'll be happy. With steel, just be sure to take care of your frame. Try not to nick up the paint a lot with posts or locks, and keep surface rust down by an occasional cleaning with soapy water and one of those little green scrubby pads or soapy steel wool. Be gentle with the steel wool; go light on the paint. As far as other materials go, you could spend big bucks on a light carbon fiber frame, but if you've got that kind of dough, you might be better off spending it on a good, custom built steel frame from an independent frame builder. There are lots of great ones out there who would love the business, and this way you'll be spending the same amount of money, only you'll be putting it in the hands of a craftsperson instead of a corporation. And it will fit you perfectly.

Where to buy

There are lots of places a person can buy a bike—small independent shops, department stores, from the newspaper or off some internet classified, yard sales, a friend, a bike recycler (like many of the community bike shops listed in the back of this book), or even from a thief off the street. As with any purchase, spend your money consciously. Think about who you are giving your business to. Bike projects are great because you can always go back and learn to maintain the bike yourself. Independent shops offer warranties and the opportunity to build a good relationship with the shop. Yard sales and friends are good because you can get some great deals, especially if you know how to make simple repairs. But, buying a bike that might be stolen is not good, for you, your karma, or for the person who got their bike jacked. Don't do it, no matter how tempting.…

IF AT ALL POSSIBLE DO NOT BUY WAL-MART OR DEPARTMENT STORE BIKES! This might sound like some kind of elitist or classist crap that implies that one bike is better than another. I don't mean it that

way.… All bikes are great, no matter what, but let me explain: The vast majority of large label bikes are made in China and we all know China doesn't have the best track record on human rights or great labor laws. This is true for department stores and for most independent bicycle shops. Buying a Chinese bike is difficult to avoid unless you are planning to spend big bucks on a new, hand-built bike by an independent builder. The best way to avoid buying a Chinese bike is to buy a used bike, therefore giving your money to a person, not to a specific company. But buying a Chinese bike is not the only issue here.

Once upon a time, during the six year stint at the bike shop in the French Quarter, our small shop was located far from any department store, in a time when New Orleans still tried to keep "big box" department stores out of the metro area. One actually had to go quite far to get to one. Our customers were transportation riders (rode less than 5 miles a day and generally did all of their chores by bike because they didn't own a car) or food deliverers. They were loyal to us for repairs, and many of them came to us regularly for a new bike for fun, or because theirs was stolen. Our shop did well with sales and really well with repairs and the work was fun and rewarding—then Wal-Mart came. It moved less than two miles from the French Quarter and our business changed radically. Regular buyers started coming in for regular repairs on bikes that were:

1) Impractical: mountain bikes with front shocks, making it impossible to put front baskets on; with knobby tires and a million gears, all unnecessary for flat city riding

2) Too small!: the sales people at those places don't know much about fitting bikes, it seems

3) Assembled poorly: You might have scored a new $89.95 bike, but paid another 40 bucks right off to get the thing running "properly" (which is never too impressive on one of those). Worse, they don't come

with maintenance plans like our bikes did (one year free tune-up and warranty!).

4) Annoying: The things fell apart right away due to inferior components like crappy shifters, and (gasp!) plastic crank arms!

5) Somehow these pieces of junk are made of, like, recycled bowling balls or something and weigh a million-zillion pounds.

While our business went up in annoying and time consuming repairs, our sales business plummeted cause somehow these folks thought they were getting a deal buying janky bikes for cheap! So we made less money and did repairs on "*NEXT...*" brand bikes all day. Anyhow, when our rent went up, the boss told me he didn't have the energy to keep fixing Wal-Mart bikes the rest of his life and we closed. So guess what? Fuck Wal-Mart. I really dislike that place, and most out-of-town, big corporate conglomerations like them. They killed our business. Just like people say, these places really, really, really do put good businesses out by selling cheap and inferior junk; just like those "Wal-Mart—proud to kill your home" bumper stickers (modeled on the ubiquitous, "New Orleans—proud to call it home"). I hope you understand why you should find a good local bicycle shop and support them, if at all possible. It's good for you and it's good for them, and in the long run, it's bad for big dumb corporations like Wal-Mart. Good.

As with any bike, treat it as well as you would any other bike, learn to work on it and be happy with it! Bikes rule! Ok! Here we go!!!

How to Do a Tune-Up On Your Bike!

These tune-up instructions are meant to be done in the order they are written. This will help you avoid unnecessary steps, like taking the wheels on and off a gazillion times, or flipping the bike over and over. You might find you can skip steps, but still try to follow the directions in a linear way, or come up with a system that works best for you.

Tune-up order

1. Gather Your Tools
2. Inspection
3. Wheels:
    A. Axles
    B. Truing
    C. Tires and Tubes
4. Brakes
5. Shifters and derailleurs
6. Bearing systems
    A. Headset
    B. Bottom Bracket
7. Drivetrain
    A. Chain
    B. Cassettes and Freewheels
    C. Cranks and Chainrings
8. Safety Check then Test Ride!

We have covered the main types of bikes and parts you will see. Occasionally, you will run across something totally wild looking, like roller cam brakes or something wack like that. Don't panic! Really! Find the part description which most closely resembles yours and use logic to figure it out. Many parts function quite similarly even if they look different. Try your best to figure it out. It will make you a better mechanic in the long run.

1. Gather your tools

A good place to start is with the tools you need. We made a list here of tools that are necessary to do the repairs in this book. Some tools are indispensable, so you should have your own. Others you will use once in a blue moon, and, really, you needn't buy it. Instead, borrow it from a friend, a local free bike project (there are many directories of bike projects found on the internet, or just ask around!), or from a nice local bike shop who will let you loosen something with their tool without charging you three dollars like one of our local shops does. So check these out and build yourself a tool kit:

Note: A lot of these tools may not be necessary for your bike type. There may even be sizes of tools listed that you will not need for your bike. Find out what sizes of things like wrenches and spoke tools you need for your bike during your first tune up and build your tool kit accordingly. That way you don't get stuff you don't need.

Essential tools

These tools are always nice to have and once you have them, you will find yourself using them more and more. If you want to do any minor repairs on your bike or other people's bikes, invest in them, you'll be happy you did...

• **Screwdrivers**: At least a small and medium size of each a flat and a Phillips

• **Tire levers:** Two, the flat black kind are my favorite!

• **Adjustable wrench (crescent wrench):** Medium size, though a small one and a large one are helpful too.

• **Allen wrenches:** A set, or at least 4, 5, 6 millimeter sizes and any special to your bicycle. Tri-tools are the best!

• **Cone wrenches:** (13, 14, 15, 17 millimeters, or special to your bike)

• **Chainbreaker!** (The tool AND the book! Ha ha)

• **Bicycle pump!** (And a Presta valve adapter if you need one or your pump is not equipped).

• **Wrenches:** Especially 8, 9, 10 and 13, 15, 17 millimeters. The smaller ones are necessary for derailleurs and brakes. Most bikes use metric wrenches (as opposed to standards). The exception to this are

old Schwinns, so be careful to check. The size of the wrenches will be stamped into the side of the wrench.

• **Sockets (or a tri-socket tool, which we love!):** 8, 9, 10, 14, 15 millimeters are good ones, but 14 is the only one really necessary (if you have three piece cranks).

• **Ratchet for sockets:** Make sure you get the right drive ratchet (3/8") to match the sockets you have. You can get a cheap socket and ratchet set with all the sizes you need at a hardware store (an independent one), or at a yard sale if you're lucky!

• **Needle-nose pliers**

• **Channel locks:** Helpful in lots of places and can replace other tools in a pinch (for example, you can use 'em in place of a proper headset wrench).

• **Cable cutters:** You can get bicycle cable cutters from bike tool makers like Pedro's, Shimano, Jagwire, or Park Tools from a bike shop. Most regular wire cutters won't work.

• **A little hammer:** Having one helps you resist the desire to use a delicate tool to really whack something with.

Good tools to have

These are great tools to have if you want to make bike repair a serious part of your life, or if you are dedicated even to doing all of the work on your personal bike. If you only plan to do the occasional tune-up, and you know someone who has these tools, borrow them instead!

• **Spoke wrenches:** To fit your wheels' spokes.

• **Headset wrench:** To fit your bike.

• **Brake adjusting wrench:** This is thin like a cone wrench. 10mm for a caliper brake adjusting nut.

• **Crank puller**

• **Chain whip and freewheel or cassette removing tool:** To fit your size.

• **Spanner tool:** For your bottom bracket type.

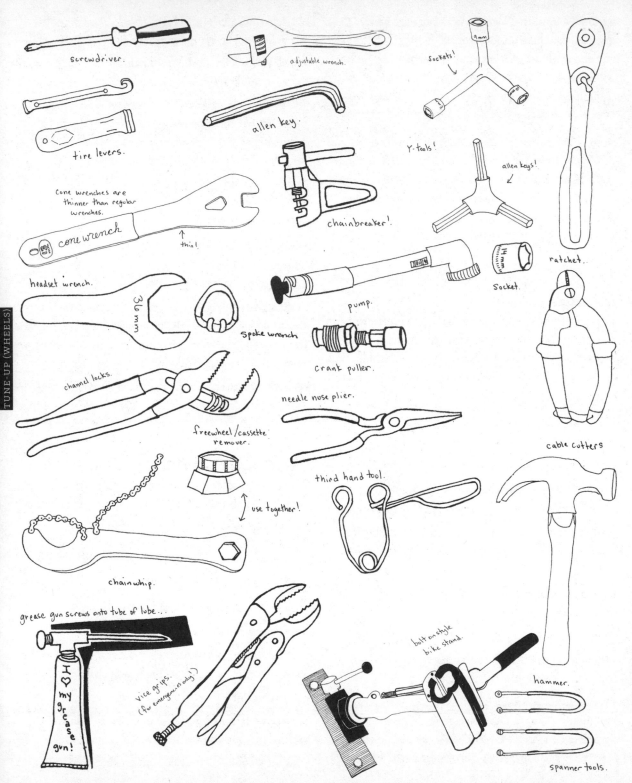

screwdriver.

adjustable wrench.

Sockets!

tire levers.

allen key.

Y-tools!

Cone wrenches are thinner than regular wrenches.

cone wrench

thin!

chainbreaker!

allen keys!

ratchet.

headset wrench.

36 mm

Spoke wrench

pump.

Socket.

crank puller.

channel locks.

needle nose plier.

freewheel/cassette remover.

cable cutters

use together!

third hand tool.

chainwhip.

grease gun screws onto tube of lube...

I ♥ my grease gun!

vice grips. (for emergencies only!)

bolt on style bike stand.

hammer.

spanner tools.

28

- **Vice Grips:** For emergency situations only!!!

- **Bottom bracket tool:** Appropriate size that fits your bike if you need one (for three-piece style bottom brackets).

- **Grease Guns** are the best!!!

- **Third hand tool:** Brake holder thing.

- **A Bike Stand:** This is not essential, but it makes all your work (especially on bikes with gears) a whole lot easier. You can usually find one for about a hundred bucks. We recommend the arm type that bolts to a stand or a wall over the collapsible kind, with the wobbly legs. They are about the same price, but the bolt-on kind has a better quality clamp.

- **Wheel truing stand:** These aren't cheap, but if you want to work on your wheels or learn to build wheels, they are indispensable.

Caring for your tools

Try to keep your bike repair tools separate from the rest of your tools. I have separate boxes for bike repair, auto repair, and wood working stuff. You should be able to fit all your bike tools in one small toolbox or bag.

Keep your tools clean and wipe them down after you use them. Respect your tools and they will serve you well.

By all means, lend your tools out, but don't be afraid to make it clear that you expect them to return to you. It's better to be honest about that and always be the one to have the tools to lend. Also, asking people to respect your shit reminds them to respect their own. Don't feel bad. Putting your name on 'em feels dorky, but is good, especially in the punk house where more and more junk is getting brought home every day. I guess this would work with lots of things!

Get good tools. Go for Park Tools, Pedro's, and fancier stuff. If a shop doesn't carry tools, they more than likely will order them for you, and if you're real nice, they won't double the catalog price on you. As for

wrenches, screwdrivers, etc, get good quality stuff. It will last you longer and often comes with a warranty that will replace something that breaks.

A word on bike stands!

I think I got really spoiled working on bikes in a shop all of the time. I mean, I learned to fix bikes in a shop with the bike clamped onto a stand and never really realized the difficulties of working without one until I started fixing bikes at home. It didn't take me long to go ahead and invest in a good stand. With one of these, you can clamp your bike down steady and flip it around into any conceivable position. Because the wheels are suspended, you can turn the crank, making brake adjustments and gear adjustments insanely easier. I mean, it's so much less frustrating than trying to keep a bike sitting upside down from falling over while you stretch to try to shift the gears while the bike is resting on the shifter mechanism. Argh! It sucks! There are a lot of different kinds of stands one can purchase or make. There are the fold-up, portable kind, or big clunky heavy ones that come with a stand and base, and there are the kind that clamp onto a table or wall. I went with the wall clamp one because you can get the higher quality clamp for much less. Most of the ones I have seen are Park Tools brand and I think that they are great. The fold-ups are a little wonky for my taste, and when comparing different models of different stands, I definitely prefer the all-metal clamp option. A shop will more than likely let you look at a catalog to choose one and even order one for you. They aren't cheap, but if you have a bike with gears, it won't take you long to wish you had one. So, if you are going to make bike fixing a habit, invest in a good stand, or look around for some nice directions on making a stand of your own. I've often thought that in a pinch, you could figure out how to rig up a car-mount bike rack to work, but I'll leave working out the details on that one for your creative mind.

2. Inspection

Before you even start, INSPECT your bicycle! Check the frame for breaks or cracks. (Do this even if the bike is new to you. There is nothing worse than doing a whole tune-up on a bike and then realizing the frame is busted.) Note items that need replacing, adjustment, repair or overhaul. Get an overall sense of the bike and how much work is worth putting into it, and what parts you will need to make the tune-up really nice.

Your question is to find out: is it worth it? If your bike has wheels that are totally jacked, bad hubs, broken spokes, warped like crazy, and has busted derailleurs, it might not make sense to fix it up. Think about the cost of new parts before you start. If you have a recycled-bike project near you, it might still be feasible for your budget. Look at what your budget is and compare it honestly to the work you need to do. Remember, while adjustments are free, overhauls and replacements add up.

DECIDING TO ADJUST OR OVERHAUL

Overhaul vs. adjustment: The distinction is very important. This is the difference in how far you want to go with a bike repair and how much time you have to do it. An adjustment usually entails nothing more than some tightening or loosening of parts, nuts and bolts to make something run smoothly. This might also involve your great grease gun, but usually is no more extensive than that. An overhaul is a complete disassembly, assessment, cleaning or possible replacing of parts, and, finally, reassembly. This can take time and a lot of patience, and more than likely a trip to the bike shop. It is almost always worth the effort though, and is absolutely necessary if you have worn or broken parts (look for extreme rust or metal falling loose out of open axles, headsets or bottom brackets especially—this means overhaul time!). Adjustments and overhauls will be explained for most repairs in this book.

OK! TIME TO START YER TUNE UP!

3. Wheels

REMOVE THE FRONT AND REAR WHEELS.

There are two ways your wheels connect to the bike: with axle nuts or with quick releases skewers.

AXLE NUTS.

Axles nuts screw onto a solid axle to hold the wheel on. If you have axle nuts, chances are they are 15mm nuts, but could also be something totally random and unusual. Use the proper wrench for the nut, or use an adjustable wrench if you have to and loosen the nuts (clockwise to tighten, counter clockwise to loosen). Take the wheel off. Put the wheel back on in reverse order, making sure to get the wheel even in the forks or chainstays, and with rear wheels, to get your chain around the rear cogs. Bolt back down securely.

QUICK RELEASE.

A quick release skewer is a long thin rod that runs through a hollow axle with nuts screwed onto the end (pic. 3). One of these nuts has an arm that when flipped down squeezes the two nuts together to hold your wheel on. If you have quick releases, flip the lever on the skewer up to loosen the wheel. This lever usually has a little curve to it. When the curve points away from the wheel it is loosened, towards the wheel is tight. The lever might even say "open" when it is opened, and "closed" when it is closed.

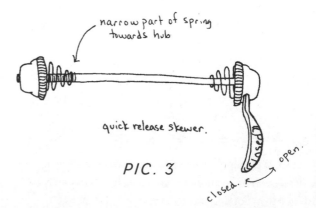

narrow part of spring towards hub

quick release skewer.

closed. closed. open.

PIC. 3

Pull the wheel off when it is opened. To resecure the wheel to your bike put the axle in the dropouts, make sure the wheel is centered evenly between the forks or chainstays, and then turn the nut on the side of the skewer that has no lever. Turn this until the wheel is just barely snug, then flip the lever closed. It should feel slightly tight to get this lever all the way down. If not, readjust the nut opposite the lever until your wheel is on well.

PUTTING A REAR WHEEL WITH GEARS BACK ON.

When putting any rear wheel on, one must be sure to get the chain around the rear cogs. With single-speeds, this is fairly easy, but with multi-speeds it can be a little trickier. First, make sure the rear gear is in the highest (smallest) gear. Pull the bottom part of the rear derailleur towards the rear of the bike. Then put the smallest gear under the top half of the loop of chain then pull the axle back into the dropout. This is especially confusing if the bike is upside down, in which case you pull the top-most part of the rear derailleur back toward the rear of the bike. Place the smallest gear on top of the bottom half of the loop of the chain and then pull the axle back into the dropout. The chain should be wrapped around the rear cogs and then form a backwards S-shape as it passes through the jockey wheels on the derailleur. When this looks right, bolt the wheel back on. Turn the cranks to make sure everything is working correctly. Re-do if necessary. If you are new at this, play around with it a little and practice so you don't get stuck somewhere weird someday.

Inspect wheels

Inspect your wheels and get a quick overview of the work that you are going to do. Check for straightness by spinning the wheels and looking to see how straight the rim looks. While the wheel is spinning also check the axles for smoothness. You don't want to hear grinding or other noise coming from the hub. Check

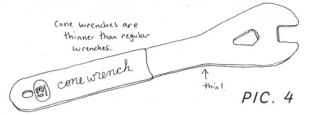

Cone wrenches are thinner than regular wrenches.

cone wrench

thin!

↑ thin!

PIC. 4

your tire pressure to discern if you might have holes in tires or tubes. Check that axle nuts or quick releases work well and are not stripped. Take note if you have any broken or really loose spokes.

To completely adjust or overhaul your wheel, follow these steps.

a. Axles

Though the axles are a bearing system and really could go in that section, we will adjust or overhaul the axles now because it makes the most sense to get the wheels taken care of first. You can't true your wheel with the axles all wobbly, and you can't adjust your brakes without the wheel trued. For more in-depth understanding of bearings and bearing systems, you could skip forward to the Bearing Systems section of this book, and then come back here and get on with the axles.

Note: There is a special tool used for axle adjustments and overhauls: the cone wrench (pic 4). This is very similar to a regular wrench, except that it is very thin. It fits into slots on the adjusting cones on your axle. It is nearly impossible to make a good adjustment without the cone wrenches that fit your wheel. They are available for sale at most bicycle shops, often in combo sizes, a different one on each side of the wrench.

The wheel includes the rims, tires, tubes, spokes, and hubs. The rims are what the tire and tube rest on, and the spokes hold the rim to the hub. The hub is where all the action happens. It is worth taking one apart just to see and understand this! The hub is basically like two cups that rest facing away from each other, much like the cups in a headset or a one-piece bottom bracket. Inside these cups are bearings, and running through the two hubs is one long axle where the cups si). The bearings are squashed between the cups and the cones, and they're rolling on this very smooth, clean track—this is what allows your bike to roll. The person who invented the wheel might have been smart, but the bearing took it to another level.

As with all bearing systems, the hubs can either be ad-justed or overhauled. An adjustment is simply relieving excess tightness or (more likely) looseness out of the axle, allowing it to run smoothly in the hub without being wobbly. An overhaul is a complete dismantling of your axle, cleaning or replacement of worn parts, and re-assembly.

If your hub is too loose, you will feel the wheel wobbling on the frame, as if the wheel isn't bolted on well (make sure it is).

On the other hand, the axle might feel tight, causing the wheel to spin sluggishly. Test this by lifting your bike and spinning the wheel forward. If it slows down real fast (and nothing is rubbing) your hub is too tight and you need to adjust it.

How do you know if your hub needs an overhaul? You will more than likely hear some loud and random knocking coming from the hub area while you are riding. If you hear grinding or notice an excessive amount of looseness in the hub, or you see little bearings or chunks of metal falling out, then it is time for an overhaul.

So decide what you want or need to do, then let's go!

Adjustment

Start first with taking the wheel off of the bike. If it is a bolt-on wheel, loosen the bolts on both sides of the wheel and pull the wheel off. If you have a rear coaster wheel, you will also need to remove the nut from the brake arm and release that brake arm from the brake arm strap and set the bolt aside. (pic. 5) Don't lose it! If

it is a quick release, loosen the skewer by lifting the lever and then pull the wheel off.Now, take a look at your axle, which goes through the hub of your wheel (pic 6). The axle is what we want to adjust. All axles (except sealed bearing axles, which we won't discuss in this book) are set up relatively the same. On each end of the axle you'll have a locknut, some washers or spacers, a cone, and some bearings. Sometimes there is a bearing cover or dust cover (which protects the bearings from dirt) attached to the cone or stuck in the inner part of the hub, holding your bearings safely in place. They pretty much all work. Please look at pic. 6. This is your first look at how a bearing works! See how beautiful it is!

Note: The exception that I can think of is on some old cruisers and three speeds. These sometimes have front wheels with a smaller diameter axle and cones without locknuts. These axles are slightly ribbed around the area where the cones sit and this ribbing holds the cone in adjustment, in theory at least. If you have these (usually they take a 13mm cone wrench), simply follow the steps of the adjustment or overhaul minus the locking and unlocking of the locknut.

Okay. The first thing you want to do is choose a side of the wheel to work on. Either side is fine, unless you are working on a rear wheel with cogs on it. If you are, you can choose to make the adjustment without removing the cogs (leaving out the step of greasing one side of the axle) or you can skip to the freewheel or cassette removing section of the book, remove the part and proceed. If you have a rear coaster wheel,

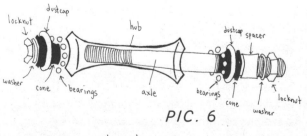

PIC. 6

axle parts.

simply choose the side that does not have that tricky little brake arm.

Now take out your wrenches (you will more than likely use a 13, 15 or 17) and your cone wrenches (again 13, 15 or 17). Put the wrench on the outside locknut, and your thinner cone wrench on the shallower grooves of the inside cone. These two nuts are "locked together" so that neither of them can move, therefore keeping the axle properly adjusted. To unlock them, hold the cone wrench still with one hand and loosen the locknut with the other, turning the locknut counter clockwise. Be careful not to open it so much that your bearings fall out!

Now the nuts are loose. It is good (but not essential) to shoot a little grease into the hub at this point. Loosen the locknut and the cone enough to cram a little grease in underneath the cone there (this is easy if you have a pointy grease gun), but not so loose that bearings are able to fall out. These bearings are pretty small, so open it a little crack, making sure that the cone on the side of the hub that you are not working on is still snug against the bearings. The easiest way to do this is by working on your wheel while it is sitting on the table, with the axle pushing into the table, keeping the gap on the topside of the wheel. Once the grease is in that side, carefully flip the wheel over and shoot or shove some grease in the other side of the hub. Carefully flip it over again, back to the side with the loose nuts, and now you can move on to adjusting the axle.

Working with the unlocked cones and locknut, tighten the cone downtowards the hub. (Note: Make sure that all the bearings are in line. Sometimes one will hop up and stack onto others, making the cone seem either way too high above the bearing ring or the bearing ring way too high above the hub. If this is happening you will either feel a lot of play or uneven tightness in the hub. Loosen it and push the bearings down with something pointy, like a spoke or a flat head screwdriver, and then start again.) Tighten the cone until you feel it bottom out against the bearings very, very gently. Now, push the washers or spacers back down against the cone, and then tighten the locknut down until it bottoms out against the cone.

Next, pick the wheel up and, holding onto the axle, make sure the hub does not have any free play. Jiggle the axle around and make sure it feels snug—no movement side to side, not even the tiniest little bit of looseness. If that feels good, hold onto the nuts on the axle on each side of the hub and turn the axle forward and backward. Does it feel like it spins freely? Not grinding, but smooth? Good. You are looking for that perfect point, where there is no free play and no binding.

Now is the tricky part. You need to lock those nuts back down without changing this adjustment! To do this, hold the cone with the cone wrench with your left hand and do your best not to move this adjustment at all. Put your wrench on the locknut and hold it with your right hand and tighten the locknut down (turn to the right) onto the cone. Your left hand shouldn't move, while your right hand turns clockwise. Tighten snugly, but don't rail on it 'til it strips. Now re-check the adjustment. Wiggle the axle side to side, and turn it forward and backward.

Quite often, the tightening of the locknut will change the adjustment slightly. If it loosens, try again, only start with the adjustment slightly on the tight side. If it tightened, start with the adjustment slightly on the loose side. This can take like ten tries the first time! Try to stay with it and be real conscious of the little nuances involved. Soon, you'll be a pro and do it in one or two tries. Great! You adjusted your axle!!!

Overhaul

Now, as I said, overhauling is basically the same thing, only more steps. To begin with, if you are working on a rear wheel, you definitely will need to take off the cogs (either the freewheel or cassette, depending on the wheel). This is covered in the "Drivetrains" section of the book. Skip to it and remove the part. If you have a

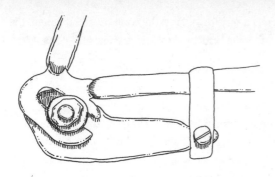

PIC. 5

THE COASTER BRAKE ARM STRAP
KEEPS THE HUB FROM UNSCREWING
ITSELF WHEN YOU ARE BRAKING.

quick release wheel, now is the time to unscrew the skewer completely, remove it, and set it aside.

Once you have done these things, again, choose a side of the axle to start with. If you have a rear wheel, choose the side that did not have the freewheel or cassette. If you have a rear coaster brake wheel (pic 5), choose the side without the brake arm to work on. Completely remove the locknut, washers or spacers, and the cone on this side, unlocking them as described in adjustments. Set aside the nuts and washers and cones (onto a clean rag or something) carefully and in the order you removed them in so as not to confuse the original set up. THIS IS VERY IMPORTANT and will save you a headache in the end.

Now the bearings are completely exposed. They will either be in a bearing ring (cage) (pic. 7) or packed loosely (free packed), and may be hidden under a neat little bearing cover (dust cover). If your bike has one of those, carefully and gently, a little at a time, working in a circle, pry that bearing cover out of the hub, being careful not to bend or pinch it. Then, carefully take all those nasty little grease covered bearings out with your fingers, tweezers, or a screwdriver and also set them aside. Now, slide the axle, with a cone, washers or spacers and a locknut locked onto the side you were not working on, out of the hub. Remove the bearing cover if you have one and the bearings from the other side of the hub.

The next step is to clean the grease off of everything so you can get a good look at what you have to work with.

Use a rag or old t-shirt or something. Start wiping down the parts that you removed. Clean the axle and other parts on it of all the grease that is stuck to it. Clean the cone and locknut that you removed from the axle, and clean well all the bearings and the bearing retainer, if you have one, leaving the bearings in the retainer of course. Clean the bearing covers. Clean the inside of the hubs really well, wiping out all the grease until they are shiny and smooth.

Now you can really get a look at all of the parts of your hub! Check to see that the bearings are smooth, round and unpitted (pits look like little rough, black spots). Check that the cones are smooth and unpitted, unchipped, and without any deep grooves worn into them. Check that the hubs are smooth and unpitted. If any of these parts are worn, they should be replaced. If you are feeling like being really great to your bike, replace them anyway, especially the bearings because they are pretty cheap and, man, bearings are the most important mechanism on your bike! You can get the parts from a local shop. It helps to bring your old parts and the wheel with you, especially to get the correct bearing ring size (they come in a lot of sizes!) if you mangled them and need to replace them.

Hubs, unfortunately, aren't so easily replaced. If the wheel is cheap and the hub is toast, get a new wheel. If it is a real high quality rim, you could consider putting a new hub on it, which requires re-spoking

PIC. 7

bearings in cages.

the whole thing and we don't explain that here. It is not impossible, but you need either a good manual or good friend to show you, or you can pay a shop to do it.

Note: If you are replacing cones, you will need to unlock the cone and locknut that are still left on your axle as well. When you do this take note of how far down those parts are on the axle. You can put the axle down on a piece of paper and mark the ends of the axles and then the starting point of your locknut. This will really help you with the spacing when you put the new parts back on. And, again, keep parts in order as you remove them. Spacers all must go back onto the places they were taken from or this job will get really confusing!

So, now all your parts are cleaned up or brand new! Put your bearings back in one side of the hub. Make sure you put them in a nice, thick bed of great, new grease—white lithium grease, Park Tools grease, or green Phil Wood grease, your choice. If they are in a ring, simply put the ring in with the bearings facing down into the grease covered hub. If they are free packed, place them in one at a time until the hub is full, then remove one. Replace your bearing cover if you have one. Put your cone, spacers, and locknut back onto one side of the axle, being careful to space

them exactly as they were before. Then slide the axle back into the hub, up to the cone. Make sure you put the axle back in the same direction you took it out. If you have a freewheel hub, the side of the axle with the most spacers, or largest spacers, goes on the side of the hub that is threaded (this makes space for the gears). Now, flip your wheel over while holding the axle, letting the bottom of the axle rest on the table you are working on to keep those bearings from falling right back out. Replace the other bearings cage, or put the bearings back in, again in a thick layer of new grease. Replace the bearing cover if you have one and put the cone back on the axle all the way to the bearings. Add the spacer and screw the locknut all the way down against the cone. Now adjust and tighten your axle as described above in the axle adjustment section. And heck yeah—you overhauled your axle! You completely restored the most important working part of your bicycle. Your wheel should spin freely and quietly and, wow, will you feel a difference when you get back on the road!

OH!!! And make sure you do this for BOTH WHEELS!!!

b. True wheels

Now it is time to true your wheels! Starting on the next page is a reprint of Ethan's mini-zine called, "A Little Guide to Truing Bike Wheels," that will walk you through it perfectly step by step!

INTRO: WHAT IN THE @#☆※! IS "WHEEL TRUING"?

IF A WHEEL IS BENT IT'S CALLED "OUT OF TRUE". THE PROCESS OF STRAIGHTENING IT IS CALLED TRUING. TRUING IS DONE BY TIGHTENING AND LOOSENING THE SPOKES TO PULL THE WHEEL BACK INTO SHAPE.*

WHEEL TRUING IS ONE OF THE MORE DIFFICULT PARTS OF BIKE MECHANICS, BUT THE BASICS ARE SIMPLE. THIS BOOKLET WILL GET YOU STARTED, BUT PRACTICE ON WHEELS YOU DON'T CARE ABOUT (FROM BIKE SHOP TRASH OR SOMETHING). AFTER A FEW TRIES YOU'LL BE ABLE TO TRUE YOUR OWN WHEELS WHEN YOU NEED TO.

* FOR EXTREME BENDS, MORE DRASTIC MEASURES MAY BE NEEDED. MORE ON THAT LATER.

1: KNOW WHAT'S WHAT

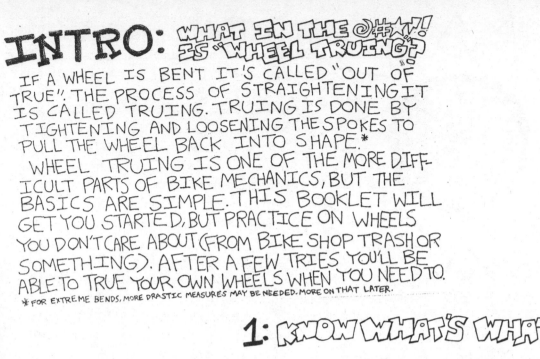

THESE ARE THE PARTS OF A WHEEL:
— TIRE
— TUBE (INSIDE TIRE)
— VALVE
— SPOKE NIPPLES
— RIM
— SPOKES
— HUB
— AXLE

THIS IS A WHEEL

GOT IT?

2: TOOLS YOU NEED

SPOKE WRENCH-THE ONLY TOOL YOU ABSOLUTELY HAVE TO HAVE. THEY COST ABOUT SIX BUCKS AND COME IN A FEW DIFFERENT SIZES. YOU CAN GET ONES WITH SEVERAL SIZES IN ONE (THEY LOOK LIKE THIS) BUT THEY'RE A LITTLE DUBIOUS BECAUSE IF YOU USE THE WRONG SIZE SPOKE WRENCH IT'LL TEAR UP THE SIDES OF YOUR SPOKE NIPPLES. DON'T SAY THAT I DIDN'T WARN YOU.

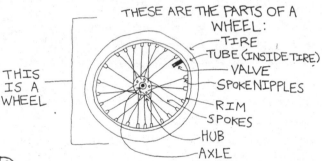

TRUING STAND-THIS IS THE MACHINE USED FOR PROFFESIONAL WHEEL TRUING. YOU PROBABLY DON'T HAVE ONE LYING AROUND, BUT IF YOU CAN GET ACCESS TO ONE, IT IS CERTAINLY NICE TO HAVE.

IF NOT, THOUGH, DON'T DESPAIR. YOU CAN STILL DO A PRETTY SPIFFY JOB BY USING YOUR BIKE FRAME AND A SHARPIE MARKER OR A PIECE OF CHALK.

LUBRICANT-GET A DRY PENETRATING LUBRICANT LIKE TRI-FLOW.

3: GETTIN' STARTED

FIRST LUBE THE SPOKE NIPPLES. JUST GO AROUND THE WHEEL AND PUT A DROP OF LUBE ON EACH ONE, THEN SPIN THE WHEEL. IF THE SPOKES ARE RUSTY, SPRAY THEM WITH SOME WD-40, THEN

WIPE IT OFF AND LUBE THEM.

NEXT, CHECK YOUR SPOKE TENSION BY SQUEEZING THEM BETWEEN YOUR THUMB AND INDEX FINGER. KEEP TRACK OF ANY OBVIOUSLY LOOSE SPOKES AND TIGHTEN THEM.

4: TIGHTENING (AND LOOSENING) SPOKES

TO TIGHTEN OR LOOSEN A SPOKE, JUST SLIDE YOUR SPOKE WRENCH SQUARELY OVER THE SPOKE NIPPLE. IT SHOULD BE AN EASY FIT. SPOKE NIPPLES HAVE NORMAL THREADS (RIGHTY-TIGHTY, LEFTY-LOOSEY), BUT THERE'S SOMETHING CONFUSING ABOUT IT.

THE CONFUSING THING:

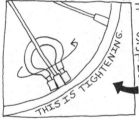

THIS IS TIGHTENING.

WHEN WORKING ON A TRUING STAND, THE NIPPLE YOU'LL BE ADJUSTING IS AT THE BOTTOM OF THE RIM. THIS MEANS THAT THE NIPPLE IS UPSIDE DOWN. SO, FROM YOUR ANGLE, IT WILL SEEM BACKWARDS.

IF YOU TAKE OFF YOUR TIRE, YOUR INNER TUBE AND THE

CLOTH OR RUBBER STRIP THAT COVERS YOUR SPOKE NIPPLES, YOU'LL SEE THAT THE HEADS OF THE NIPPLES LOOK LIKE NORMAL SCREW HEADS.

TWIST ONE OF THE SPOKE NIPPLES BACK AND FORTH WITH THE SPOKE WRENCH. AS YOU DO IT, TURN THE WHEEL SO THAT THE SPOKE YOU'RE MESSING WITH IS FACING DOWN. YOU'LL BE ABLE TO SEE THE CONFUSING UPSIDE-DOWN EFFECT. THIS IS WHAT CAUSES THE MOST TROUBLE TO NEW WHEEL TRUERS,

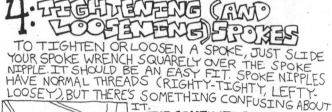

BUT IF YOU NEVER TIGHTEN A SPOKE MORE THAN ONE TURN AT A TIME, THEN YOU CAN'T DO TOO MUCH DAMAGE.

5.TRUE!

IF YOU DON'T HAVE A TRUING STAND, FLIP YOUR BIKE UPSIDE-DOWN (BE CAREFUL NOT TO DAMAGE YOUR SHIFTERS. HOLD A PIECE OF CHALK OR MARKER NEAR THE BENT RIM. BRACE YOUR HAND AGAINST THE FRAME AND SPIN THE WHEEL. THE MARKS ON THE WHEEL WILL SHOW YOU WHERE IT IS BENT.

DO THIS ON BOTH SIDES OF THE WHEEL. AFTER YOU TRUE IT, RUB OFF THE MARKS AND DO IT AGAIN.

IF YOU DO HAVE A TRUING STAND...

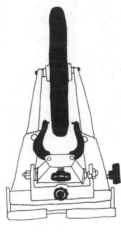

... PUT THE WHEEL ON IT. CENTER THE RIM BETWEEN THE CALIPERS ON THE STAND. TIGHTEN THE CALIPERS UNTIL THEY ALMOST TOUCH THE RIM. IF TRUING A REAR WHEEL, ONE CALIPER WILL PROBABLY TOUCH BEFORE THE OTHER, BECAUSE THEY ARE CENTERED DIFFERENTLY. IN THIS CASE, WEDGE A SPOKE OR SOMETHING BE-NEATH ONE CALIPER, THEN WORK ON TRUING THE OTHER SIDE. WHEN FINISHED, SWITCH SIDES.

SKRRATCH!

NOW, SPIN THE WHEEL AND LISTEN TO HEAR IT RUB AGAINST THE CALIPERS. IF YOUR WHEEL IS HITTING AGAINST THE CALIPER ON THE RIGHT, THEN, OBVIOUSLY, YOU WANT TO PULL THE RIM TO THE LEFT. IF THE BEND IN THE RIM IS BENEATH A SPOKE COMING FROM THE FAR SIDE OF THE HUB, THEN YOU WANT TO TIGHTEN THAT SPOKE, AND LOOSEN THE TWO NEIGHBORING SPOKES. THE REASON FOR THIS IS THAT WHEN YOU TIGHTEN A SPOKE, IT NOT ONLY PULLS THE RIM FROM THE LEFT TO THE RIGHT, BUT ALSO TOWARDS THE

TIGHTEN THIS

LOOSEN THESE

PRETEND THERE ARE MORE SPOKES HERE!!

CALIPER RUBS HERE

HUB. BY TIGHTENING ONE SPOKE AND LOOSEN-ING TWO, IT KEEPS YOU FROM MAKING A FLAT SPOT ON THE RIM. IF THE BEND IS LOCATED BENEATH A SPOKE COMING FROM THE SAME SIDE OF THE HUB AS THE BEND, THEN LOOSEN THAT SPOKE AND TIGHTEN THE TWO NEIGHBORING SPOKES. ALWAYS WORK IN ONE-TURN INCRIMENTS (OR LESS)

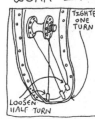

TO KEEP YOURSELF FROM MAKING ANY DRASTIC MISTAKES. EVERY TIME YOU ADJUST A SPOKE A CERTAIN AMOUNT, ADJUST THE NEIGHBOR SPOKES HALF THAT. THIS WILL INSURE ROUNDNESS. PLUS, DON'T FORGET "THE CON-FUSING THING"!

6. NOT-SO-BASIC-TRUING

OKAY, WHAT YOU JUST READ ABOUT WAS THE PRIN-CIPAL OF BASIC WHEEL TRUING. UNFORTUNATELY, IT'S NOT ALWAYS SO SIMPLE. HERE'S SOME OTHER STUFF THAT YOU MIGHT RUN INTO.

OUT-OF-ROUND WHEELS- REMOVE YOUR TIRE AND TUBE AND HOLD A RULER AGAINST YOUR FRAME OR ADJUST YOUR STAND CALIPERS SO THAT THEY ARE JUST BELOW YOUR RIM.
SPIN THE WHEEL. IF THE RIM HAS A "HOP" IN IT AND RUBS, THEN YOU WANT TO TIGHTEN THE SPOKE RIGHT ABOVE IT. TIGHTEN IT HALF A TURN, THEN LOOSEN ALL THE OTH-ER SPOKES ON THE WHEEL A QUARTER

TURN. SPIN THE WHEEL AGAIN, RE-PEAT IF NECESARY.
FOR FLAT SPOTS, DO THE OPPOSITE, LOOSEN THE SPOKE ABOVE AND TIGHTEN ALL OF THE REST, THEN TRUE THE WHEEL.

BULGES AND DINGS- IF YOUR RIM IS BULGING OUT IN A SPOT (WHICH COMES FROM HITTIN' STUFF WITH LOW TIRES), REMOVE YOUR TIRE AND LAY IT ON A FLAT (PREFERABLY WOODEN) SUR-FACE. WITH A SOFT FACE MALLET (ONE OF THEM PLASTIC-COVERED ONES) OR OTHER BIG, FAT, NON-METAL OBJECT (TWO-BY-FOUR, FLAT ROCK, ETC.), WHACK THAT MUTHA' FLAT.

IF THERE'S A DING IN YOUR RIM, OR IF YOU GET TOO WHACK-HAPPY WITH THE MALLET, PULL IT INTO SHAPE WITH AN ADJUSTABLE WRENCH. WORK THE WRENCH AROUND THE DING; DON'T PULL TOO HARD IN ONE SPOT. CHECK THE SPOKE TENSION AROUND THE DING. ALSO, IF THE RIM IS CRACKED OR SPLIT, THEN **DON'T RIDE ON IT!!!**

MAN, IT'S BENT- IF YOU DON'T THINK YOU CAN FIX THE WHEEL BY ADJUSTING THE SPOKES, TRY THIS: REMOVE THE TIRE AND HOLD THE POOR WHEEL IN BOTH HANDS.

TELL IT THAT EVERYTHING WILL BE OKAY, THEN PLACE THE BOW IN THE RIM OVER A FLAT, SOLID OBJECT (WORKBENCH, TREE TRUNK, CINDER BLOCK), AND PUSH REAL HARD. CHECK FOR CRACKS, CHECK SPOKE TENSION, TRUE WHEEL.

STRIPPED NIPPLES- IF YOUR SPOKE NIPPLES ARE WORN, USE VICE GRIPS TO REMOVE THEM, THEN REPLACE.

O.K., THAT'S IT (AT LEAST FOR THIS LITTLE BOOK)! LIKE ALL THINGS, TRUING WHEELS TAKES A LOT OF PRACTICE TO MASTER, BUT STICK WITH IT!

GOOD LUCK + HAPPY RIDING, ETHAN 02/04

c. Tubes and tires

Inspect tubes and tires. Replace or repair as needed. (Directions for removing the tubes and tires are found below under "How to Fix a Flat.")

Inspect tires

Check out your tires first for holes, gashes, bald spots, or cracking and dry rot on the sidewalls. If they have any of these things, replace them. If they look ok, then inspect them for glass, rocks, nails, staples, etc. Rub your fingers through the inside for anything sticking through and remove any offending items. Pinch the outsides and look for foreign objects like rockachaws or goat's heads or other pointy things with strange colloquial names.

Repair holes in sidewalls ("booting")

Holes in the tire sidewall can be repaired by "booting" the tire. This is great to know, 'cause people often throw out real decent tires because maybe a brake pad or something wore a small hole in the sidewall.

To do this, find a small piece of cardboard, a small piece of tire liner (or the famous folded up dollar bill— or Tammy says energy bars wrappers work great!), and put it over the hole on the INSIDE of the tire (pic. 8). Tape it in place if you need to hold it to the tire until you put the tube in, and then replace the tire normally. When the tube is pumped up all the way, it will hold the boot in and keep your tube from squeezing out the hole. Great! You saved a good tire!

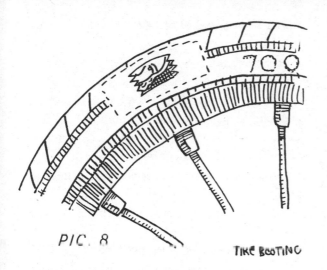

PIC. 8

TIRE BOOTING

Choosing a good tire

A friend once told me that no matter what shape your clothes might be in, you can never underestimate the importance of good shoes. I think this applies just as well for tires. Your tires bear the brunt of your ride. They support you and give you ground. They make you stable and they stick you to the earth. Having good tires, good tubes, and good tire pressure prevents flats and saves you so much time and labor! After working for years in a bike shop, there is nothing I dislike more about bike work than having to fix my own flat. Boring! Because of this, I ride good quality high pressure tires with tire liners (these go between the tube and the tire for puncture resistance) and I always keep the air filled to the top. I get a flat about once every two years—and in a city where broken oyster shells are considered perfectly legitimate paving material, no less! By the time they puncture it is usually time to get new tires! So get good tires now! Splurge on this one thing. Touring tires are great—anything that has a built-up ridge down the center part of the tire and says "puncture resistant." Ask a nice salesperson at a shop which ones they think are the best.

The first thing you need to know is your tire size. This will be written on the side of your tires. It will say something like 26 x 1 3/8, or 700 x 23 c, or something. If it is worn off, look for your wheel size stamped into the inside of your rim, maybe near the valve stem hole, or it may even be written on your tube. General tire sizes are listed under "Bicycle Types," but be careful for special sizes- especially on old Schwinns, which use their own sizing schemes altogether (often you will see S-5 or S-6 on these tires and may have to special order them from a shop). Also beware of misleading measurements, and those weird Canadian sizes. On the tire will also be written the ISO (International Organization for Standardization) number. This is the actual measured size of your tire, but is really not used so much for getting the tire you need. Next, choose a good tire for your needs. Tread is important (pic. 9). Get a tire with tread to fit your type of riding. For example, get knobbies for rougher or off-road riding. If you ride a mountain bike in the city, get yourself some good city slicks or something less knobby to reduce friction on the road. You'll feel a big difference in the amount of effort it takes to move. Slicks may seem more puncture prone, but one with a good bit of rubber down the middle that holds a high air pressure will be surprisingly tough. Even on tiny 700x23 slicks you can go a long time on rough streets if you keep the pressure up. If you live somewhere hilly, you might want to get some treaded tires to keep the bike from sliding out from under you when cornering.

Which brings us to air pressure. Always keep your tires properly inflated!!!

Good tire pressure makes you faster and more efficient and helps to prevent flats! Check your tire pressure often, especially during drops in temperature. The amount of air to put in will also be on the side of your tire. It will say something like 55 psi (pounds per square inch) or 110 psi. Use a gauge when you fill up.

slick.

knobby.

PIC. 9

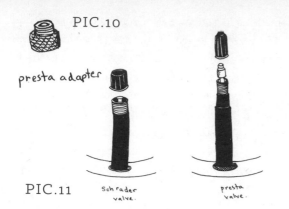

PIC.10

presta adapter

PIC.11

Schrader valve.

presta valve.

Topping off your air is a great excuse to pop into a shop and let the folks see your face regularly.

Rim strips

Don't skip the rim strips! These are the thin little strips of rubber or fabric tape that cover the tops of the spoke nipples inside your rim. They make the space between the tube and the rim soft so the spoke nipple tops that are slotted for screwing in don't eventually wear holes in your tubes. If your rim does not have a rim strip, get one. Or tape that area with electrical tape for a temporary solution.

Inspect tubes

If you are not sure if your tubes are good, you can do a couple things. One, air them up properly and set them aside for a while, then come back and check the pressure again. If they haven't lost any air pressure, then move onto the next step. If you are still unsure, pull the tubes out and put a little air in to see if there are any holes. Listen for a tell tale "pssss" or fill them up pretty good and then run your hands over the tube with your fingers around all sides of it. Or run the tube in front of your face and feel for tiny streams of air leaking out. You can also put the tube in a little pan of water or your toilet tank and look for bubbles. If they are good, use them. If not, patch or replace them..

Presta vs. schrader

Schrader is the standard valve stem that one sees on most bicycles. The valve stem is fat and the top is threaded, and any standard pump, including the type at gas stations, will work with it. Presta valves are thinner and have a little part under the valve cap that must be unscrewed before you can put air into the tube. They require a different type of pump or a Presta adapter that will allow you to use a standard pump (pic. 10 and 11). Presta valve tubes generally hold higher pressure and many road bikes and newer mountain bikes have these. Be aware that the your rim's valve hole diameter is specific to the type of valve, so use the correct tube! Don't use a Presta tube in a rim with a Schrader size hole or the stem will wobble around and the valve will more than likely puncture. If you need to do this, ask a shop for a valve hole adapter.

How to fix a flat

First things first! Know proper wheel vocabulary!

Remove wheel from the bicycle. Deflate tube of remaining air.

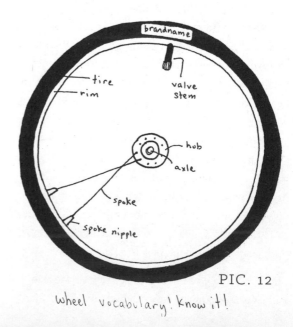

brandname

tire

rim

valve stem

hub

axle

spoke

spoke nipple

PIC. 12

wheel vocabulary! know it!

Remove one side of the tire (the bead) from the rim. Do this either with your hands (if the tire is loose) or with tire levers. Never use a screwdriver, as you risk ruining a repairable tube or even your tire! If you have no tire lever, use something soft, like the blunt end of a spoon. Remove tire completely from the rim.

PIC. 13

Take tube out of the tire, pulling the valve stem out of the hole in the rim. Fill the tube with some air to find out exactly what caused the hole (you can pump the tube quite full, huge even, to help find tiny holes). If you have a single puncture, it was probably caused by something poking through the tire. A slit in the tube could be caused by a rim bruise (under-inflated tires cause these). Two slits in the tube (snakebite!) are also caused by hitting bumps or curbs on under-inflated tires. A huge gaping hole is probably a blowout (or the handiwork of an enemy—a spurned lover perhaps) and you should inspect your tire for a corresponding tire-ruining hole, or a busted tire sidewall or exposed bead. A hole on the underside of your tube (on the part laying against the RIM not the TIRE) indicates a spoke sticking out too long, which can be filed down, or a broken rim strip, which should be replaced. File down any rust or nubs that may cause holes as well. Holes can also be caused by tire levers during a hasty tire removal, or a tube seated poorly in the rim or pinched by the tire.

Inspect your tire for holes, glass, nails, thorns, staples, dead mice, crawfish claws, etc... (pic. 13) THIS IS THE MOST IMPORTANT PART FOR PREVENTING FUTURE FLATS! Run your fingers through the inside of the tire and feel for things poking through. Squeeze the tire and look for tiny pieces of glass poking out. Pick out every last piece. Decide if you need to repair your tire or get a new one.

things we've pulled out of tires! really!

Repair tube according to the instructions on your patch kit. If your kit does not have instructions, this is the general system: 1. find the hole. 2. lightly sand or rough up the area around the hole with sandpaper, or in desperate situations, on a patch of cement. 3. put glue in a thin layer around the hole, slightly larger than the diameter of the patch you are going to use. 4. LET THE GLUE DRY! Really! It is not actually glue, it creates a chemical reaction with the patch to stick and to do this it must be dry (this is called "vulcanizing," though it doesn't involve knocking people out by pinching their necks or anything that cool). Blow on it, sing a song to pass the time. (Or as a Plan B bike project customer once said: "First you put your glue on, then you drink your beer, then you smoke your cigarette, then you put the patch on.") Whatever you do, wait until it is dry! 5. Peel the foil back off of the patch, being careful not to touch the bottom of the patch with your fingers! 6. Stick the patch onto the glue and press down firmly all the way around it to flatten it and get air bubbles out. 7. Wait a minute and then peel the little plastic layer off, though this isn't really necessary, making sure not to pull any part of the patch up. 8. Put some air in and check to see that there are no leaks! DONE!

If you don't wanna do all of this, go ahead and buy a new tube (though patching is cheaper!) and move on! The next steps are putting the tube and tire back on your rim.

9. Put just enough air in the new or repaired tube so that it holds the shape of a loose circle. Lay the semi-inflated tube inside of the tire with the valve pointing to the inside of the circle. Put valve stem through the valve stem hole in the rim as you put the tire on the rim, one side (bead) first, making sure the tube is not kinked or sticking out. Then put the other bead on (inside the rim). Be careful not to pinch the tube. Let some air out if you need to. Be sure tire is seated, meaning, that both beads are entirely and evenly on the rim. Add air slowly, watching closely to make sure that neither bead pops off the rim (otherwise the tube will poke out and explode and scare the hell out of everyone around you!).

10. When the tire is inflated to the proper pressure (this will be written on the side of your tire—45–60 psi for fatties and 80-100 for skinnies, generally, though these days, fancy-assed racing tires can go up to like 175. Fucking scary!). Spin the wheel in your hand and look for any eggs or bumps or tube popping out. If there are, let the air out of the tube and go to step 9 again. (Note: If you have a bike with brakes you cannot release, you can wait to inflate the tire fully until the wheel is back on the frame. That way you can get the thing back in between those brake shoes.)

11. Bolt or quick release your wheel back on to your bike being sure that it is evenly spaced in the fork (for front wheel) or chainstays (for rear wheel). Make sure you have your chain around the rear cog, too. This is simple with single speeds, but with multi-speeds, getting the rear wheel on is a little trickier. Refer to the wheel section above for putting your rear wheel back on with the chain in place.

12. Done!!! Now remind yourself that you rule because you can fix your own flat, which saves you money and makes you more self-reliant. Teach others how to do this, too! Now go ride your bike!

NOW THAT YOUR AXLES ARE ADJUSTED, WHEELS ARE TRUE, AND TUBES AND TIRES ARE IN ORDER, PUT WHEELS BACK ON SO YOU CAN PROCEED WITH BRAKES AND DERAILLEURS!

4. Brakes

There are a few different types of brakes: coaster, caliper (side or center pull), v-brakes, cantilever. There were also, once upon a long time ago, drum brakes, and now we have fancy hydraulic and disc brakes. This is a simple manual and we won't discuss those here. It's actually pretty easy to hurt yourself adjusting hydraulic brakes. Ethan cut a chunk of finger and fingernail off—twice! Let gearheads at the fancy shops hurt themselves instead (they like it).

If you have a brakeless track bike, write me a description of how YOU stop and I'll put it in the next edition. Ethan says the best way to do this is to rear-end a courier, then have her angrily show you how to do it. For her response, see "Stopping a Track Bike" at the end of the brake section.

Types of brakes

Coaster: these are kick back brakes found mostly on old single speed cruisers. For the most part, when one of these begins to lose its braking power, it is probably easiest to simply get a new wheel. If you choose this option, get a Shimano rather than a Hystop brand (brand name is stamped on the brake arm) if you can—it's worth the extra few bucks.

Rebuilding an internal coaster break is not commonly done, and parts are difficult to find anywhere but a recycled bike parts joint, or a shop where the proprietor still keeps heaps of shit sitting around. Also each make and brand can be quite different and finding interchangeable parts is a problem. But, if you want to give repairing it a try, you can look that up in an old

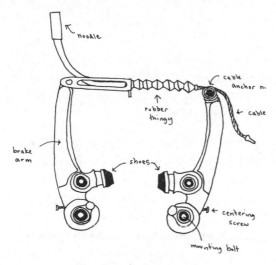

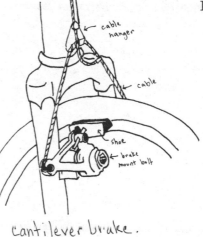

Cantilever brake.

V- brake.

school manual like *Glenn's Complete Bicycle Manual* (a great book!) or the *Sutherland's Manual*. By all means, take the little thing apart; you have nothing to lose. Take it apart very slowly and carefully, paying very close attention to where all the parts go and reassemble it back to the way it started, with new grease in all the right places, and you might just be in luck! Refer to the "axles" section in "wheels" for help with bearings and tightness of the axle and such.

Caliper: Calipers are possibly the most common brakes out there these days. They're the kind you see on most

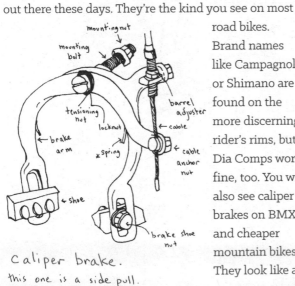

Caliper brake.
this one is a side pull.

road bikes. Brand names like Campagnolo or Shimano are found on the more discerning rider's rims, but Dia Comps work fine, too. You will also see caliper brakes on BMX and cheaper mountain bikes. They look like an

upside-down "U". They can be side pulls or center pulls (like the Weinmanns on old 10-speeds), and are mounted by a center bolt on the brake bridge between the seatstays (rear) or fork (front).

V-brakes (linear pull): These are the type of brakes you see on most mountain, hybrids, and comfort bikes these days. (I always wondered why they are called v-brakes, because, to me, the cantilevers look more like v's and v-brakes look more like lines, and should really just be called linear-pull!) They are good brakes and stop strongly. Pads are easy enough to replace, so long as you pay special attention to the spacers and match them up. They are much easier to adjust than the below-mentioned cantilever.

Special note: V-brakes have their own type of brake lever which has a longer pull than a caliper lever! You can run most brakes on these type of levers but CANNOT run v-brakes with a cantilever or a caliper lever! Make sure you get the correct one.

Cantilever: These are really old school these days, though there are loyalists out there who swear by them, and some are still in production. They are found on some older models of mountain and hybrid bikes. They work fine and can be upgraded with good pads, but are not as easy to work on as

brake cable in cable stop.

the new v-brake types as the cables are awkward to adjust. But you can do it! They bolt to mounts brazed onto the forks and seatstays. (pic. 14)

Adjusting brakes

In this description I will only refer to v-brakes and side pull calipers. If you have cantilevers, treat them like center-pull calipers. They are very similar, and with a little logic, you will see which parts are the same even if they look a little different. For these center-pull style calipers, the only difference from side pulls is in the tightening of the cable. I will address that when the time comes.

Step one: INSPECT! Look for broken housing or fraying cables. If they are broken, cracked, or frayed they should be replaced to prevent water seeping in and causing rust. If they need replacing, see the special cables section. Be sure ferrules are in place and barrel adjusters are fully screwed in for finer

adjustments later. Make sure the brakes themselves are intact, that all the parts are there, and that the brake shoes are usable. Are the levers functional and tight on the handlebar? Are your rims clean? If not, give them a quick (light!) sanding to get gunk off and clean them with some degreaser. If everything is cool, move on to step two.

Step two: LUBE (or replace!) your cables. The best cable is a fresh, un-grimey one with no lubrication, because lube can attract gunk and slow cable movement. But if you're strapped for cash and trying to get an old bike road-worthy, lube will help

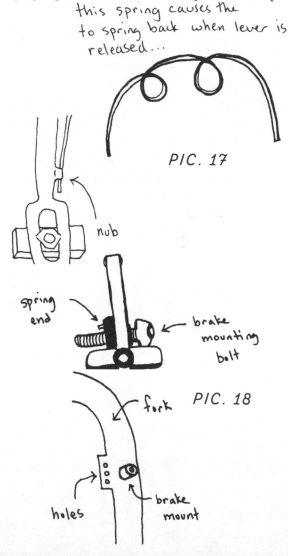

this spring causes the to spring back when lever is released...

PIC. 17

nub

spring end

brake mounting bolt

fork

PIC. 18

holes

brake mount

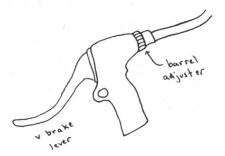

barrel adjuster

v brake lever

PIC. 16

ferule

side pull style brake lever

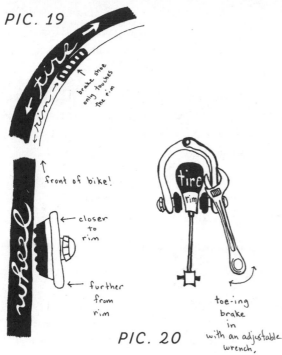

PIC. 19

tire

rim

brake shoe
only touches
the rim

front of bike!

wheel

← closer
to
rim

← further
from
rim

PIC. 20

tire
rim

toe-ing
brake
in
with an adjustable
wrench.

defend against rust and crappy cable movement that already exists. So to remove the old cable, clip the cable tip off of the cable with cable cutters (not wire cutters, but the bike kind). Loosen the cable anchor nut to slack the cable. Carefully pull the cable out of the housing. This can be difficult if the end of the cable is kinked. Either try to get the kink out with some good pliers and some patience or pull out as much of the cable as possible.

LUBE the cable and slide it in and out of the housing a couple times to get it in there. Rethread the cable back into the housing and then into the cable anchor bolt. Retighten (see next section for help). Spray some regular Tri-Flow on moving parts on the brakes, like around the pivot points on the brakes and the springs.

Note: if it is really hard to get the cable back into the housing because it is kinked or rusty, opt for a new one. You'll save some time and frustration for just about two bucks.

If your cables and housing are totally jacked, like cracked or split, it is definitely time to replace them! Go to the special cable section of the book—there we'll walk

you through replacing cables, cutting cable, ferrules, all that stuff. Brake cables are much like derailleur cables. So check that section out. Do what you need to do and then come back here.

Step 3: TIGHTEN CABLE! Squeeze the brakes with your hands so the shoes hit the rim (if the shoes are not exactly hitting the rim, skip to step 6, adjust, then return here). You can hold the brakes down with a third hand tool, if you have one, or just try holding with one hand and loosening the cable anchor nut, pulling the cable tight and then tightening the cable anchor nut with the other hand. Easy, right?

Double check that the ferrules on the levers are still in place and on the housing and brake cables are in their stops on the frame (pic. 15). When you release the shoes they should be about 1/8" from the rim. (If your wheel is real straight and true, that is! If you did not true the wheel first, do it now.) If the pads are close to the rim, but could get closer, make up the difference by turning the barrel adjuster on the brake lever or brake itself. The barrel adjuster pulls the cable tighter, allowing for a fine tune without having to loosen the cable anchor nut again. If the brake shoes are too far off the rims (you have to pull the levers really far before the brakes work), try the adjustment again. Sometimes it takes a couple tries (pic. 16).

This is where cantilevers are different. They have a cable hanger with a bolt that attaches to the brake cable and holds up a middle cable called a straddle cable. They are pretty awkward to adjust so be patient with yourself. Hold the brake shoes down with a third hand tool. They are especially helpful with these type of brakes. You can do it without one, but it is pretty frustrating, unless you have a friend to help! Loosen the bolt on the hanger and pull the cable tight. Tighten the bolt. Your pads should be right next to the rim when you remove your third hand tool. Reloosen the bolt on the hanger and loosen the cable a tiny bit, until, on removing the third hand tool, the pads are about 1/8 inch from the rim. Trick! If you have a brake with a barrel adjuster on your brake or on the brake lever, twist one of them until it is almost as far out as it will go. Adjust the brake so the cable is all the way tight, bringing the pads right to the rims. Remove your third hand tool and then twist your barrel adjuster in! This will bring your pads out from the rim! Twist in until the pads are about 1/8 inch from the rim.

Once the cables are tightened, give them a few tough squeezes. Most new cables will stretch a lot in the beginning and this can help get some of them out right away and let you do a quick re-adjust. Put new cable tips on by pinching them on with pliers.

Step 4: Check SPRINGINESS! Squeeze your brake lever and then release it and make sure the brake shoes easily spring back away from the rim (so they don't rub). If they don't spring back, try lubing the brake pivot points if you haven't already. If they still don't spring back, adjust the springiness.

On side pulls, slightly loosen the tensioning nut and lock nut. Adjust them so that when you squeeze the brake with your hand it should move freely and release freely, but should not wiggle or feel loose. The brake should still feel firmly attached to the bike (play with this and feel the difference between too loose and too tight to see what I mean). When it is where you want it, hold the locknut down with your skinny 10 mm brake adjusting wrench to keep it from turning and then tighten the tensioning nut against it. Recheck and make any adjustments. Make sure spring arms are behind the little nubs on the brake arm, too. If the brake still isn't springy enough, you can pull the spring arm from behind one

of the nubs using your fingers or a flathead screwdriver and pull on it *gently* to widen the spring and increase its springiness. Then put it back behind the nub. Remember, do this gently!

On v-brakes, loosen the mounting bolt and set the spring end into a higher hole on the fork (for more springiness) or down one lower (for less springiness). Retighten the mounting bolt.

Step 5: CENTERING! Squeeze the brake lever. If the wheel is centered in the forks or chainstays, both shoes should end up about the same distance away from the rim when the brake levers are released. If they are not, or if one side is pulling more than the other, it is time to center your brake!

On side pulls, loosen the brake-mounting nut and move the entire brake until the shoes are equal distance away from the rim. Tighten the mounting nut. Squeeze the lever to test and re-do if necessary. Sometimes it takes more than one try.

On v-brakes, use the centering screws to center the brakes. (Sometimes there is one, sometimes two. It is usually a small screw with a Phillips head, but occasionally is a tiny screw turned by a tiny Allen wrench. Tighten to pull shoe away from the rim, loosen to allow it to come closer. Pretty cool, huh? Adjust so that both shoes are equal distance from the rim, and so both brake arms pull with the same force when the brake lever is pulled. Squeeze the brake levers to test, and re-do if necessary.

Step 6: Line up yer SHOES! If your shoes are missing the rim they will wear unevenly and cause bad braking (if they are already worn like this, replace or file them down a little, but not past the wear line on the brake shoe, to flatten them out again). If they hit the tire, you'll burn a hole through it in no time, so make sure the shoe hits only the rim (pic. 19).

To adjust: Loosen brake shoe nuts (on v-brakes these are often Allen bolts) and move the shoes into position. Tighten the nut. If you find your brakes are squealing,

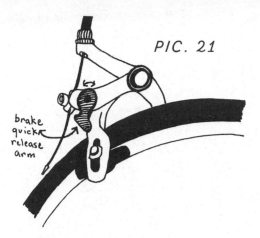

PIC. 21

brake quick release arm

TOE THEM IN by adjusting them so the front of the shoe (toward the front of the bike) hits the rim first. On side pulls, use an adjustable wrench to GENTLY bend the brake arm. Gently. On v-brakes, do this with the shoe mounting nuts loose while you are adjusting the shoes to hit the rims, then tighten mounting nuts (pic. 20).

To replace worn shoes: Remove old shoes (taking note of the placement and order of any spacers or washers) using either a 10 mm wrench or a 5 mm Allen wrench. Replace with new shoes (with spacers or washer in same order and placement), lining them up to the rim as described above. Remember that with v-brakes and some calipers, there is a right and a left shoe and that the direction they are installed is important. There is often a little arrow on the shoe itself that should point in the direction that the wheel is turning. Also, some shoes are threaded and go on with a washer and nut. Others are not threaded and are bolted on the brake arm with a 10 mm nut or 5 mm Allen bolt. Look to see which you have. This will also help you get the correct pads when you replace them.

Tips: Rough up brake pad surface with a wood file if they slip or don't stop well. If your brakes SCHREEEEEEEEEEEECH!!!!!! You need to TOE THEM IN! You and everyone else will be happy you did! If after the first pull on your levers you hear a loud click and they suddenly slack up, you probably had a ferrule slip out, or your cable and housing were not correct somewhere.

Fix that! Also make sure if you have brakes with a quick release arm on them (so you can pull the wheel off easy) and that you adjusted the brakes with that arm DOWN. Great! (pic. 21)

THAT'S ALL! Squeeze the levers real tight a few times to test and be sure the cables don't slip. Make sure that your cable doesn't bind and stop your wheel when you turn the bars all the way to the left or right. Check that all your nuts are tight, give the wheel a good spin to test stopping ability, and then make any re-adjustments. Take it for a test ride and a test stop! OK!

How to stop a track bike

My first bike that I ever relied on for transportation was a track bike, loaned to me by my courier roommate in Philly. I didn't know how to stop the thing, but being seventeen, full of bravado and with somewhat more resilient bones than I have now, I just rode around on it hoping for the best. Somehow, I didn't get run over. I just slowed to a stop whenever I needed to and never had to stop short. Then, one day, I did need to stop short, not because of a car, but because my roommate (the one who'd loaned me the bike) had stopped short in front of me. I slammed into her and she took me onto the sidewalk and gave me a tutorial on the art of stopping the brakeless juggernaut. Here's what she told me:

If you don't have a brake (which I don't encourage), you've got to learn to "skip stop," which is basically to hop the back wheel up, then pedal it backwards so that you skid to a stop. I know it sounds crazy, but it's actually pretty easy with some practice. Oh, and toe clips or clipless pedals. Those are key.

OK! Brakes are done! Let's move onto shifters!

5. Shifters & derailleurs
Shifters
How the shifter functions

All shifters do the same thing in relatively the same way. They are mechanisms that pull and release the

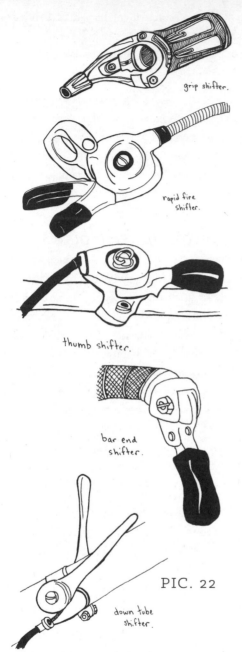

grip shifter.

rapid fire shifter.

thumb shifter.

bar end shifter.

PIC. 22

down tube shifter.

shifter itself, you are still just pulling the cable tighter and releasing it to loosen it—that's all!

Types of shifters

There are a lot of different kinds of shifters out there (see pic 22), including grip shift (twist shifters), rapid fires, thumb shifters, three speed shifters, bar end shifters, down tube shifters, and new school integrated shifters which are part of your brake levers. It would be impossible to make a manual explaining every single type of shifter and how to service each, especially because many companies change the way you remove and replace the cables with every new model. Is this a ploy to keep you at a bike shop, getting wooed into buying new stuff for your bike while it is getting repaired? Who knows. Either way, we're going to explain the basic premise of shifters here, and hopefully demystify them enough that you will feel confident to work out the nuances of your shifter type all on your own.

Friction vs. indexing

While all shifters look different in shape and size, there are basically two different ways the shifter functions. There are friction shifters and indexing shifters. Indexing shifters are the kinds that click between each shift, indicating the difference between one gear and the next. The other type is the friction shifter which shifts from high to low in one smooth movement, making a simple ratcheting sound, without stops between each gear. The latter are great, as they are much, much easier to adjust, as you will see as we move on. If you are building a bike from scratch, we suggest you find some old friction shifters. Those old Suntour thumb shifters that mount on the handlebars are just rad.

A word on gear ratio

Ok, some people have bikes with shifters and derailleurs and never really use them because they don't understand how they work. Or they use them

shifter cable in order to pull the derailleur closer to the bike frame, allowing the chain to hop up gears. When released, they drop the derailleur back to the original position. Whether this is by turning a grip and twisting the cable around the handlebar, or pulling up on a down tube shifter and wrapping cable around the

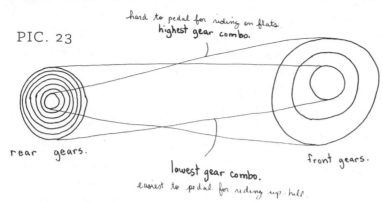

PIC. 23

hard to pedal for riding on flats.
highest gear combo.

rear gears.

front gears.

lowest gear combo.
easiest to pedal for riding up hill.

a little on the wrong side and make things more complicated than they need to be. Ever see someone riding down a flat as hell street pedaling like 100 times a minute? Man, that looks tiring! I feel like yelling over to them as I pass them in my high gear, "Hey! Shift, man! Shift!!!" and giving them a little shifting lesson right there on the road. Anyhow, this is how it works. (see pic 23)

Front gears: On the front end of the bike you will usually have between one and three chainrings. The big size is the high gear. It is the gear that requires more effort to turn and fewer revolutions to go fast. The smallest gear is the low gear. It is the gear that turns easier, but a lot more times. Riding on a flat surface or down hill you should be in a high gear. Going uphill, you should be in a low gear. Did you see Lance Armstrong whip ass over and over in the Tour de France? He did that by flying up hills in his lowest gear.

Rear gears: Ok, here is where it gets a little confusing (and we will restate this later to make sure you get it), in the back of the bike, the small gear is your high gear. When you are using the smallest cog, you will push harder and fewer times. It is the gear you use when you are on a flat or downhill surface. The biggest gear is your low gear. This one is easier to pedal and you use this to go uphill because it requires less force to turn the cranks. Got it?

Here is a good way to remember this. *The gear furthest from your bike's frame is your high gear. The gear closest to your bike's frame is your low gear.* So if you are on the big one in the front and the little one in the back, this is the hardest gear you can have. If you are on the little one in the front and the big one in the back, this is for riding straight up Mount Everest; this is your granny gear. Three speeds work the same way, only the gears are in the hub and you can't see them. Really. Same difference. Out it now?

Ok… so using your gears, you should try to keep an even pace. You can downshift and start in a low gear when you are starting out from a stop, giving you an easy way to pick up speed, and then when you get up to speed, shift it up to a higher gear and cruise. Or just downshift from a high gear when you get to a hill and you'll be able to keep your pace by simply changing the amount of times you pedal. If you've ever driven a stick shift car then think of it like that. It's more efficient to use those gears, starting low and building up as you hit your stride on the straightaway, and downshifting when you hit a steep grade. Understand?

Servicing your shifters

So we call this servicing because there is no overhaul or adjustment to make to your shifters generally. You need to simply find out if they work. If they do, great. If they don't, replace them. You can also take them to a shop to see if they can get repaired, or go crazy and see if you can figure it out and replace them yourself.

Inspect

Inspect your shifters. See if they move (meaning, do they twist, turn, pull, or whatever to change gears). If the shifter is broken, or the cable is really, really rusty, or if your derailleur (one or both) is rusty and seized, the shifters might not even move. If it doesn't move, discern if the sticking is due to the shifter being busted or the derailleur being busted. You can do that by unhooking the cable where it attaches to your derailleur and then trying again to see if the shifter moves.

Check them both out, see if they can or do run through all the gears. If they do, great. Derailleur adjustments are next and you can fine tune the shifting then. If the shifters still don't move, it might be time to replace them, or at the very least the cables attached to them. Start with removing the cable.

Removing and replacing the cable

Gosh, this can be really easy and obvious or really, really weird and difficult. Generally, thumb shifters (like the ever-ruling old Suntour thumb shifters), down tube shifters, and bar end shifters are really clear. Cut the cable from the derailleur, pull it out of the housing and cable stops and then, with your fingers, push it into the shifter. You should see a little cable end pop out of the derailleur. Pull the cable from here, completely pulling it out of the derailleur. Rapid fire shifters should work the same way, only you might need to hunt around a little for the cable end popping out. Once the cable is out, replace it (make sure you have a new one with the same type of cable end!) by sliding a new cable into the hole you pulled it out of, and put it back into the housing. If the housing needs replacing, skip up to the special cable section of the book, replace the cable and then come back here! The real pain in the booty here is the grip shift. Man, what a pain. These things have a million little ways that the cables go in, from a little hole to stick the cable through, to a little piece of the shifter shaped like a triangle that gently pries off, to a little piece of rubber in the grip that peels back to slide the cable into. Then, removing the cable is the real pain!!! You need to take the shifter off by taking off the grips and loosening

the bolt on the shifter and then sliding it off. Then you open the thing up, and again they all seem a little different. With some, you dial it all the way up and pull apart. Some you dial all the way down. When it is pulled apart, make sure you note how the cable threads in and is twisted around (careful not to let the little metal clip inside fall out cause it has to go in the right way to keep the thing ratchet-ing and holding its gear!). Pull the cable out. Put a little white lithium grease in there and then replace the cable by putting it back into the hole you took it out of and then rethreading it the same way it came. Push the two pieces back together while pulling the cable snug. Be patient, it isn't easy. When the shifter is back together, test that it dials up and down and then reattach it to the handlebar.

Once your cable is replaced into the shifter, lube the cable a little and then slide it into the housing and reattach it to your derailleur. If replacing the housing is new to you, skip to the special cable and housing section and follow the instructions on replacing your cable and housing and then come right back here. Once the cable and housing are in place, reattach the cable to your derailleur the same way you removed it. Make sure the shifter is dialed all the way down to the smallest gear and then slide the cable under the cable tensioning bolt on your derailleur, tightening it down. This usually takes a 5mm Allen wrench or a 9mm wrench. Great! Now remember, your shifters aren't going to run through the gears smoothly yet. You still have derailleur adjustments to make for this. We'll get to that next.

Replacing the shifter

Now, if you have replaced the cable and lubed the pivot points on the derailleur and found that the shifter is still totally seized, you will for sure need to replace the shifter. To do this, you need to figure out how the shifter is attached to the bicycle. First you may need to remove your grips and anything else in between there and the shifter (bells, computers, little headlight brackets, blah blah). To remove grips, gently pry a tiny bit of the grip up with a flathead screwdriver and squirt some soapy water under it. Slowly twist back and forth, working the soap in until the grip slides off. (If this is a real pain, you can cut the grips off. Just know you'll need to buy new ones to replace them!) With grip shifts, rapid fires, thumb shifters, and three speed shifters, you will find an Allen bolt (this can be very tiny) or a nut that tightens the shifter to the bike. Loosen this and slide the shifter off. Bar end shifters will twist out of the bar once the cable is removed. Down tube shifters are simply held onto the frame with a screw, usually fitted with a ring on the top that can be held and unscrewed. Whatever the case, bring the broken shifter to a shop to get the same or similar part to replace.

Compatibility

There are some shifter-to-derailleur compatibility issues you should be aware of. With indexing shifters, you must make sure that any shifter you get matches the amount of gears you have, both front and rear, to assure good shifting. If you have 6 speeds in the back, make sure you get a shifter that accommodates 6 speeds. Simple enough. Here is the tougher part: friction shifters are compatible with almost any derailleur, but indexing ones are not. For example, Shimano indexing shifters won't necessarily work with Sram derailleurs, as they have a different amount of space between each click, making shifting imprecise. Also, newer manufactured parts sometimes don't work with older stuff. This can be true of Suntour and Shimano parts. When in doubt, bring your bike with you when purchasing new parts, or, if you are working on your own bike with recycled parts, be patient and try to match your parts as well as possible on the first try. For less hassle, stick with friction style shifters. They're great.

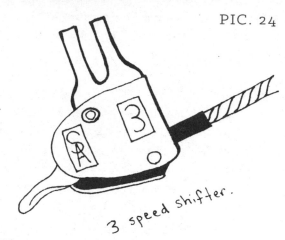

3 speed shifter.

Three speed shifters

Three speed shifters are really different than the others. To begin with, these shifters run gears that you can't see. They are internal gears housed inside of the hub on the rear wheel. They are often found on old style bikes from the 70s and 80s, but there are also the new Nexus shifters and hubs.

The old kind of shifters usually work fine, though they feel kinda funny to use. To shift, you simply push or pull on the shift lever. Some rear hubs require you to stop pedaling while making the shift, others do not. The parts for these shifters are surprisingly still available in shops! You can get a new shifter with the cable all ready to get hooked up to the shifting mechanism on the rear wheel. Sometimes it is best to take your bike into a shop to make sure you get the right parts. Replacing them is basically the old, "take-it-off-put-it-on-the-same-way" method, but the connection to the rear wheel can be different. To connect the cable to the shifting mechanism on the rear wheel, some screw onto a tiny little bike chain looking thing that is attached to a rod that slides and screws into the axle, which makes the gears shift. Some screw onto a rod that is attached to a little chain that is attached to a little arm that screws onto the axle which pushes onto a rod which makes the gears change. Whew! Sounds complicated, but they are actually not really that weird. They are really easy to get at bike recycling joints, and these three speeds are resilient and reliable. And pretty fast, too. We'll talk about adjusting these gears later.

Nexus shifters

I put these in here because I like them. Nexus is a new internally geared hub, made by Shimano. I put one on my old, old cruiser and I like it a lot. They are not difficult to find these days; lots of new cruisers come equipped with them, and they are pretty easy to work on. If you have a Nexus shifter and rear hub (3 or 7 speed), the shifter again simply bolts onto your handlebar with a little Allen head screw. The shifter cable is a special solid, stiff wire that runs through the housing and down to the wheel. These cables and housing come in one piece, with or without the shifter, and are available in shops, usually special ordered. With patience and attention they are as easily replaced as other shifters. To disconnect the cable from the rear shifting mechanism, follow the cable and housing down to the wheel. On the axle is a little shifting mechanism that sits on the end of the axle, just like some old three speeds. The cable runs through this shifting mechanism and bolts down very similarly to other derailleurs. Pay attention to how you remove this cable and, when replacing it, rethread and tighten it the same way.

Once your shifters are in order, you can get the shifting really tuned in by adjusting your derailleurs.

Derailleurs

This section is about adjusting your derailleurs so that shifting is smooth and even—no skipping, no rubbing.

Come on baby, don't fear derailleurs. Derailleurs are, for something so small and with such a French-sounding name, pretty intimidating little gadgets. Many a New Orleans cyclist has scrapped their derailleurs entirely, converting their bike to one speed just to never deal with the things. If you live somewhere flat and want to turn your bike into a one speed, that's your prerogative, but don't do it just

because you're scared of your derailleur! They're not that hard. We'll walk you through it.

Derailleurs (or de-rail-er, if you prefer) are the things that move the chain from gear to gear. You have one in the front (front derailleur) and one in the back (rear derailleur). They are shaped very differently, but both do the same thing and work in the same way. When you shift, the shifter tugs on (or releases tension on) the shifter cable, which in turn moves the derailleur up or down, pushing the chain up and down on the cassette in the back or the chainrings in the front. If your bike isn't shifting properly (i.e., it's slipping out of gear, not hitting all of the gears, or not shifting at all) it is probably a derailleur issue. Before you start turning screws or beating on the derailleur with a wrench, take a close look at your derailleurs. Are they bent? They should both be in a straight line with the chain, meaning that if you look at the rear derailleur from behind, the chain should come straight down and pass through it, not going off all wonky (pic. 25). In the front, the derailleur should be almost perfectly straight

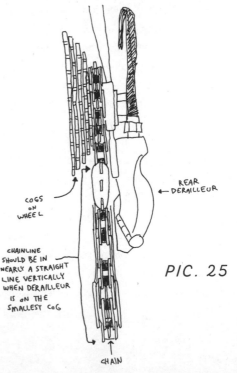

COGS
ON
WHEEL

REAR
DERAILLEUR

CHAINLINE
SHOULD BE IN
NEARLY A STRAIGHT
LINE VERTICALLY
WHEN DERAILLEUR
IS ON THE
SMALLEST COG

PIC. 25

CHAIN

with the path of the chain. If it is all the way up (on the low gear) or all the way down (high gear), it shouldn't be pushing or rubbing on the chain at all. Also, if you have a second-hand bike, look at the bike as a whole. Do the derailleurs match (same brand and model like XLR or LX or whatever)? Are they the same brand name as the shifters? Or something similar looking, like two different brands with Japanese names and similar logos? They don't need to match, but it is good to be aware of differences when you move onto adjusting and possibly getting parts. Assuming they're not bent and not set up wrong (if they are, we'll come back to that later), let's adjust them.

Cables

If the cables are not frayed and the housing is not split or cracked, and the gears are running well, you just need to lube your cables.

To start out, do the fancy cable slackening trick! Shift the shifter all the way to the largest gear while turning the pedals. Once the chain is on this large gear, STOP turning the crank and then down shift the shifter all the way down. This will slack the cable for you and allow you to take the housing out of the cable stops

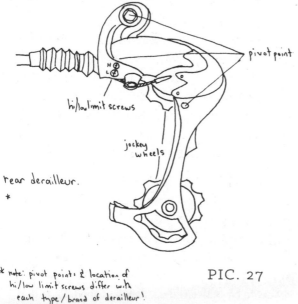

hi/low limit screws

jockey wheels

pivot point

rear derailleur.

*

* note: pivot points & location of hi/low limit screws differ with each type/brand of derailleur!

PIC. 27

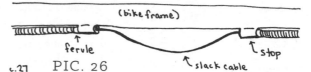

(bike frame)

ferule

slack cable

stop

c.27   PIC. 26

that are brazed onto your bike's frame so that you can lube the cable. Pretty cool huh?! (pic. 26) Lube the cable with dry lube (like Tri-Flow) and then put it back into its stops. If the cables are rusted or frayed, or the housing is split or cracked, replace cable and housing for both the front and rear derailleurs. If your gears rub or the chain falls off, adjust the derailleurs. Follow the next steps!

Now, we will go through the process of how to set up a derailleur from scratch, which will explain the mechanics of the thing.

Rear derailleur

The rear derailleur (pic 27) should be adjusted before the front, because the chain's positioning in the rear affects the shifting in the front. First things first: give your derailleur a look-over. If you have it off of the bike, check the pivots (the parts on the derailleur that pivot and move) by tugging the thing around. Does it feel all loose and wonky? If so, it might not ever shift quite right (especially on old or cheap derailleurs) so maybe you should get a new one. If it seems time for that, take your old one down to the shop and get one that is compatible, runs the same amount of gears, pulls from the same direction, etc. Then, let's move on.

Setting up the rear derailleur

If you feel like your derailleur's pivots are good and it doesn't look bent, go ahead and give it a little clean up with some degreaser, paying special attention to get any gunk or chunks off of the rolling jockey wheels, and then let's install it. Some old derailleurs will either bolt to a little eyelet on the rear of the dropout with a little bolt, or they will have a little u-shaped bracket on a bolt that slides into the dropout (pic. 28). If you are missing either of these bits of hardware, they can be cheaply replaced at a bike shop. Otherwise, your

PIC. 28

pic. derailleur hangers.

derailleur should have a big bolt that attaches to the derailleur hanger with an Allen wrench. Grease the threads on the bolt and attach it.

The derailleur is a pretty fragile, intricate piece of machinery, and because of its placement on the bike, it, and the hangar it attaches with, are easily bent. So much so, in fact, that lots of newer bikes have replaceable derailleur hangers (that little loop on the rear dropout where the derailleur bolts to the frame—this is the part that usually bends when your derailleur takes a whack, sometimes even breaking it off and ruining your frame). Look at the hanger and the derailleur from the rear. Is it bent? The chain should be pretty much straight up and down, parallel with your frame or leaning slightly inward at the bottom of the derailleur.

If your derailleur or derailleur hanger is bent, you should probably get a new one. If it seems straight, you're ready to adjust the derailleur. There are three different adjustments, listed in order below.

Cable

If you are setting your derailleur up from nothing, now would be the time to run the cable. See the sections on "shifters"and the special "cable section", then skip to the section below. Or, if you just took the cable off for lubing like I said above, now would be the time to put it back in the stops (easier to do with the cable slacked, using the slackening trick). Then, when you are in the high (in this case, the smallest) gear, the cable should be taut but not over-tight, and it shouldn't be pulling the derailleur when your shifter is all the way to high. If there is a barrel adjuster on your shifter, derailleur, or

down tube cable stops, set it to the middle of its range so that you can use it to fine-tune the cable tension later.

Now it's time to connect it to the derailleur. There are lots of different kinds, but your derailleur will have a little bolt with a washer on it. This washer should have a little groove on the underside. The width of that groove will be suspiciously similar to the width of your shifter cable. That's because the cable fits into the little groove. If there's no little groove, then there should be a small ledge or something to hold the cable. Slide the cable under the washer and, pulling it taut (but without moving the derailleur), tighten the bolt so that the derailleur is held in place. Now your rear derailleur should move when you shift. Booyah. Once the cable is clamped in, you'll probably have a lot of excess cable hanging off. Eventually, you're going to have to cut that off and put a cable end on it to keep it from tattering, but for now just leave it 'til you're sure you want it bolted like you have it.

Limit screws

There are two "limit"or "set" screws located on your rear derailleur. They are small and probably next to each other on the back of the thing, but if not, you'll find them. It's a pretty small contraption. There are two, one for the high limit and one for the low limit. This means that one keeps your derailleur from throwing the chain off of the low (big) gear, one keeps it from throwing them off of the high (small) gear. If the screws are too loose, that's what happens, which can be really dangerous. If the screws are too tight, then your derailleur won't shift to all the gears correctly.

Limit screw—high: Unless you have a newer reverse-tension type derailleur (which is set up the opposite of the old style—with the derailleur springing to the largest gear when there is no tension on it from the cable), when you let all of the cable tension off, it will fall to its high (small) gearsetting. That's where it wants to be. So let's adjust it so it is good. First, dial

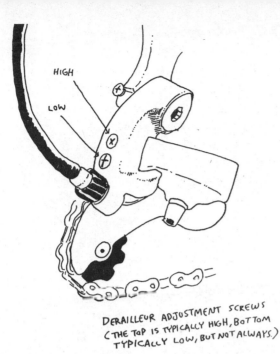

HIGH

LOW

DERAILLEUR ADJUSTMENT SCREWS
(THE TOP IS TYPICALLY HIGH, BOTTOM
TYPICALLY LOW, BUT NOT ALWAYS.)

are helpful because they break and slide around.) Instead, tighten the low limit screw (the one you didn't adjust before) until your chain can easily shift onto the low gear but won't go further than it should. If your derailleur won't quite make it up onto the gear, either your screw is too tight, or your cable needs to be tightened.

Test shift

Now your rear derailleur should be adjusted properly. Try running the gears all the way up and all the way down and make sure all of the gears are engaging. With friction shifters, the limit screws should be all you need to adjust to get them running smoothly up and down. With indexing shifters, dial it down to the highest (smallest) gear. You can double check here that your cable is tightened correctly by loosening the cable tension bolt and then making sure the derailleur is still in the same position, gently pull the cable taut, and retighten the bolt. Now, dial up one gear and the cable should jump up to the second smallest gear. If it does, count yourself lucky. If it doesn't, turn the barrel adjuster on either your shifter or your derailleur to get it to hop smoothly to that second gear. When it does that, dial back down to the smallest gear, and then see if you get one gear per click and dial up to the biggest gear. If this isn't perfect, run though your directions again. When you got it, cut the cable's end (with your bike cable cutters!), leaving about two inches after the bolt and squeeze a cable tip onto the end!

Again: lube yer cable, high limit screw, low limit screw, check cable tension, barrel adjust. Do this until you get it. Great!

Front derailleur

To set up the front derailleur (pic 29), start out by bolting the derailleur collar onto the seat-tube. Before you tighten the collar all the way, pull the derailleur up (meaning, pull it out towards you and towards the big chainring) with your hands. The bottom of the

the shifter all the way down to the high (smallest) gear. Now look at the derailleur from the back. The chain-line should be a hair to the outside of the smallest gear. If it is further (or if your chain has fallen off and gotten all jammed in-between the gears and the frame), your high screw is too loose. If your screws aren't labeled (with a tiny H and L next to them to tell them apart), you'll have to guess which one is the high. Do an eenie-meenie and pick one. Tighten it one turn. If you didn't see the derailleur move at all, loosen it back to where it was and try the other screw. When you find the right screw, turn it until the chainline and jockey wheels are in line with the high (smallest) gear.

Limit screw-low: Now, go ahead and shift the rear derailleur all the way up to low (I know, it's confusing), or the biggest gear. Again, if the chain wants to fall off of the gear (between the cassette or freewheel and the wheel), don't let it 'cuz it's kind of a pain to pry it out. (Your bike might have a little plastic thing there to prevent your chain from falling off. This is so that stores (department stores usually) can slap the bikes together without any real skill or attention to how it shifts. They're usually more annoying than they

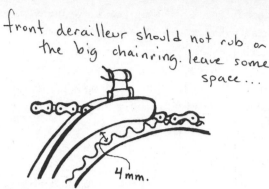

front derailleur should not rub on the big chainring. leave some space...

4mm.

derailleur should be about three or four millimeters (just under half a centimeter) from the top of the teeth on the chainring. The line of the derailleur should also run parallel to the line of the chainring, so they are parallel to each other. Bolt it down when it seems right. You will usually need either a 9mm wrench or a 5 Allen wrench.

Cable

Basically, running your cables varies a lot from bike to bike, as is discussed in the special cable section. But the cables especially vary on the front derailleur. The main difference with the front derailleur is whether you are using a top-pull or bottom-pull front derailleur. Derailleurs are traditionally "bottom-pull," with the cable coming up from under the bottom bracket and pulling the arm of the derailleur down to move it. Mountain bikes now often use "top-pull" type derailleurs, with the cable coming from above to avoid getting the cable sprayed with mud all the time. Make sure you have the right type of derailleur for your frame. When running new cable, just be sure you pay special attention to how the cable was run before you clip it all off to put on your new stuff. If you get confused, refer to the special cable section for instructions and advice. Once your cable is run, lead it all the way up to the front derailleur, and then let it be for a minute. We're gonna set the low limit screw before we clamp the cable down onto the derailleur.

Limit screws

Limit screws (pic 30; sometimes called "set screws") control how far your derailleur can move in either direction. These are two tiny screws located somewhere on the top or sides of the derailleur. I don't care if your bike is some beaten old department store grocery-getter or some hill-bombing pseudo-spaceship-looking mountain bike, if it has a front derailleur, that derailleur has limit screws. They are either philips head, flathead, or hex wrench screws (little bitty ones). Find them. On the front derailleur, the set screw closest to the frame controls how far the derailleur can move down, towards the small chain-rings, at least on older derailleurs. On new ones, it might be the other way around. Most derailleurs will be labeled high or low, otherwise some experimentation might be necessary. If the screw is too loose, the derailleur will move too far down and drop the chain in between the chain-rings and the frame. If the screw is too tight, the derailleur won't shift onto the small rings right. So when you set up the derailleur, before worrying about the cable at all, you want to adjust the inside screw. This is so that it will hit the gears where you want without any interference from the cable pulling on it, which can mess it up and keep it from ever really shifting right.

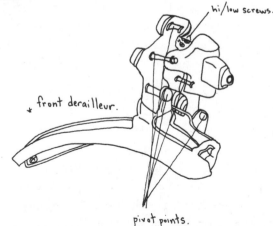

hi/low screws.

* front derailleur.

pivot points.

* note: pivot points & location of hi/low limit screws differ with each type/brand of derailleur!

PIC. 29

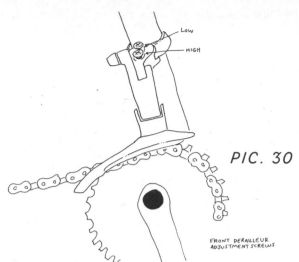

PIC. 30

FRONT DERAILLEUR
ADJUSTMENT SCREWS

Now loosen the limit screw closest to the frame of the bike. Loosen it a lot. Watch the derailleur closely. If it wasn't already loose, you should be able to see the derailleur moving inward towards the frame as you loosen it. Now, the chain should be on the little chain-ring. Adjust that limit screw until there is about one millimeter of space between the edge of the chain and the inside lip of the derailleur (on the side closest to the frame of the bike). When you pedal, ideally, the derailleur should not rub on the chain, or should only rub very slightly. Once you have the cable properly hooked up at the shifter and run down to the derailleur, you can hook up the derailleur. There will be a little bolt with some sort of a washer where the cable bolts in. The washer should have a little groove running down it. That's where the cable should get clamped down. Don't over-tighten. If there is a barrel adjuster on either your shifter or your derailleur, set them in the middle, so that you will have some range of adjustment after you have everything set up. Once the cable is clamped to your hub, which is pretty darn easy, look on the hub itself for a little cap that you can either take off or flip open. Pour about a tablespoon of oil in there. You can use 3 in 1 oil, motor oil, or Phil Oil. Cap it back up. Do this every time you do a tune up (which is like twice a year, right? Every three months? At least do this that often, ok?). Now, let's adjust your cable.

There are a couple different types of these shifting mechanisms.

1) One looks like this: It has a little rounded nut-like thing that screws onto the axle. Out of the end of that you will see a little rod that goes into the axle. Attached to that rod is a thing that looks like the tiniest little bike chain, which is attached to the cable. When the cable is pulled, the rod moves in or out of the hub, changing the gears.

2) The other type is a nut-like thing that screws onto your axle and has a little lever attached to it that is attached to your cable. As the cable pulls, that lever adjusts and moves a rod that, again, changes the gears. The way either of these attach to the cable can be different; either it screws on or it is bolted on with a tiny bolt, similar to the way a brake cable at-taches to a brake. You can adjust the cable tension by either twisting where this screws on, or loosening that nut and adjusting the cable.

So! While pedaling, set your shifter on second gear, then stop pedaling. With shifting mechanism type 1, adjust your cable tension until the end of the rod (which you can do through the end of that rounded nut thing on the axle) is flush with the end of that rounded nut thing. With shifting mechanism type 2, adjust the cable until the indicating mark (often red) on the end of that rod can be seen through the little viewing hole or window on that little lever. Good!

Now, run through your gears (again, with some, you may need to stop pedaling between shifting to get the gears to change). You should get three different gears. If you don't, try making some minor adjustments with the cable tensioning screws located where the cable attaches to the shifting mechanism. Test again. Try and try again. It takes a little tweaking here and there sometimes, but keep at it. Many shops don't like to deal with these at all, but we did a lot at French Quarter bikes. As there are no standards with these and all of them look different, I only had one rule—deal with second gear. If this doesn't work or you can't deal at all, you can do one of a few things. 1) Turn the cable tension adjuster until you find a gear you like and then treat it like a 1 speed. 2) Find a new three speed wheel somewhere, or 3) My favorite option: These great little 3 speeds are even greater as a single speed! Simply strip off the rear wheel, the brake levers and brakes themselves, and the shifting stuff all together and get yourself a good 26 x 1 3/8 coaster wheel for the back! Put that baby on and now you have yourself a sweet, simple, lighter little single speed. Yay!

NEXUS HUB ADJUSTMENTS.

Again, Nexus hubs are internally-geared three speed hubs made by Shimano. As with the Nexus shifters, Nexus hubs are fairly easy to service; beautifully easy actually. The cable must be attached to the shifting mechanism on the hub while the shifter is set to first gear. Then, simply set the shifter on second gear, as above, line up the red indicator between the lines in the little window and you should be good to go. If you

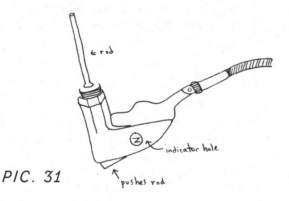

← rod

indicator hole

PIC. 31

pushes rod

pic. types of 3 speed mechanisms.

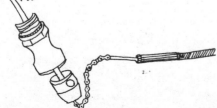

rod

hear any minor clicking, adjust this out by adjusting the barrel adjuster. Rad huh?

Converting to one-speed

We are putting this little extra bit in here with derailleurs because it seems like a good time to mention the alternative of taking your shifters and derailleurs off and making your multi speed into a single speed. These days, there are a lot of fixed gear, track bikes on the road, and we see a lot of people being wooed by them. A lot of the appeal of riding a fixed gear is the idea of taking any so-so road bike frame and turn into a really light street machine. An alternative, though, is to just make your bike a one speed with brakes, or just one brake to lighten and simplify your ride. A lot of folks use only a front brake, which provides better, skid-free stopping. If you do this, just be sure to invest in a decent brake! You can do this a few different ways. 1. Getting a BMX single speed freewheel that will screw onto your rear wheel in place of a freewheel with multiple gears. Be aware that, in order to do this, you will have to "re-dish" your wheel, which means re-truing in a way that moves the whole hub over so the new bmx freewheel is perfectly in line with your front chainring. This is not an easy job, and I would leave it to a shop to do this for you! You can't run the bike if the chainline is not straight, so be aware! 2. By setting your rear derailleurs set screw to keep the chain on one rear cog that is in line with your front chainring, then taking off the excess (shifters, shifter cables, front derailleur, and all but one front chainring). Again, this will only work if you keep your chainline straight from front chainring to rear cog! 3) Getting a rear chain tensioner to replace your rear derailleur and doing everything you just did in option 2. (pic. 32)

There are lots of ways to do this, but please don't do the old "shorten the chain and just wrap it around one of the rear cogs on your cassette or freewheel"! It will eventually bind and you'll go flying off your bike before you figure out what happened. Really! You might think it will be fine, and it may for a while, and then one day, wham!

PIC. 32

a chain tensioner is kinda
like half a rear
derailleur.

Whichever way you do choose, it's a fair amount of
work, but if you've got crappy derailleurs that you're
sick of struggling with, and you live somewhere where
it's flat enough to make a lot of shifting unnecessary, go
for it. We would suggest going to your local bike shop
and getting advice on what you need to make your
specific bike into a one speed, because there are so
many variables (cassette or freewheel, type of dropouts
you have, etc.). If you are going to do it, be prepared to
spend a day on it, and to do the following: Remove and
shorten chain, replace freewheel or remove cogs on
cassette (optional), possibly install a chain tensioner (if
needed), possibly add spacers to your axle and re-dishing
your wheel. Center the rim by loosening the spokes on
one side and tightening them on the other side. This is
necessary to keep your rim centered between the brakes.
If all of this sounds do-able to you, get a mechanic's
opinion and, hell, go for it. Or get a friend or shop to do
it for you. One speeds are a lot simpler and far lower
maintenance, and are great in the right conditions!

Troubleshooting

DERAILLEUR WON'T SHIFT INTO GEAR
Tension screws misadjusted, cable too loose or too
tight, derailleur bent.

DERAILLEUR SLIPS OUT OF GEAR
Shifters need tightening. Depending on the type, there
will be some sort of screw on the outside of the shifter
that you can tighten, either by hand or with a flathead
screwdriver.

CHAIN IS FALLING OFF THE GEARS
Limit screws too loose.

DERAILLEUR IS SKIPPING GEARS
Cable tension is wrong. If it's skipping gears from small
to big gears, it's too tight. If it's the opposite, then it's
too loose. Adjust with barrel adjusters, or if that doesn't
work, tighten cable on the derailleur.

SHIFTING IS UNRELIABLE
If your shifter seems to be doing something different
every time, it could be that your cable is gunked up
(replace it) or that the pivots on your derailleur are
worn out (replace the derailleur), or that your derailleur
is bent. If it's bent, see if you can tell how. You can
try to bend it back, but be careful not to bend your
derailleur hanger. A bent derailleur hanger can also be
causing poor shifting. The fancy tool for fixing this is a
derailleur hanger alignment gauge, which they'll have
at any bike shop. Or if you can tell how it's bent you
can probably fix it with a big-assed adjustable wrench.

Changing brake and gear cables

Cables are kind of like the tendons and ligaments
of your bike. Just like the thin tissue of the Achilles
tendon moves your foot around, your shifter cable
has the task of forcing your derailleur up and down
on the cassette and chainrings. And your brake cable,
well, your life might depend on it working well. So it's
important to make sure that they're installed correctly.

Types of inner wire and housing

What we're calling the "Cable" is made up of basically two parts, the inner wire and the housing. The inner wire is the steel wire, which is made up of lots of tiny little wires and, these days, usually coated with Teflon to prevent rust and help it move through the housing easily. The housing is the plastic coated sleeve that the inner wire moves through, which isn't made of plastic but of plastic-coated steel.

The only difference between the brake and derailleur inner wires is in the little anchor on the end that holds into either your brake or shifter lever (pic. 33). As for the cable housing, there are two types: brake housing and shifter housing (pic. 36). The difference is the construction of the inner steel tubing. In brake housing, the steel is one long coil like a spring. If you were to take it and pull on it, it would come unraveled, but it can't really be compressed. That's why it's used for brakes, to withstand all of that sudden force when you get cut off by a cab and slam your brakes on. In shifter housing, the steel core is made of long strands side by side like a tiny, rolled-up sushi mat or something. This is to create less friction on your shifter cable and insure smooth shifting. It doesn't need to withstand a bunch of pressure, so it isn't built to. Because of this, you should never use shifter housing for brake cables, because it will split when you apply pressure. If you're in a pinch, though, you can use brake housing for your shifter cables.

Cutting cables

You shouldn't cut the inner wire of your cables until you've got 'em all set up, to make sure the length is right. Once you're ready, the inner wire of your cable can be cut with a sharp pair of good snips or dykes, as they're called. You just have to make sure that you get a good clean cut without any stray strands of wire sticking out because these will give you problems if you need to take them out and re-insert them in the housing. To cut the housing, you will need a special housing cutter. This is a heavy-duty pair of snips with a rounded area that fits the contour of the housing so as not to crush it (which it still sort of does, as we'll discuss in ten-to-thirty seconds, depending on how fast you read). Park Tools makes a pretty standard version of this tool, but it got crappier in the last few years. Jagwire used to make one with a little reamer on the end (pic. 35). This was a rad feature, so if you can find one like that, get it.

Dressing brake housing

When you cut the brake housing, it usually crushes the steel spiral that runs through it (pic. 36). This leaves little jagged edges that will shred your cable in no time if you don't clean it up. By far the best way to do this is with a grinding wheel and scribe (you can make one by grinding down an old screwdriver or using a spoke, spoke nippple and some brake housing like the one in pic. 37), though if you don't have that, a file will work. On a grinding wheel, simply take the end of your housing and twirl it as you touch it to the wheel. This

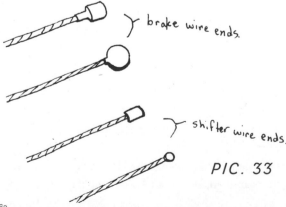

brake wire ends.

shifter wire ends.

PIC. 33

← REAMER

CABLE CUTTERS- BIKE CABLE & HOUSING REQUIRES A SPECIAL TYPE OF CUTTER. SOME, LIKE JAGWIRE BRAND, COME WITH A BUILT-IN REAMER FOR CLEANING UP THE HOUSING AFTER IT IS CUT.

PIC. 35

NOT GOOD   GOOD!

PIC. 36

BRAKE   SHIFTER

should grind it down smooth in no time, but it will leave a little chunk of molten plastic stuck in the middle. Using your scribe to drill this out will flare the hot metal a little bit too, leaving a perfectly clean opening for your cable to slide through. If you don't have access to a grinder, file the end of the housing (remember that files only cut in a forward direction), until the same effect is achieved. Shifter housing doesn't need to be dressed.

Ferrules and end caps (cable tips)

(pic. 38) Ferrules are the little metal or plastic caps that go on the ends of cable housing. Pretty much every piece of housing should get a ferrule of some sort (they've come in lots of different shapes over the years and variety packs are available), though some bikes have cable stops that don't require ferrules.

"End caps" or "cable tips" are the little metal things that get pinched onto the ends of your cables. All inner wires should have these to keep them from unraveling, which they'll do quite quickly without a tip.

Cable length

These days, there are so many types of brakes and shifters, and so many configurations of cable stop on frames, that it can be pretty confusing to run your cables. There are, however, a few basic rules of thumb to help you make sure your cables are set up correctly.

The most important thing to look out for is not cutting your housing too short. It should be long enough that you can turn the handlebars all the way to either side without pulling the housing out of the stops. You wouldn't believe how easy it is to make this mistake, and thus how many people there are out there on bikes that suddenly downshift every time they turn left. The easiest way to avoid this is to cut all of your housing, before running your inner wire through it, and making sure it fits right. If you are re-placing housing that is cracked or worn out but seems to be cut right, simply cut new housing in the same lengths.

PIC. 38

ferrules.

cable tip.

While longer is definitely better than shorter, you don't want it too long either, because this leads to inefficient (and possibly unreliable) shifting or braking. The rule of thumb for this is that the cable should be routed away from its destination (the brake or derailleur) as little as possible. If your housing is bowed up off your frame and then back down, it's going to affect the cable movement, especially between the chain-stay and rear derailleur. Once you've run the inner wire through the housing, and through the bolts that will attach it to the brakes or the derailleurs, cut it off with about two inches of extra cable sticking off.

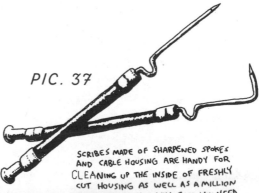

PIC. 37

SCRIBES MADE OF SHARPENED SPOKES AND CABLE HOUSING ARE HANDY FOR CLEANING UP THE INSIDE OF FRESHLY CUT HOUSING AS WELL AS A MILLION OTHER THINGS YOU WILL FIND YOU NEED A LITTLE POKEY THING FOR.

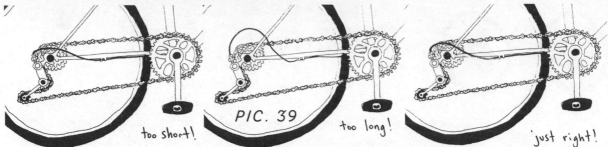

too short!

PIC. 39

too long!

just right!

Replacing cable and housing for brakes or derailleurs

Clip the cable tip off the one you are removing. Loosen the bolt holding the wire down to the brake or derailleur. Pull the wire and housing away from that bolt, out of any cable stops on the bike (this is easy for the kind with the slit cut out of the bottom of the cable stop, requiring more pulling to get real rusty cable out of the solid cylinder type). Pull the wire and housing out in one piece if you can, all the way up to the brake lever or shifter. Pull the housing off of the wires and then carefully get the wire out of the brake lever (usually very self explanatory and visible) or shifter (which can be tricky, refer to the shifter section for different wire set-ups). Be careful not to lose ferrules or cable ends. And again, be aware of the original configuration of things before you take them apart! Memorize it or draw it out or take a picture of it so you don't get stuck when you try to put it back together later.

Now, you can either take your wire and housing to a shop and have the wire matched and the new housing cut to match the length of the old housing, or you can just buy a wire with the proper end to fit your brake lever or shifter, and buy a big length of housing by the foot and cut it yourself when you get home. Whichever the case, be sure you get the proper ferules for your housing, cable tips if you need them, and even new barrel adjusters for your brake levers if yours are munched up. When you got all the stuff, go home and put the wires and housing back the way they were, first threading the wire into your brake lever or shifter, then into the housing, or first piece of housing. Stop in any cable stops using the proper ferrules and make it all the way down to your brake or derailleur, bolting the wire back on when you get there and cutting off the excess after leaving about two inches after the bolt! Whew! That was easy, huh!? And really satisfying after you see how much smoother your cables run!

Note: I know this seems silly, but sometimes this can be confusing. Once your cable is all gone you might forget which brake lever attached to which brake and which shifter to which derailleur! Oh no! Ok. With shifters, the left generally runs the front gears and the right the rear gears. The left has three chicks and the rear maybe has seven. Cool. The brakes are the same! Left—front, right—rear! For safety's sake. Well, this is only true, for some odd reason, in countries where people drive on the same side as these front brakes. I mean, that's not important, but it's hella weird, and pretty interesting. I always install mine opposite so it is easier to ride my bike with a cup of coffee in my left hand, but when I have to stop fast with only a front brake it is a little scary! Flip over! But I've done it without spilling a drop of joe! Don't try this at home.

6. Bearing Systems

The beautiful bearing! I had an old friend who once said that bearings remind her of pearls in an oyster when she opened up her bottom bracket. They sit there, shiny and perfect in a bed of grease waiting to be uncovered! They are so small and delicate, yet strong enough to carry the entire weight of you AND your bicycle (and the mounds of junk you might be carrying with you!). They are the base of all machines,

...overhauling...

and create smooth, low-friction movement in things all around us in a totally world-transforming way. They are movement creators. And all they are, are little, tiny, super strong, metal balls. Wow.

Ethan was the one who pointed out to me the similarity in all of the moving parts of a bicycle—the axles, bottom bracket, and headset (and even some pedals). They all are composed of the same basic system, built up with cups, bearings, cones and lock nuts. They each require a precise adjustment and lots of lube. These adjustments are the most core part of your tune up. When these, most essential, moving parts run well, it really is, essentially, like getting a brand new bike! So don't skimp here!

The best place to start with a bearing system is with an inspection. Again, you want to determine whether you want an adjustment or an overhaul. Cracking all of these babies open, shooting in a bunch of grease and adjusting them is an adjustment. Pulling the whole thing apart, cleaning the parts, inspecting them, replacing what is worn, then greasing the hell out of them and reassembling the parts is an overhaul. Often,

all of the moving parts are in about the same state of wear, and you can choose between doing a tune up for maintenance (adjustments), or giving the whole thing an overhaul, either cause it needs it, or because it is winter and you are bored, or you just want to learn a bunch of fun new stuff... For overhauls, you'll have your grease out, a clean space to work in whether you do just the axles, or the axles, headset and bottom bracket, so if you have the time, give your old bike a serious bit of love and affection and do the whole damn thing. Though, it may be that your headset needs an adjustment while your bottom bracket needs an overhaul, and you just don't feel like dealing with more than you really need to. That is fine, too. If an axle has been ridden out of adjustment for a long time, or a headset has dropped some bearings, you really should do the overhaul. Same with extreme cases of rust or broken parts, little pieces of metal falling out, gritty sounds or rough or sticking movements. Waiting too long to fix this stuff will wear out your components, cost you more money, and make riding no fun. Besides these things, the decision to adjust or overhaul is really your call.

We'll try to give you a good description of both adjustments and overhauls here. In either case, make sure first that you have the necessary tools. Most bearing adjustments require special tools. You will need the correct size cone wrenches for your wheels, a headset wrench to fit your headset, and a bottom bracket tool specific to your bottom bracket. These tools are explained in the tool section of the book. You can find out your size by trying different wrenches out at a shop, or asking a friend or a nice person at a shop. A shop shouldn't have an issue with doing this for you, especially if you intend to buy the tool from them. Be sure to have a lot of grease ready! White lithium (in a pinch, though thicker stuff definitely lasts longer), or Park Tools grease, or Phil grease in a tube with a nice grease gun attached is the best way. Grease in a tub is fine too. There are lots of kinds. Ask your shop what they use. Get some rags too, and cultivate a little patience and you are ready to go! Great!

a. Headsets

To begin, headsets come in two different types, threaded and threadless. The distinction is in how the stem attaches to the fork within a system of bearings that make the handlebars turn so you can steer your bike. In this explanation, we will take you through how to make simple adjustments to your headsets, and the stems that work with them. We'll also give you some idea of how to do a simple headset replacement, though we do not explain certain parts of a full overhaul, as the replacement of parts such as cups and races require special tools that are a little over our heads for this manual. Sorry. We'll give you an idea how these parts work and walk you through what we can. Ok! Let's go!

Threaded headsets

A lot of bikes have threaded headsets—older bikes, like three speeds and cruisers, most road bikes, and lots of lower end mountain bikes. Threaded refers to the fork.

It means that the top of the fork has threads on it and the headset parts screw onto the fork. With this system, tightening or loosening those parts makes an adjustment. Though the stem is separate from headset it is often helpful, if not necessary to remove the stem to properly adjust the headset.

LOOSENING OR REMOVING THE STEM

The stems for these types of headsets are called quill stems, and they have a bolt, which runs through them with a "wedge" screwed onto the bottom of it that holds your stem tight into the steerer tube (pic. 40). To loosen the stem, you need to loosen the bolt on the top of the stem. It is usually a 13 mm wrench or a 6 mm Allen wrench (be careful… with some of the better quality stems, these Allen bolts may be standard size, not metric). Loosen this bolt a bunch of turns and then get a little hammer and hit the top of the bolt. Sometimes is just takes a little tap, but sometimes it takes a real good whack. When you "get it" the bolt should fall back down towards the stem and the stem should be loose. Now you can pull the stem out (sometimes this takes a little wiggling and pulling). If you have shifters or brakes attached to the handlebars here, it is best not to just drop the stem and let this stuff just hang around. Instead, take some tape, or a zip tie, and attach the stem to the top tube or something on your bike so that it is stable but also out of your way. Now, you can work on your headset.

PIC. 40

stem bolt & wedge.

Note: If you simply need to adjust your stem height, loosen the stem bolt as shown above. Pull your stem up and, for good measure, put a little grease on it, and then adjust the height. Make sure you don't pull the stem above the "max height" which should be stamped onto your stem. Then, hold the stem in place, make sure the handlebars are centered over your front wheel, and then tighten the bolt back down.

Adjusting

An adjustment needs to be made if the handlebars bind or don't turn freely, or if there is play in your headset. You can test for play by checking to see if there is side to side movement of the fork in the steerer tube. If it is loose, the headset needs tightening; if it is tight, it needs a little loosening. That makes sense, right?

You can remove the stem if you want or need to (if you have a front basket, it is helpful to get it out of the way). Removing the front wheel is helpful here as well, as it makes the fork a little lighter to hold into place. Loosen the top nut (the locknut) on the headset just enough to free up the adjusting cone. Pull the washer underneath it (a keyed washer that helps hold the adjustment) up away from the adjusting cone. Now, while pushing up on the fork, screw the cone down to tighten the headset, or unscrew it to loosen it. Let go of the fork and check the adjustment. You want the fork to turn smoothly, but also not be loose or wobbly. Do this until the adjustment feels good. When it does, push the keyed washer back down against the adjusting cone and then screw the locknut back down. Now is the tricky part (the same tricky part you will find in any bearing system adjustment). Hold the adjusting cone in place either with a headset wrench (pic. 41) that fits your bike, or with channel lock pliers (if the cone edge is the round ribbed edge type that looks like the edge of a quarter), while tightening the locknut down against it. I usually jam my knee between the forks to hold it still while I make the adjustment. The key is to lock the adjusting cone in place by tightening the locknut on top of it. Tighten it 'til it sticks and then check the adjustment. Re-do if necessary.

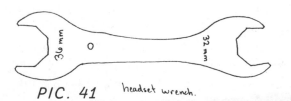

PIC. 41   headset wrench.

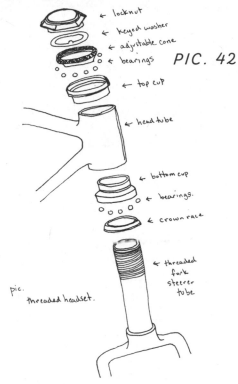

← locknut
← keyed washer
← adjustable cone
← bearings   PIC. 42
← top cup
← head tube
← bottom cup
← bearings.
← crown race
← threaded fork steerer tube

pic.
threaded headset.

Overhauling

With an overhaul, it is necessary to take the stem out as described above, and, again, it is helpful to take the front wheel off. Loosen the locknut and remove it. Remember—set these parts aside in the order and position that they were removed so you can reinstall them in the same exact way!

Remove the keyed washer, and then while holding the fork up, unscrew the adjusting cone and remove it completely. Pull the fork out of the steerer tube, being careful not to drop loose bearings or the bearing cage from the bottom cup on the steerer tube. Pull the bearings (these are quite small, don't lose any!) or bearing cage out of the top cup, taking note of whether the cage is facing up or down, and do the same with the bottom bearings or cage. Now, with all of the parts removed, taking note not to lose the order in which they were removed, clean all the parts of grease and dirt until the little things look shiny and new! Don't forget to clean the race on the fork! Then, replace all of the parts in the order in which they were removed, being sure to fill those cups full with plenty of grease and with the bearings facing in their original direction, and then make the adjustment as described above! Great!

Note: If any of those parts look worn, or you have pitted bearings, pitted cups or cones, they should be replaced. If you don't replace them you won't have smooth turning forks. To replace the parts, bring your old parts to a shop, including bearings, and have them match your old parts. Get the parts and then reinstall them in the order they were in and adjust as above. If the cups or the crown race are worn, you should take the bike down to the shop to get these parts replaced. Installing and removing the cups and installing the crown race require special tools. You can sometimes get away without using them, but to make sure they are all real straight, bring it to a shop for this. Ok!

Threadless headsets

Most new bikes have these. Where the old-style threaded headsets were separate from the stem, the stem and headset are integrated on these newer models (see pic 43). The steerer tube is stuck through the head tube, the stem is bolted to the steerer tube, usually via a star nut that is sunk into the steerer tube, then the stem is clamped to the steerer with pinch bolt(s) on the side. It's pretty simple.

Threadless headsets are available in a few different sizes, but mainly 1" (usually road bikes) or 1 1/8"

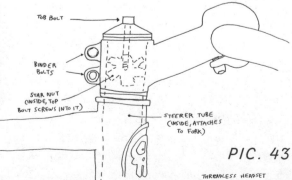

TOB BOLT

BINDER BOLTS

STAR NUT (INSIDE, TOP BOLT SCREWS INTO IT)

STEERER TUBE (INSIDE, ATTACHES TO FORK)

PIC. 43

THREADLESS HEADSET

(usually mountain). This measurement is the outside diameter of the steerer tube.

Adjusting

If your headset is too loose, you will probably feel it wiggling if you stand over the bike and press down on the handlebars, with your weight holding the frame in place. It will also make an odd clunk if you pick the front wheel up and drop it. If it is too tight, the wheel won't flop to the side when you pick up the front of the bike, or it will feel as though the wheel is sticking in one position when you're riding.

To adjust the headset, loosen the binder bolts on the sides of the stem. These generally take a 5mm Allen wrench. Tighten (or loosen, depending on your issue, but usually you'll be tightening this) the bolt on top of the headset. Sighting down the headset from riding position, line the stem up with the front wheel and tighten the binder bolt(s) on the side of the stem. Turn the handlebars side to side and test the adjustment. The bars should move smoothly with no binding, but not feel loose. If it feels good, you're done. Voila.

Overhauling

This is pretty much the same as a threaded headset. (See pic 44.) Remove the top cap of the headset and loosen the binder bolt(s) on the stem. The stem should slide off easily, followed by some spacers, the bearing race, and the bearings. Set these parts down in the order and position they were removed in so you can put it together the same way you took it apart. If the bearing race gets stuck, whack your steerer tube with a rubber mallet. Your threadless headset probably has bearing cages in it, and these aren't really standardized, so don't lose 'em. It's hard to replace one, especially if you don't have the old one to compare it to. If there aren't cages, be careful when removing the bearings, especially from the bottom. If you have a work stand, it's easiest to remove and reinstall your bottom bearings with the bike clamped in upside down.

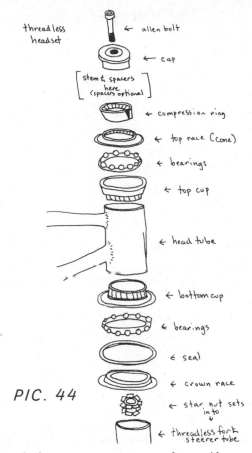

threadless headset

← allen bolt

← cap

[stem & spacers here (spacers optional)]

← compression ring

← top race (cone)

← bearings

← top cup

← head tube

← bottom cup

← bearings

← seal

← crown race

← star nut sets in to ↓

← threadless fork steerer tube

PIC. 44

Clean the bearings, cups, cones and races (the one on the fork too!), and use lots of grease when reinstalling. Put it back together the same way you took it apart, making the adjustment as described above.

Note: Again, if your cups or crown race are worn you should take it to a shop to replace them. Read threaded headset note above.

Troubleshooting

TIGHTNESS IN STEERING

Loosen headset (see "adjusting" previously)

HEADSET LOOSE

Tighten headset (see above)

HEADSET WIGGLES LIKE IT'S LOOSE AND STEERING IS TIGHT

Bearing cages might be upside down. There is no set way that these face, you just have to look and figure out which way to put them so that the cages aren't touching anything, just the bearings—or the steerer tube might be bent, which means you need a new fork. Bummer.

GRITTY, GRINDY OR SLUGGISHNESS WHEN TURNING

Parts need a good cleaning. Follow "overhauling" above, making sure to thoroughly clean and relube all parts.

TIGHT SPOT AND A LOOSE SPOT IN TURNING

Cups are pressed in crooked, crown race is not on straight. Check that these look pressed in or on well and level. Or fork is bent, or steerer tube is worn. Check fork for straightness, look at steerer tube top and bottom for evenness

b. Bottom Brackets

All of the rotational systems on a bike, that is, the parts that spin: wheels, headset, and bottom bracket (and even some fancy pedals), work the same. They all have bearings, some sort of cone (the thing that holds the bearings in place and spins along them), a cup (what the bearings sit in) and an axle or spindle that goes through the whole thing. These days, a lot of the stuff you buy from the bike shop tends to be a little different. Sealed bottom brackets are just a sealed cartridge that screws in and that's it (and now, the newer, fancier thing is the outboard bottom bracket, which is what high end mountain bikes have. We won't be getting into that. Sorry). They have all the same parts as a traditional three piece bottom bracket, but you can't access them. So when it's done, it's done. It'll start creaking, or grinding, or rubbing, and you just take it out and buy a new one. Some people love these because it's zero maintenance, and they do last a good long time, even on the cheaper end of things—especially if you're just tooling around town on the bike and not going out on trails or anything. Some people hate them because they want to open up

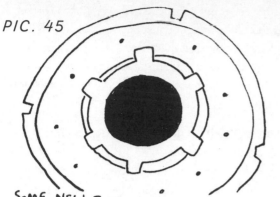

SOME NEW BOTTOM BRACKET SPINDLES ARE SPLINED ON THE ENDS, NOT SQUARE

and overhaul everything and keep their parts from the seventies alive forever. This makes sense, too.

Whether you want to go for a sealed bb or not is entirely up to you. If your bike has the old style bb with the spindle and cups, this chapter will walk you through working on them.

The different types of bottom brackets

THREE-PIECE—the traditional type of BB found in road and mountain bikes. The "three pieces" refers to the spindle (axle) and the two cranks. Traditionally the spindle has a tapered square end that the crank arms get pressed on to when you tighten the crank arm bolts. Nowadays lots of people use fancy "splined" cranks, like the Shimano Octalink or ISIS, which aren't square but are shaped more like a cog (pic. 45).

ONE-PIECE—most single speed cruisers have these. The crank is one big, sort of S-shaped piece of cast steel that slides through the bottom bracket shell.

TWO-PIECE—new super-high end stuff that we're not going to get into, though they do work well, it seems.

Bottom bracket and spindle widths

If you are replacing or rebuilding your bottom bracket, take note that they come in different shell widths (the width of the actual bottom bracket shell on your frame) and a (pretty much endless) variety of spindle lengths. This has to be taken into consideration if you are replacing parts on them. Most newer bikes have a bottom bracket width of 68mm, with some mountain bikes having oversized shells of 73mm. Older bikes have all sorts of different sizes, and the spindles need to match up with these. I once met a guy who was a frame-builder in the seventies, who told me a story about how he was rebuilding some old three-speed, I believe a Robin Hood. He and his pals couldn't find a replacement bottom bracket, so they rebuilt the one they had with molten steel and then tempered it in their oven. Hopefully, if you're replacing yours, it will be more common.

The length of the spindle you need is determined by your chainline, that is, how many gears you have in the back and how many chainrings you have in the front.

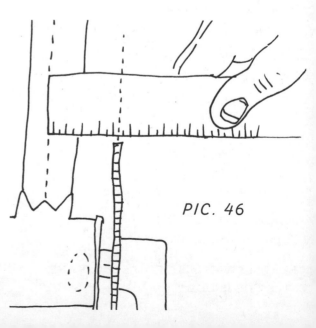

PIC. 46

CHAINLINE. (pic. 46)

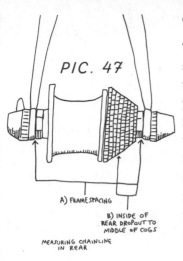

PIC. 47

A) FRAME SPACING

B) INSIDE OF REAR DROPOUT TO MIDDLE OF COGS

MEASURING CHAINLINE IN REAR

To get your chain straight, you need to figure out what your exact chainline is. This means that the front chainrings need to be the same distance from the middle of the bike frame as your mid-most cog in the back, so that the chain is in a straight line and won't pop off the gears. This is especially important with one speeds. Most people just eyeball it, and sometimes that's okay, but with a little bit of measurement, you can get it exactly right, then change the spacing accordingly with spacers in the front, on the chainrings. To get the chainline measurement, use a ruler or calipers (if you got 'em) and figure out first what the spacing of your rear dropouts is (sometimes called the over-locknut distance). Some common rear dropout spacings:

120 mm—5 speeds and newer track hubs

125 mm—6 and 7 speeds

130 mm—7 speed mountain bikes, 8, 9, 10 speed road bikes

135 mm—rear 7, 8, 9 speed mountain bikes

Measure from the inside of the drive-side (on the right if you're looking from the back) dropout to the middle of the cogs (or cog on a one-speed). (pic. 47) Double this and subtract the overall dropout-spacing. Then divide this number by two and that's your chainline-measurement.

Let's say you found an old seven speed in your mom's garage and live in pancake-flat Iowa. So you want to turn it into a one-speed. The dropouts are 125mm (A) apart and your dropout-to-middle-cog measurement is 19mm(B). So:

$$19 \times 2 = 38$$

$$125 - 38 = 87$$

$$87 / 2 = 43.5$$

43.5 is your chainline measurement, so that's how far the middle of your front chain-line should be from the middle of the seat-tube. You want it to be within a millimeter or so of this number. If it's close, you can get little spacer from a bike shop that goes between the crank spider and the chainring. You can also sometimes put the chainring on the other side of the spider. If it's way off, though, you need a different bottom bracket spindle.

When to adjust or overhaul

Here are some signs that your bottom bracket might need adjusting or over-hauling: Sluggish pedaling, clicking, grinding (tight or needing an overhaul) or if you take your cranks in your hand and can wiggle them from side to side (too loose, needs adjustment) (pic. 48). You can give your bottom bracket a good test by taking the chain off of the chainring and then giving your pedals a little spin while the chain is off. This way, you'll be able to better see if it is running too tightly or too sluggishly. If it is running tight or feels like it is wonky and loose, it is time for an adjustment or overhaul.

Three-piece cranks

So you've decided to open up the bottom bracket. OK. Let's do it! First things first, you're going to have to remove the cranks. For that you will need a crank

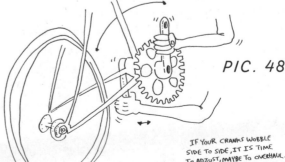

PIC. 48

IF YOUR CRANKS WOBBLE SIDE TO SIDE, IT IS TIME TO ADJUST, MAYBE TO OVERHAUL.

puller and some sort of wrench for loosening the crank arm bolt (some of these have a handle and others are used with a crescent wrench, see tool drawings at beginning of "How to do a Tune Up" section). Take a look at it. It is probably either a 14mm or an 8 hex wrench bolt. So use your 14mm socket (bike companies make handy little wrenches specifically for this, but you can use any socket) or your big 8 mm Allen wrench and take the bolt out. Make sure you get the washer out, too! If it's stuck, spray some lube in there and try again.

Next, take your crank puller and carefully thread the outer shell of it into the hole in the crank (the little well that the bolt was down in). I say carefully because it really sucks when you strip these threads (which is what happened to the bike I'm riding now, and I've been putting off fixing it for months). Your cranks are most likely aluminum, which strip easily. So thread it in by hand as far as you can, checking from every angle that it's going in straight, then tighten it a couple of times with a wrench so that it is taut, but not over-tight. Spraying some lubricant on the threads, and down into the hole, helps a lot. Once you are confident that the crank puller is in well, with about half of the threads in, take a deep breath and spin the handle around clockwise. You should feel some resistance after several turns, then it will start to force the crank arm off the spindle. If it feels wrong at all—too tight, or crunchy, or like it is stripping the threads of the crank arm, then stop, unscrew the tool, and check it out. Are there signs of stripping, like little scraps of aluminum? Do the threads look damaged? If so, stop immediately. If not, rethread the tool and give it another shot. Once it gets harder to turn the thing, it should only take a couple of full turns before—plop, your crank falls off, hanging from the end of your crank puller. Repeat on the other crank.

PIC. 49

cottered crank.

Cottered cranks (pic. 49)

I'm not a fan, and sort of wish that I could forget about cottered cranks. I would have already forgotten except that our boss at French Quarter Bikes used to have this big crush on a girl who had a very distinct way of saying "Kah-TER pins," and he walked around repeating "Kah-TER pins, kah-TER pins" for a week, and it still cracks me up every time I think about it. But I digress.

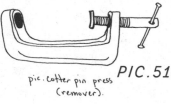

pic. cotter pin washer & nut.

PIC. 50

pic. cotter pin press (remover).

PIC. 51

These things can be a total pain. A cottered crank is an old-style, three-piece crank with crank arms held on by a tapered cotter pin (pic. 50). The pin is forced in by tightening a nut, similar to the way that other three-piece cranks are forced onto the spindle. Removing these can often be difficult since they've probably been stuck on there a long time. There's a tool for it, the Park Tools Cotter Pin Press (pic. 51). If there's one of these around, try it first, but I wouldn't suggest buying one. In theory, this thing works just like a chainbreaker (yay, chainbreaker!). Just remove the nut of the cotter pin and thread the tool down onto the pin—but in practice it always seemed to me like the tool was too big to press the pin all the way out. One trick I've used is to put a bearing between the press-part of the tool and the cotter pin (pic. 52). If you don't have a cotter-

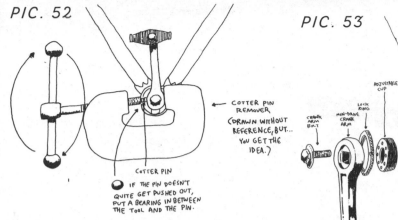

PIC. 52

COTTER PIN REMOVER (DRAWN WITHOUT REFERENCE, BUT... YOU GET THE IDEA.)

COTTER PIN

IF THE PIN DOESN'T QUITE GET PUSHED OUT, PUT A BEARING IN BETWEEN THE TOOL AND THE PIN.

PIC. 53

DOWN TUBE

SEAT TUBE

ADJUSTABLE CUP

LOCK RING

SPINDLE (AXLE)

FIXED CUP

DRIVE-SIDE CRANK ARM

CRANK ARM BOLT

NON-DRIVE CRANK ARM

OTHER BOLT

BEARINGS

B.B. SHELL

THREE-PIECE BOTTOM BRACKET (TRADITIONAL SQUARE SPLINE)

STAYS

pin remover, you are probably going to have to use a hammer. Remove the nut of the cotter-pin (that probably seems obvious, but I've seen someone try to do this with the nut on.). Oh, it takes a 10 mm wrench. Really whack the living hell out of the pin. Really, on the first try, whack it. It's really easy to either smoosh the pin or break it, so you want this to work on the first try. If you end up smooshing the pin or breaking it, next try a punch. If that doesn't work, you're going to have to drill out the pin with a drill bit smaller than the hole (the hole isn't round and you don't want to drill into the crank, nor would you probably even be able to since they're really, really hard), then pound out the left over pin bits. Once you have the pin out, the bottom bracket comes apart same as a typical three-piece BB. Replacement pins for putting it back together are available at most bike shops. Be careful, though, they come in at least a couple of different sizes and the cranks come with holes in a ton of different sizes, so you might have to file one down. Good luck. To put the crank back on, slide it onto the spindle and then push the cotter pin into the hole, flat side towards the spindle. Put the washer on and then crank the nut down on there. Oh and hey—make sure one crank arm points up and one points down. Getting the cotter pins cranked down and then realizing both cranks arms point down may seem funny, but really, it's just more work....

Three-piece bottom brackets
Adjusting

If you have a conventional (non-sealed) cup-and-bearing type bottom bracket (pic 53), there will be a lock-ring on the non-drive (left) side of the bottom bracket (the adjustable cup). This is a ring on the outside of the threads of the bottom bracket shell with notches on the outside. The notches are there so that you can put a bottom bracket lockring remover into them and remove the lockring, thus letting you adjust the cup (pic. 54). If you don't have the right tool, you can carefully tap the lockring off with a hammer and a screwdriver. You might want to spray lube behind the lockring if you do this, so as to help avoid munching up the notches on the ring. The lockring is LEFT HAND THREADED, and will come off clockwise as will the non-drive side cup itself. If your bottom bracket has just come loose and the spindle

PIC. 54

removing lockring

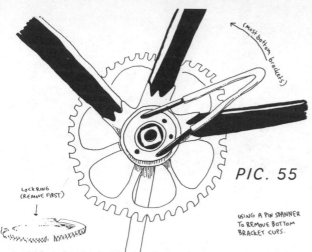

(most bottom brackets)

PIC. 55

LOCKRING
(REMOVE FIRST)

USING A PIN SPANNER
TO REMOVE BOTTOM
BRACKET CUPS.

is wobbling back and forth a little, then you may simply need to tighten the adjustable cup a bit. This happens most frequently if you have an Italian or French bottom bracket (on an Italian or old French bike, probably), because the non-adjustable cup spins the same direction as the adjustable cup, and they loosen up if not cranked down super tight.

Once you have the lockring loose, tighten the adjustable cup a hair with a pin spanner or wrench, depending on what tool fits (pic. 55). If you leave the non-drive side crank on while you're doing this, you can use it as a handle for leverage and see if the spindle is still loose. Once it feels okay, hold the cup in place with the wrench or spanner you used to loosen it. As you hold it there, tighten the lockring down around it. Check the looseness/tightness of the spindle again. Spin the cranks and see if they are dragging. This might take a couple of tries to get right, and if you're tapping the lockring back on with a screwdriver, you might need a helping hand to hold the cup in place.

Overhauling

If your bottom bracket feels really loose or really sluggish, you probably need to fully overhaul it. In that case, take both cranks off and remove the lockring (as described above). Lay the bike down on the right side and remove the adjustable cup with a pin spanner. As

you do this, pull up on the bottom bracket spindle. The spindle has a flanged part that spins in the bearings, so pulling up on it like this will keep all of the bearings (if loose) from falling out and flying everywhere. Spreading a rag out under the bike as you pull the spindle out is a good idea, too, so that if the bearings fall out of the other side they won't all roll away. You shouldn't have to take the fixed cup out to overhaul it. If the bearings are loose you'll be able to get them out through the hole in the fixed cup. If they're in cages, you can pull 'em out the opposite side once the spindle's out. Be sure to clean the inside of the fixed cup, rub your fingers around in there and check for wear.

Once the bottom bracket is out, inspect the bearings and spindle. Are they dry? Full of gunk? Are there loose bearings or cages? If cages, are they all chewed up? (pic. 56) Look at the spindle on the flanged part. Is it smooth or chewed up? If anything looks worn and pitted it should be replaced. If all your parts seem to be in good shape you'll just need to clean them up and repack them. The cleaning can be done with some sort of degreaser, or even WD-40

and a rag. Wipe all the parts down really well, making sure to get any of the black crud that builds up on bearings. Steel wool really helps get this stuff clean.

Putting the bottom bracket back together is basically the same as taking it apart, but, uh, in reverse. Take a bunch of grease and smear it in the cups and all over the bearings. Use a good quality thick grease if you can, like the green Park Tools stuff. If not, lithium grease from an auto parts store will work, but won't last as long. Don't use Vaseline, like our friend did when he

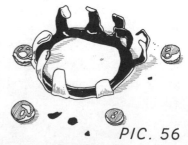

PIC. 56

TUNE-UP (BOTTOM BRACKETS)

was drunk once. It doesn't work. If the bearings are in cages, make sure they are facing the correct way when you put them back in, with the open side against the cup and the metal back of the cage around the flange of the spindle, not touching anything. Once you have everything back together, you have to get the tension of the cups adjusted. This can be a little bit tricky. It's a lot like adjusting the cones and bearings of a wheel, but a little bit trickier. Tighten the adjustable cup until it feels right. You shouldn't be able to wiggle the spindle all, but it should still spin smoothly. With all that grease in there and without the cranks on there giving you leverage, it might feel more sluggish than you would expect. That's normal. When you feel satisfied, hold the cup in place with your pin spanner and tighten the lockring as described in the section above.

Here are some specs about bottom brackets. The thread pitch is the number of threads per inch. Sometimes it seems like one will fit, but the pitch is off, and you can screw up your bb threads this way.

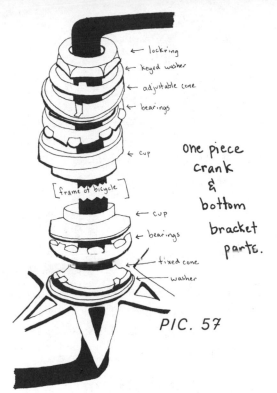

← lockring
← keyed washer
← adjustable cone
← bearings
← cup
[frame of bicycle]
← cup
← bearings
← fixed cone
← washer

one piece crank & bottom bracket parts.

PIC. 57

Diameter	Pitch	Right Cup	Left Cup
Italian	36 mm x 24F tpi*	right	right
British	1.370" x 24F tpi	left	right
French	35 mm x 1mm	right	right
Swiss	35 mm x 1mm	left	right

*tpi (threads per inch)

Sealed bottom brackets

A sealed bottom bracket is sealed and not serviceable. So you don't adjust it or overhaul it, you simply replace it.

If you have a sealed bottom bracket, follow the above steps for removing the cranks. You will need a big, splined removing tool to take the bottom bracket cartridge out. This thing looks like a big socket that attaches to a ratchet. Turn the cartridge from the drive side of the bike. Turn counter clockwise to remove and

when you get it all the way out, either write down the numbers on the cartridge to get a new one, or take it to the shop with you. Clean up the threads on the frame where your cartridge screws in, lube it with a little grease, and then install your new cartridge in reverse order.

Note: That is the simplified version if this repair. There are lots of different configurations and tools to use these days. Some basic advice to help you through the differences: Once your cranks are off, you will be more clear on what tool or tools you will need to remove your bottom bracket cartridge. There is usually a fixed cup on the opposite side of the side you work on to remove the cartridge. This can be difficult to remove, so be patient. Also, DO NOT FORGET that usually the non-drive side part of the bike is reverse threaded. SO! If you have an adjustable cup, or fixed cup on that side of your bike, remove it by turning clockwise! This is very important! Also, be sure to put your cartridge in correctly. It should be marked "right & left" with arrows.

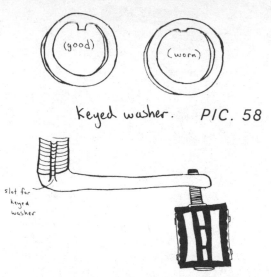

Keyed washer.   PIC. 58

slot for keyed washer

And, always, clean your bottom bracket threads and lube them before replacing any bottom bracket type into it! This will save you a lot of time later. Same with your crank bolts. OK?

One-piece bottom brackets

Adjusting

Adjusting a one piece bottom bracket is super easy! It is the greatest way to really understand the type of adjustment one makes in a bearing system. Simply loosen the locknut (Left hand threaded! Remember, loosen clockwise!) on the non-drive side of the crank, then pull the keyed washer back. It is good here to actually loosen the cone a bit so that you can shoot a little grease into the bottom bracket cups, being careful not to open it up more than a few millimeters so you don't lose any loose bearings! A grease gun rules for this job. Squirt the grease in both sides of the bottom bracket. Now, adjust that on the non-drive side. Tighten it down (by turning left, remember!) until the bottom bracket turns freely (it is easiest to test this with the chain off of the chainring) but also has no free play from side to side. Ah, that perfect little adjustment you are looking for again. The middle way, not too tight, not too loose. When you got it, push the keyed washer

back on with the key in the little slot on the crank and retighten the locknut. Test the cranks for free turning and no free play again. Sometimes tightening the locknut can change the adjustment slightly, though unless the key on the keyed washer is worn, the keyed washer should prevent this (pic. 58). If the adjustment changed, try again. Done!

Overhauling

If your sweet cruiser feels sluggish (and your wheels are spinning fine), or if your cranks wobble significantly when you pull them from side to side, or you are hearing grinding or see bits of metal hanging out of your bottom bracket, it's time for an overhaul. This is fairly easy on these things, and doesn't require as much precision as more complicated bottom brackets do. First, take off your left pedal. A pedal wrench is ideal for this (hence the name) but if not, a box end wrench will work. It will be either a 15mm or 9/16, and remember, the left pedal is reverse (left-hand) threaded and comes off clockwise. Next, remove the locknut on the bottom bracket. This, too, is left-hand threaded, and comes off clock-wise. After that, there is a washer to remove. Notice that it's keyed, with a little tooth that fits into a little notch on the threads. This is so that when you're torquing away, tightening the locknut (in a few minutes), the cone won't tighten with it and smoosh your bearings. If the little tooth is

PIC. 59

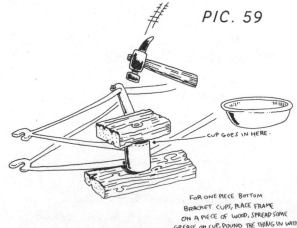

CUP GOES IN HERE.

FOR ONE PIECE BOTTOM BRACKET CUPS, PLACE FRAME ON A PIECE OF WOOD, SPREAD SOME GREASE ON CUP, POUND THE THING IN WITH ANOTHER HUNK OF WOOD AND A HAMMER.

PIC. 60

IF A ONE-PIECE CUP IS TOO LOOSE IN THE B.B. SHELL, WRAP THE INSIDE OF THE CUPS WITH A LAYER OF ELECTRICAL TAPE.

worn off, replace the washer. Under the washer is the cone. It'll have a couple of notches in it and can be loosened either with a pin spanner or tapped off carefully with a screwdriver. It is, like the other stuff, left-hand threaded. Now you should be looking at your bearings, either in a cage or loose (in which case they probably all just fell out). Take those out. With all that stuff out, you should be able to slide the cranks out through the drive side of the bottom bracket shell.

As with all overhauls, inspect all parts for wear. The cones on these things are usually old and get thin pitted rings around them. These will never feel that great and should be replaced if you can. Check out the cups themselves, too, inside the bottom bracket shell. Do they feel rough and pitted? If so, tap them out from the inside of the frame with a screwdriver and replace them. The new cups can be installed by putting a piece of wood, like a two-by-four, over the cup and whacking it in with a hammer (pic. 59). If the cups are really loose and won't stay in, wrap them in electrical tape and

pound them in (pic. 60). At least that's what our boss at French Quarter Bikes used to do, and though he did have some fairly dubious practices, this always seemed to work.

When you're done cleaning everything, pack the bearings with grease and re-install. Adjust as described above!

Bottom bracket odds and ends

Bottom bracket spindles have one side that is longer than the other. Make sure the longer side goes on the drive side of the bike to make space for the chainrings and cranks, so they don't hit the frame. Some spindles and sealed bottom brackets are marked right and left to help you get them in correctly.

Caged bearings are easier to deal with than loose bearings, though it is generally accepted that they don't work as well. If you are using them, however, remember to always install them correctly with the bearings facing into the cup (pic. 61). If you want to install loose bearings, get new ones that are all the same size, and the same size as the ones you removed. If they are off even a few millionths of an inch, you're probably thinking, "so what?" but think

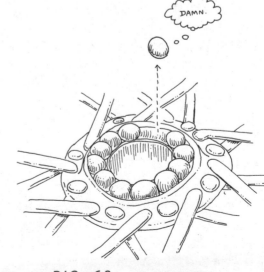

PIC. 61

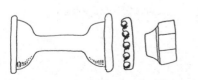

WHEN INSTALLING BEARING RINGS, BE SURE THAT THEY ARE FACING THE RIGHT WAY. YOU WANT THEM TO GO IN SO THAT THE BEARINGS ARE IN CONTACT WITH THE CONES AND CUPS BUT THE CAGE PART IS NOT TOUCHING ANYTHING.

PIC. 62

WHEN INSTALLING BEARINGS, PUT IN AS MANY AS WILL FIT AND TAKE ONE OUT.

about it—if all the bearings are one size except one that's a little smaller, that one is not going to do a damn thing except sit in there, and might as well not even be there. So get the same size bearings. Ok?

When you put the bearings in, there are (in a three piece bottom bracket) normally eleven bearings per side. If you don't know how many should go in, you can put them in until no more will fit, then remove one. This is standard practice for all bearing systems (pic. 62).

7. Drivetrains

The drivetrain is what makes the bike go. It includes: the crank (crank arms and chainrings), the chain, and the cogs on the rear wheel.

Note: The front "cogs" are called chainrings. Some chainrings can be removed individually from the crank arm, by loosening little chainring bolts that hold them together. For multi-speeds, the rear cogs are called the cassette, or the freewheel depending on the type of wheel you have. A freewheel screws onto the wheel and is one piece. A cassette comes apart into individual cogs which slide onto a freehub body on the hub of your rear wheel, and then lock on with a lockring. Most lower and medium end bikes have freewheels while cassettes usually (but not always) come on higher quality bikes. Single speeds either have a single cog which is either clipped onto the hub with a retaining ring (like on a coaster brake wheel), or a single speed freewheel or fixed gear which screws and locks onto the rear wheel like the above mentioned freewheel.

Chain

It is quite common, especially with people who are just starting to monkey around with bikes, that the bike chain is taken for granted. "I'll just slap some old chain on this thing and off I go" might work, but also might feel like total crap. See, the chain is made up of hundreds of precision made parts, all moving together

as one unit, kind of like your spine does. Not only that, but all these parts are being yanked and jerked and pushed around by chainrings, by the rear cogs, by the derailleurs. That's a lot of pressure on all those little plates and pins, so making sure that you have the right chain, and making sure that you take care of it and keep it lubed, is crucial. Wicked crucial.

Get the right chain

Chains come in several different sizes for different numbers of speeds. This refers to the width of the cog teeth, which are wider on one speeds and narrower the more speeds you have. So if you have a one-speed (or a bike with internal shifting like a three-speed), you need a one-speed chain. If you have a BMX or a track bike, don't go for the cheapo one-speed chain, either; get a good, burly one. These are 1/8" wide.

Multi-speed chains come in 5/6/7 variety, and specific ones for 8, 9, and 10 speeds. Usually a thinner one will work on a bike with less speeds than it is intended for, but it's not the best because they wear out quicker (and cost more), but if you're in some weird position and need to slap one on, an 8 will probably work with 7, a 9 for an 8, a 10 for a 9, etc.

When to replace your chain

Chains don't last forever. Slowly, as you ride, the rubbing of the chain parts wears down the little rollers inside each link, creating tiny gaps in how the parts interact with one another. This phenomenon

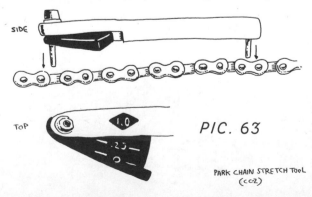

SIDE

TOP

PIC. 63

PARK CHAIN STRETCH TOOL
(CC2)

MEASURING CHAIN WEAR
WITH A RULER, THE PINS SHOULD
LINE UP WITH THE ONE INCH MARKS

is normally called "chain-stretch" because the chain seems to get longer as it happens. As this stretching occurs, the chain begins to rub differently on the teeth of the cogs, wearing them down. The angle of the teeth is called the tooth pitch. Ideally, you don't want to change the pitch of your cogs' teeth because, if you do, when you replace the chain with a new, unstretched one, it won't sit right on the teeth. It will skip around or create "chain-suck," which is what it's called when your chainring doesn't let go of the chain and tries to pull it back up on the rear of the cog. Both skippage and chain-suck can be annoying at best and really dangerous at worst (when you're really cranking on the pedals in a traffic jam perhaps). So, for the most part you can usually get away with keeping your chain lubed (more on that below) but it's also important to change your chain regularly.

How do you know when it's time for a new chain? Park Tools makes a handy tool for this called a chain wear gauge or something like that. It has pins that go into the chain links and measure the width of the gaps (pic. 63). A bike shop will usually let you use one of these, because it means you might buy a chain off of them. Another method is to measure the chain with a metal ruler or tape measure. You can leave it on the bike. Simply line up an inch mark on the ruler with a rivet on the chain. Now look down the ruler one foot away from the rivet. The one foot mark should also line up with a rivet. Does it? If it is more than 1/16" away, you need to replace the chain. If it is more than 1/8" away, you'll probably have to replace your cogs in the back, too.

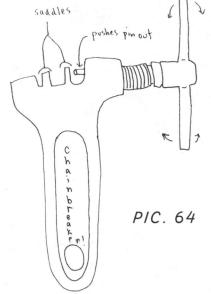

saddles

pushes pin out

chainbreaker!

PIC. 64

Removal and installation
Chainbreakers

A small note on chain tools, or as we at *The Chainbreaker Bike Book* like to call them, chainbreakers! Yay! Anyhow, chainbreakers usually have two places you can place the chain into. These are called saddles (pic. 64). The lower saddle is for breaking or reattaching the chain. The upper saddle is for loosening tight links. Ok? So use the lower saddle here. Also, while most chainbreakers are universal and work on all chains, the Park Tools chainbreaker that is regularly used in shop situations comes in two sizes! One for single speeds (blue rubber handle) and one for multi speeds (black metal handle). Weird huh? So be careful of all that.

Pins

Spray the chain with lube and lay it in the slots of the chain tool. Make sure they are flat in there. Tighten the handle of the chain tool so that the pin of the tool is pushing on the pin of the chain. Make sure that it is pushing straight in there and not ramming against the side of the chain link. If you are going to reinstall this chain, push the pin almost all of the way out. Do not

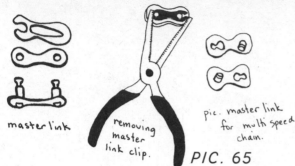

master link

removing master link clip.

pic. master link for multi speed chain.

PIC. 65

push the pin out! If you push the pin out, it is nearly impossible to get back in. I have seen it done, once, and have tried for a long-ass time to do it myself, to no avail. You should be able to pull the chain apart now, working the inner piece out from the brackets, gently. If not, ease the pin out a little bit more. This takes doing a few times before you really get a feel for it, but eventually you'll be able to feel a little click when the pin clears the small length of the chain and is just stuck in the outer part.

Master links (pic. 65)

New chains will frequently have some sort of link that doesn't involve using the chain tool. If so, use these, because sometimes the chains won't react well to the chain tool and will be stiff. Also, the chain tool is going to sheer off a little bit of metal every time you use it, which isn't a huge deal but eventually can lead to increased chain wear or failure. Shimano uses something called a master link. SRAM uses one called a power link. These come with instructions and both require needle nose pliers for installation. Some chains now come with a chain pin attached to a little breakaway pin. With these you just slide the breakaway pin in, use the chain tool to push the real pin through, then snap the breakaway pin off with pliers. Voila.

Installing a chain

If you are installing a chain with the chain tool, follow these steps:

Figure out the proper length of the chain. If you are confident that your old chain was sized correctly, spread the new chain out next to the old one and size it this way. Otherwise, see the section on sizing chain at the end of this section.

Shift your derailleurs to the smallest gears in both the front and the back. Thread your chain through your derailleurs, making sure that it is beneath any metal guides on the rear derailleur. If your bike is a single speed, simply wrap the chain around the rear cog. Either way, when you do this, be sure to do it so that the pin (the one you'll be pushing back in, unless you are using a master link) is facing you on the drive side of the bike. It's a huge pain in the ass to try and do it from the other side. It will also be easier if you thread it through so that the disconnected ends are at the bottom of the loop of chain. Now, lay the chain on the bottom bracket, off of the chain-ring in the front so you will have some slack to reconnect the chain with. Now reconnect the chain.

With a pin: Put the chain ends in the gaps on the chain tool. Make sure they are lined up really well. Squirt a little bit of lube on the pin or in the hole. Tighten the pin in, making sure that it goes in straight. It will be tight, but should go in smoothly. If you feel any resistance, stop. Be sure that, when the pin comes out on the other side, that it doesn't bend the outer plate. Make sure that the pin is in there evenly (with the same amount of pin sticking out of each side) (pic. 66). Check for tight links and loosen them if needed as described below. Yay!

With a master link: Place the master link pins in the ends of the chain so you now have a continuous loop of chain. Put the master link plate over the pins, then clip the master link clip on with a needle nose plier.

when the chain is connected, all the pins are in evenly.

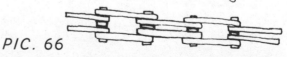

PIC. 66

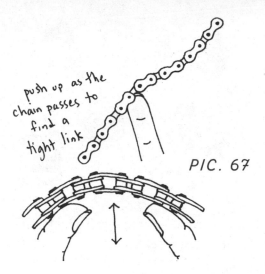

push up as the chain passes to find a tight link

PIC. 67

loosening tight links.

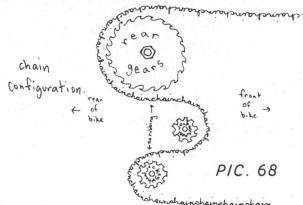

chain configuration.

rear gears

chainchainchainchain...

← rear of bike

front of bike →

PIC. 68

...chainchainchainchainchainchain...

Loosening tight links

If you have a tight link in your chain, you will probably notice a skipping sound in your chain that makes an even sounding rhythm, like once per revolution. First find the tight link (probably caused when putting your chain on) by running your finger under a portion of the chain and pushing up (pic. 67). Watch all the little link pivots move one at a time until you get to one that doesn't move. Here is your tight link. To loosen it, take the chain in both hands on either side of the chain and move and bend the chain back and forth to loosen the link. Check it and try again. If this doesn't work, you might need to use the chainbreaker on the upper saddle to adjust the pin a little bit. Yay!

Sizing your chain

It is important to get your chain length right so that you will be able to hit all the gears when shifting. If you are trying to figure out what length to make your chain, do this:

Shift your derailleurs so that they are both on the largest gear (low in the rear, high in the front).

Thread your chain through the derailleurs, making sure that they are going through all of the metal guides on the rear one (not sitting on top of them). Thread the chain so that it is lying on top of the gears and the loose ends are at the bottom. Pull the chain ends together (and past one another) until the rear derailleur is pulled tight, but the chain still curves over the jockey wheels of the rear derailleur (pic. 68). Figure out which links you are going to join (keeping in mind that you have to join a wide with a skinny link unless you are using a master link or similar linking device.)

Shift to the smallest gears in front and back. Rest your chain on your bottom bracket shell and use your chain tool to join the links (as described above).

Once you have the chain put back together, make sure that when you are in your small gears, the chain doesn't sag. If the chain sags, but your measurement while on the big cogs was correct, your derailleur probably isn't the right one for the number of gears you have. If you have to make do with it, shorten the chain to the point where it won't sag and keep in mind while riding that you won't be able to shift into certain gear combinations (pic. 69).

Freewheels and Cassettes

The rear cogs on a bike are attached to the wheel by one of two systems: cassette or a freewheel. Most newer road and mountain bikes use a cassette, while older bikes and lower end bikes (like comfort bikes) still

CHECK CHAIN LENGTH ON
THE SMALLEST COG & CHAINRING.
MAKE SURE THE CHAIN IS TAUT,
BUT NOT TOO TIGHT OR TOO SLACK.

PIC. 70

VARIOUS
FREEWHEEL
REMOVERS

have freewheels. Both work fine, more or less, with the cassette having an advantage for harder riding (see fancy stuff section for an explanation of why). At some point though, you will need to remove them, like when you need to repack the bearings on the drive side of your hub (see section on axles), if your cogs have broken or worn out teeth, or if you replace your chain and experience skipping from worn out cogs (see section on replacing chains).

Freewheels

Removal

A freewheel is a little easier to remove (well, in theory anyway) than a cassette. Take off your back wheel and remove the quick release skewer if you have one, or the axle nut if you don't. Determine which type of freewheel tool you need by looking at the inner ring of the cogset (pic. 70). There will be a number of notches for tool placement, probably either two or four, or it will look splined inside. A bike shop can help you with this and sell you the right tool for your wheel. Then, with the axle nuts or skewers

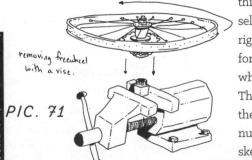

removing freewheel
with a vise.

PIC. 71

removed from the axle, slide the removing tool into the notches on the freewheel. Now, if you have a solid axle, thread the axle nut down onto the tool (not too tightly) or if you have a quick release, remove the springs from the skewer and tighten it down onto the tool. This will keep the tool from slipping when you're torquing the hell out of it in a few moments. With either a large crescent wrench, box wrench (there's one on the end of the Park Tools chainwhip that fits perfectly), or by clamping the tool in a vise, torque the hell out of the tool (pic. 71). It is a regular right-hand, counter-clockwise thread (note that if you are using a vise this can be somewhat confusing since you will be torquing on the wheel, and thus will be looking at the whole set-up upside down. (Hint: turn the wheel counter-clockwise.) Sometimes these things have been on there for a really long time, frequently in someone's back yard getting rained on, and can be seized up pretty good. If you're using a wrench you might need a pipe on the end for leverage, or you might want to whack your wrench with a rubber mallet (pic. 72). Or have a friend hold the wheel while you step down

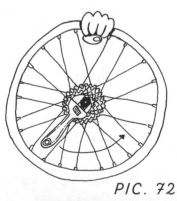

PIC. 72

REMOVING FREEWHEEL WITH A
WRENCH. A PIPE CAN BE PLACED
OVER THE WRENCH HANDLE
FOR EXTRA LEVERAGE (NOT
SHOWN).

TUNE-UP (DRIVETRAINS)

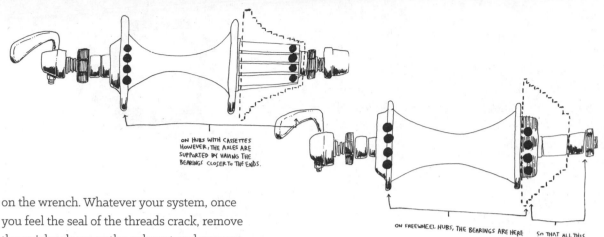

ON HUBS WITH CASSETTES HOWEVER, THE AXLES ARE SUPPORTED BY HAVING THE BEARINGS CLOSER TO THE ENDS.

ON FREEWHEEL HUBS, THE BEARINGS ARE HERE

So THAT ALL THIS AXLE IS UNSUPPORTED, WHICH LEADS TO BENT OR BROKEN AXLES

on the wrench. Whatever your system, once you feel the seal of the threads crack, remove the quick-release or the axle nut and remove the freewheel. If you are overhauling the wheel bearings, follow the directions in the axles section. If you are replacing the freewheel entirely, clean off the threads of the hub and grease the threads of the new freewheel.

Installation

To install the freewheel, simply thread it on by hand, making sure not to cross-thread. When you get on the bike to ride it, the force of the chain will tighten the freewheel down. Most likely what will happen is you'll thread the freewheel on then forget about it and go do something else. Then when you get on to ride, you'll have forgotten all about the freewheel and feeling it twist beneath the chain will totally freak you out. But it's ok.

Cassettes

Cassettes are the new style of cog system. They look similar to freewheels but, unlike freewheels, they aren't one piece. A cassette is actually a bunch of cogs that slide onto the freehub body, a ratcheting spindle that is attached to the hub of the wheel (pic. 73). Look at the smallest size cog of your cassette. In the center is a splined ring that, upon close inspection, you will see is not attached to the cog itself. That's the lockring, which is what holds all those cogs on there. (Note: If you have an older cassette, the smallest cog might act as the lockring. If that is the case, you need two chainwhips to remove the cassette. More on that in a minute.) To remove the cassette, you have to remove the lockring. To do that, you will need a cassette tool and a chainwhip, as well as a wrench to turn the cassette tool (either a larger box end wrench or a crescent wrench, or if you have two chainwhips, there is a wrench on the end of the Park Tools version that fits on the tool).

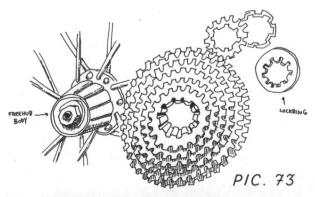

FREEHUB BODY

LOCKRING

PIC. 73

CASSETTE

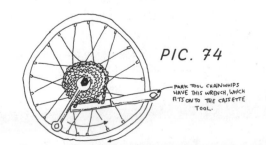

PIC. 74

PARK TOOL CHAINWHIPS HAVE THIS WRENCH, WHICH FITS ONTO THE CASSETTE TOOL.

Stick the cassette tool in the splines of the cassette. Wrap the chainwhip around one of the larger cogs in a clockwise direction, so that when you twist the lockring to the left the chainwhip will hold the cassette in place (pic. 74). Take your wrench and turn the lockring while holding the cassette in place with the chainwhip. The lockring should unscrew. Unscrew it all the way, and then slide the rest of the cogs off of the freehub body.

Installing

Reinstalling the lockring is just the same process in reverse. Clean off your freehub body, slide the cogs onto the freehub body (notice that the splines have different widths and there is only one way you can put the cogs on). Thread the lockring in by hand, then torque on it with your cassette tool and wrench while holding the cassette in place with the chainwhip.

Older cassettes

There are some old variations on the modern cassette, most notably the Shimano Hyperglide and the Helicomatic. The Hyperglide works the same as a modern cassette but the lockring is the smallest cog. To remove these, hold the cassette in place with one chainwhip while torquing on the cog with another whip.

The Helicomatic is rarer, a seventies cassette that takes a special tool, a nifty little lockring wrench/ spoke wrench/beer opener. If you encounter one of these hubs, you'll probably want to just replace it whenever it has a problem, since the cassettes aren't interchangeable with regular cassettes. If you do want to remove one for some reason, go find the oldest and coolest bike mechanic in town and ask them to borrow their Helicomatic tool. They'll probably have one, and you'll probably get some raised eyebrows. (We go to Donny, in New Orleans. Thanks, Donny!)

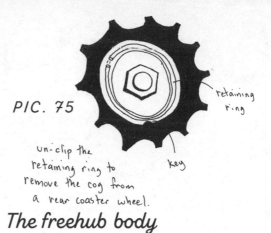

PIC. 75

retaining ring

key

un-clip the retaining ring to remove the cog from a rear coaster wheel.

The freehub body

The ratcheting spindle that your cassette slides onto is called the freehub body. If this thing starts to feel gritty or not spin right, you can pour a thin grease like Tri-Flow down in it to try and flush out some of the crap, or spray it out with a good lubricant (NOT WD-40, but T-9 or something that actually promises long-lasting lubrication). The other option is to replace the whole thing (which is also what you do if the splines are badly damaged), which is done by sticking a 10mm Allen wrench in the center of the freehub body and unscrewing it.

Removing cog on a rear coaster wheel

If the cog on your coaster wheel needs replacing due to wear, or you just need to remove it to get into the axle or to replace some spokes, follow these steps: Take the wheel off. With a very small flathead screwdriver, or the threaded end of a spoke, pry off the retainer ring holding the cog on. This can be really challenging and may take some patience and time and a really thin flathead screwdriver or even a scribe to get under the retaining ring. Once you have gotten the retaining ring off, then pull the cog off (pic 75). There is usually a thin but tallish spacer ring that fits around the hub end underneath the cog. You will usually get a new one of these when you get a new cog, so replace them together. That's all! To replace it, make sure the spacer is under the cog, place the cog on the hub with the

shark toothing

little key in place (the cog has a key similar to a keyed washer), then put the retainer ring back on by prying it open with, again, a tiny screwdriver or the threaded end of a spoke, and then popping it back onto the hub. This holds the cog down.

Chainrings

Another important part of your drivetrain is the front cogs that pull your bike forward. The chainrings are the actual rings with the teeth on them. They are attached to the cranks. Some chainrings can be taken off of the cranks, while others cannot. We talked about removing the cranks back in the bottom bracket section. Here, we will only discuss the removal and the replacement of chainrings.

When to replace

There are two reasons to replace your chainrings. One, because you want to change the gear ratio of your bicycle. We discussed gear ratio back there in the shifter section. If you want to change the ride of your bike and you have only a single chainring up there in front, sometimes the easiest way is to just change that chainring. This is especially true with single speeded road bikes, track bikes, and cruisers. The amount of torque is up to you, but remember: if you want to pedal less and harder, get a larger ring; if you want to pedal more and easier, get a smaller one. Two, if one or more of the teeth are worn (or just because you want to). To check for wear, look for broken, bent or jagged teeth on your chainring(s). If your teeth look busted or worn on the sides resembling shark's teeth (pic. 76), it is time for replacement. (Note: There are teeth on some chainrings called droptooth that are smaller or may appear different than the other teeth. These assist in dropping the chain down during shifting. Try not to confuse these for busted teeth.)

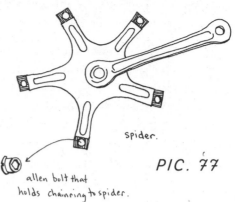

spider.

PIC. 77

allen bolt that
holds chainring to spider.

Also check for straightness of your chainrings. To do this, look at your chainring from above, close one eye and take note of the placement of the teeth compared to something like your bottom bracket or derailleur. Now, turn your crank slowly and look to see if your chainring is moving side to side, indicating that it is bent. If it is and is not too extreme, you can straighten it with the help of an adjustable wrench. No, don't whack it with the wrench! With the chain off, gently clamp the wrench onto the chainring (get down low on the ring, don't just clamp onto the teeth!) and gently, gently, slightly bend the thing to the right direction to make the chainring straight. Do a little section at a time, and BE GENTLE! Put your chain back on and pedal the bike softly and then fast to make sure the chain isn't binding. Ok! If your chainring is real bent, take it off and get a new one. Once they bend a lot, they lose their strength, so it is better to replace them. Here's how you do that:

Removal and installation
Three-piece crank chainrings

Ok. there are two types here. There are chainrings that are permanently attached to the drive side crank, and others that attach to what is called the "spider" on the drive side crank (pic. 77). You can tell the difference here by looking at how the chainrings attach to the crank. With the permanent type, the chainrings are held on by rivets, or something like rivets. With the removable type, the chainring(s) are attached with small Allen bolts called chainring bolts.

For the permanent type: Remove the drive side crank as described in "three piece crank removal" in the bottom brackets section. This type usually has three chainrings and, sadly, the whole darnn piece must be replaced even if only one chainring is ruined. Take your crank down to a shop, find a matching one, and replace it. Reinstall it as described in the "three piece crank removal" in the bottom brackets section.

For the removable type: With this type, the chainrings are individually Allen bolted onto the crank's spider. This is great, because you can remove them individually to replace an offending chainring. Remove the crank as described in "three piece crank removal" in the bottom brackets section. (Note: If you have a bike that has been converted to a single speed, you can usually remove the one chainring by taking the chain off of the chainring, unbolting it, as will be described, and then sliding it around and over the crank spider.) Remove the chainring bolts with a 5 Allen key. You may need to hold the nuts on the rear of the crank to make these bolts turn. There is a special tool for this, but you can usually get away with using a really big screwdriver. Remove the chainring from the spider. Reinstall chainrings in the opposite order, being careful to put any washers from your chainring bolts, as well as the chainring itself, in the same position (they can go on the front or backside of the spider).

Important!!! When reinstalling your chainrings, make sure you tighten the Allen bolts really well! Loose bolts are not just dangerous, but will cause the most annoying creaks when you are riding! If you ever hear creaking coming from your bottom bracket area, and the bottom bracket is ok, check these bolts for looseness and give each a turn for good measure! Reinstall your crank as described in "three-piece crank removal" in the "bottom brackets" section. Done!

One-piece crank

Follow the directions on removing your one-piece crank as described under "one-piece bottom brackets overhaul" in the bottom bracket section. When you have the crank out, you will notice that the chainring is held onto the crank itself with a big nut. These are removed in different ways depending on the nut. Some have three little slots on the outer part of the nut. With this kind, there is a wrench that fits into those little slots which removes this nut. Note: this tool is also sometimes used on cottered crank lockrings and fixed cups (pic. 78). Some are rounded with flat spots on each side of the center. You can turn this type with a special wrench (see illustration) or with a really big adjustable wrench or channel lock pliers. Some are just rounded and are hard as hell to get off with a channel lock. All of them turn to the left (regular threaded) to remove, and all of them will require a lot of muscle and maybe a good bit of something like liquid wrench. It is easiest to do this with the crank clamped into a vise for support if you can get to one.

Once that nut is off, lift the chainring off of the crank. You will notice it has a little hole in it. A little nub on the drive side of the crank sits in that hole to keep the chainring from spinning free of the crank. (Good to know, because if this thing breaks off it might take a while to figure out why pedaling doesn't move your bike anymore. Yikes!) Replace the chainring in the

One piece crank chainring locknuts & removing tools.

PIC. 78

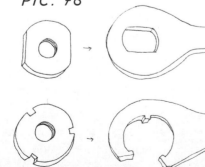

opposite order, making sure to tighten that nut down pretty well and to get the little nub in the hole. Replace your crank as described in the "one-piece crank overhaul" in the "bottom bracket" section. Done!

Cottered crank

These usually have a chainring, which is permanently attached to the drive side crank. Remove the drive side crank as described in the "cottered crank removal" in the bottom bracket section. Bring it to a shop, find or order another one, replace in the opposite order.

Drivetrain troubleshooting

Lots of weird noises come from your drivetrain! They can give you a good clue about what might be wrong with your bike.

With your drivetrain there can be a few different problems. Skipping is one of the big ones and can be diagnosed by watching HOW the chain skips. Does it slip forward on the push down of the pedal? Probably your cogs or chainrings are worn. Does it happen on EVERY gear in the back? Probably the front gear you are riding on is worn. All the gears in the front? Probably the gear you are riding in the back is worn. One skip or hop in regular intervals? Tight link in the chain? See "loosening a tight link" in the chain section. The sound of catching or constant rubbing? Derailleur limiting screws need adjusting. Chain hopping off the chainrings or cogs. Same. General creakiness? Tighten Allen bolts on your chainrings, crankbolts and pedals, and lube them! Always! General sluggishness? Replace your chain. Excessive amounts of grinding or metal falling out around the cranks? Bottom bracket needs adjusting, or, more than likely, an overhaul (go to bottom brackets in the Bearing Systems section).

Note: As chains and cogs wear together, unless you regularly replace your chain, you can have some serious problems when you try to put a new chain onto an old cassette or freewheel. If you put a new chain on an older bike and you suddenly get lots of skipping,

your cogs (and maybe your crank or chainring) need to be replaced. Do this, or put your old chain back on if it is something you can't deal with right away, though eventually you will need to.

So now your drive train is in order and your bike is totally tuned up. Turn the pedals a bunch while the bike is still on the stand and make sure everything is running well on the stand. Squeeze and check the brakes. Run through and gears. Listen for rubbing or knocking, etc.

Now let's do a last little check over.

Ok, this is the end of your tune up! You've gotten everything cleaned up and adjusted by now. All that is left is just going over your bike for a safety check and fixing or adjusting any little things that might be left.

8. Safety Check & Test Ride
Safety check

Start with a safety check and make sure that your wheels are on tight (remember! lube those axle nuts before you put them on!) and all bolts are tightened well. Are your handlebars on tight? Headset bolt tight? Seatpost bolt tight? Brakes functioning? Did you leave the brake noodle out or forget to attach any cables? Make sure nothing is going to move that is going to put you in danger. If everything looks good, move on.

Now you can check for all the little things. If you have a basket, is it on all janky and rattly? If yes, tighten it up; unless you're cool with it, then leave it. Bottle cages on tight? Brake levers bolted on level? Tires still inflated well? Pedals greased up a little? Anything squeaking or squealing? Fix it now....For example:

Seat

There are a few different things you can adjust on your seat. You can adjust the height by raising or lowering

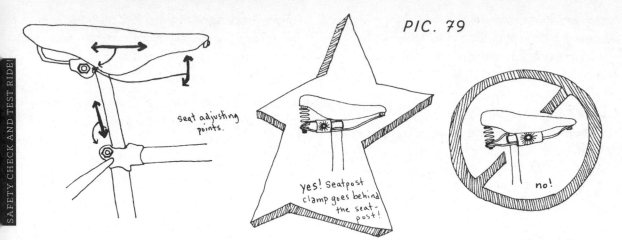

PIC. 79

seat adjusting points.

yes! Seatpost clamp goes behind the seat-post!

no!

your seatpost. You can adjust the seat forward or backward by loosening the seat clamp and sliding it back or forward on the rails of the seat. And, you can adjust the tilt of your seat by, again, loosening the seat clamp and then tilting the front of the seat up or down. Here are the different adjusting points for your seat:

Seatpost

The seatpost clamp can be a standard or metric sized bolt or an Allen bolt. The bolts are usually 13, 14 or 15 mm, and the Allen bolts are almost always (but not every time!) a 6mm. Simply loosen the bolt and the seatpost should slide up or down to adjust the seat. This might involve a little strength and wiggling the seat side to side, but it should work. If it is really, really tight, try squirting some lube in there, something that is for loosening things up, like WD-40 or Liquid Wrench. If this loosens it up, do yourself a favor and go ahead and pull the seatpost all the way out. Rub the seatpost down with a little grease so it won't get stuck again. Put the post back in and then adjust it to the preferred height, then tighten the bolt back down. Tighten it 'til it sticks, but don't make it impossible to loosen again. Ok?

As a note: If you want to replace your seatpost, take it out and bring it with you to a shop. There are a gazillion little sizes of these, usually in millimeters, and you want the right size. So bring the post with you

so they can measure it with a caliper. If your seat and post got stolen, or it seemed the wrong size for your bike, bring your bike down to the shop with you so you can get the right size. Someone at the shop will measure the inner diameter of your seat tube to get the size of your seatpost. Great!

Adjusting or replacing your seat

When adjusting your seat, you will want to loosen your seat clamp. This will be one of a couple kinds. It will either be a clamp, which is both separate from the seat and the post, that is usually loosened by loosening a bolt (13, 14, 15 or sometimes 17) on the side. Loosen it a little but not so much that the clamp starts to fall apart into separate pieces. The other type is one that is integrated into your seatpost. These are usually loosened from way under the seat with an Allen wrench. Loosen this until the seat gets a little loose and then make the adjustment. Simply slide the seat forward on the rails to bring the seat closer to the bars, or back to make it further from the bars. To adjust the tile, pull up or down on the front of the seat. You will probably feel a little ratcheting type feel as the seat finds a position in the little grooves in the clamp, which help the seat stay in place. Get the seat into the position that feels best for you (seat should be parallel to the ground, or tilted slightly down from there), then tighten the seat clamp and bolt it back down.

Another note: make sure your seat clamp is on in the right direction (pic. 79). The clamp should be behind the post. If it is in front of the post, the seat will be placed slightly in front of the cranks, making pedaling just a little more awkward. This happened to be my bike shop boss's biggest pet peeve, and I didn't understand it until after a vacation from home. I returned to my bike and just felt like biking was suddenly way harder! It felt like I suddenly got really out of shape. It wasn't 'til my boss disgustedly mentioned that my seatpost clamp was on backwards that I realized what was up. Apparently someone at my big house of roomies had borrowed my seat or something weird and switched the thing around. I put it back to its rightful position and on my ride home felt like a real biker again. Whew.

Pedals
Replacing or lubing pedals

If your pedals are all squeaky and loud or not turning smoothly, it might be time to lube 'em up or replace them. With some, you can take them apart and relube the little bearings inside of the pedal. We aren't going to get into that here, but if you wanna try it, they are basically the same system as your axles. Give it a try! I usually just shoot a little Tri-Flow around the bearing area and give 'em a spin and, more often than not, they loosen up and quiet down just fine. If they don't, and they just seem like they have lost their spin, or some other part of the pedal is broken, it is time to replace them. They are usually easily loosened with a 15 mm or 9/16 wrench, but the length and angle of a pedal wrench makes the job a little easier. The pedals can get a little stuck sometimes, so give them a little lube and read the section in this book on leverage if you have some problems. Either way, remove your pedals by turning the drive side pedal counterclockwise, and by turning the non-drive side pedal clockwise. Again! The non-drive side pedal is left hand threaded! (pic. 80) Don't forget this! When you go to get new pedals, take an old one to the shop with you as the threaded

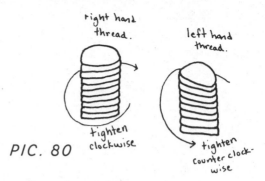

PIC. 80

right hand thread.
tighten clockwise

left hand thread.
tighten counter clockwise

spindle on the pedal comes in two sizes, either 1/2 or 9/16. Make sure you get the right size, then put your pedals back on. They will be labeled either on the end of the spindle or somewhere on the pedal. It will say "R" and "L" for right and left. Easy huh? Make sure you put the pedal on the correct side and tighten them down really well! Really well, ok, tight 'til they stick. A loose pedal will only get looser and end up stripping your nice little crank. A pain in the booty, so make sure they are tight, alright? And again! Drive side tightens clockwise and non-drive side counter clockwise! A good way to remember is that both pedals will tighten when you turn towards the front of the bike. Both loosen when you turn towards the rear of the bike. Got it? Great!

A Story about Pedals with a Handy Trick, by Ethan. Once, when Shelley and I were at work at the bike shop, a friend of ours (who we'll call, uh… Bumps) came in stressing out. He was working, delivering food for the shwaggy po-boy shop up the street, and while out riding with a ton of deliveries piled up in his basket, his pedal had broken off on the drive-side of his beefy cruiser. Bumps is a pretty big guy, and the pedal had just sheered off, leaving the threaded spindle still screwed into the crank, so there was nowhere to put a wrench on it and get it out. At first we said, "Sorry dude, you need a whole new crank," but he didn't have the thirty-five bucks to spend on that, nor did he have the time for us to do it, because he had all these shrimp po-boys and whatnot piled up in his basket, waiting to be taken to the hungry masses of the French Quarter. "Ok," we said, "Walk the deliveries that are close enough to walk, leave your bike here, and we'll try to figure something out." So he took an armful of the translucent, grease-soaked bags and took off, looking pretty bummed to be reduced to the rank of pedestrian on this mind-numbingly hot New Orleans summer day. When he was gone, we scratched our heads for a minute, then got out the Dremel Tool. With a cutting disc, I ground a slot into the offending nub of steel, then used a flathead screwdriver and a lot of lube to twist it out. Booyah! By the time Bumps was done loafing around with the sandwiches, we had a new pedal in. We'd even found one that matched his old one. It was awesome. When he walked in, it looked like we'd just traveled back in time to before the thing had broken. "What do I owe you?" he asked, and I said, "Nothing, but from now on, whenever you see me, you have to call me daddy." He agreed, took his bike, and brought us some fancy beers later. He kept the agreement, too, and every now and then I'd be riding my bike down the street and suddenly have the living crap scared out of me when this huge dude came running out yelling, "HEY DADDY!" Once, years later, I was sitting in a bar in Portland with an old friend when, randomly, Bumps came in, snuck up behind us and yelled, "THERE'S MY DADDY!" and bear-hugged me. I think my friend and I both choked on our beers.

Yay! You are finished with your tune up!

Test ride!

Lastly, if everything seems cool, take her for a test ride; a safe test ride, on a street not covered in fast moving cars. Make the block a few times and make sure the gears (if you have them) are all running well (these often need little readjustments here and there), brakes are stopping well and quietly. If everything worked out right you should notice how much BETTER it feels! Isn't a new, or greased, chain nice! Don't great brakes make a big difference in your ride?! Notice all these little things, take note, and remind yourself of this stuff next time you are feeling too lazy to work on your bike! And, again, remind yourself how rad you are for doing your own work on your bike. Now that you are more experienced and more confident with tools and repairs, share the knowledge. Help a friend fix a flat, walk someone through their own tune up, volunteer at a community run bicycle shop. Whatever! Keep working on your bike and it will never let you down, and you will learn more and more with each repair. Ok! Now, go ride your bikes!!!

The random, and (hopefully) helpful information section
Wrenching tips
1. Screwing and stripping

Sounds kinky huh? Well it isn't. The important thing here is: DO NOT STRIP PARTS!!! This is a really big deal and we see people do it all the time! Here are some tips on how not to strip a part:

1) Use the right tool for the job! Examples: 15mm wrench, not a vice grip; the right size screwdriver, as well as cable cutters, not wire cutters; etc. The right tool will do the job better and not strip something that will take you hours longer to repair.

2) Never use excessive force! This will avoid breaking bolts. And if you are screwing in a nut or a screw onto your bike, HAND-TIGHTEN IT FIRST! Get a few threads in with your fingers to make sure it fits right. You can lube the nut to help this along, but absolutely STOP turning the thing if it gets HOT or difficult to turn. If this is happening you are stripping threads and you will regret it. Don't do it!!!

3) Be patient. Especially with lining up threads on things like bottom brackets, axles, pedals. Be sure you are threading the right way! Not everything on a bike is righty tighty/lefty loosey! (See list below of things that are left hand threaded for exceptions.) Do your best to never cross-thread a bottom bracket because it is a real pain to fix.

4) Lube up all your nuts and bolts! Yes! Before you screw in any nut or bolt, or anything with threads, put a little grease on the threads! This will allow it to tighten better and will keep it from seizing after it's been on for a while. Do this with things like pedals, crank bolts, quill style stem bolts, bottom bracket cups. It will really help later down the road.

THINGS THAT ARE LEFT HAND THREADED.

Generally anything you screw in will tighten when screwed to the right (righty tighty) and loosen when screwed to the left (lefty loosey). There are a few exceptions on a bike to keep things from automatically loosening by the forward movement of parts. These are the parts you tighten to the left and loosen to the right:

THE LEFT SIDE PEDAL

Internal parts on freewheels (which we don't discuss in this book), non-drive side bottom bracket parts, such as: the cone and locknut on a single speed crank, and fixed cup threading on all EXCEPT French and Italian cartridge style bottom brackets. A good trick is if your bottom bracket has a swooshy cursive logo that ends in an 'i' or an 'o' (Italian!) then it's probably counter clockwise on the non-drive side. Giant is not Italian.

WHY are things left hand threaded? Well, if you notice, a lot of things on the non-drive side of the bike are left hand threaded. This is because the natural forward rotation of these parts on that side of the bike would cause regular threads to loosen themselves. The forward movement causes friction to pull the part to the left, which would cause it to come loose. The solution? Left hand threads! Got it!?

2. Leverage

Using leverage when you are working on bikes, or with any tool, is something that doesn't always come naturally, but can make the hugest difference working with stuck parts or certain tools. I always understood the idea of leverage as a concept, but it took me a long time of mechanicking to figure out how to apply it to my work and make my job a lot easier. The actual definition of leverage is "the useful work done is the energy applied, which is force times distance" or something like that. The important words here are force and distance. Important because, as the definition confusingly states, you get a lot more done when you have a lot of distance and a lot of force. How do you apply distance to your work? When you are turning a bolt, for example, try to find a position to put your wrench or whatever on the nut where you will have the most space to turn. This will lessen the amount of work you will have to do, the amount of pressure on your body and excess turning and turning which can be real hard on the hands and wrists. Find a place where you can make one good long turn, and turn the part there. Also, to get greater distance, you can use a longer tool. Try a big adjustable wrench instead of a little one. Or put a "cheater bar" on the end of a ratchet or wrench to get more distance. This is not cheating. You'd be surprised how a real tight axle nut will practically fall off when you turn it with a long bar. It's crazy.

Force is another matter. In fact, it may be the most important matter. In order to get a nut to turn or a

solid part of wrench on top for less slipping

tighten

PIC. 81

push down to help hold wrench tighter as you turn.

tighten

screw to loosen you need force. It is important to find a way to maximize the amount of force you are putting on the tool. Here are ways you can do that:

Get a good grip. Make sure the tool is not going to slip! This can sometimes be a little tricky. For example, some tools have directions they should go on a part in order to minimize the possibility of slipping. Sometimes I'll grab a screwdriver with both hands (Wait guys, don't laugh—mine just happen to be particularly small girl's hands and, believe it or not, in the man's world we live in, most tools are sized for a large hand. So stop your laughing!) to be sure I am really pushing in on a potentially stripped screw, and turning real hard at the same time. Also, some tools need to be placed in a specific way to get a good grip on a nut. Adjustable wrenches and channel locks are like this (pic. 81). They have a fixed and stable part, and a looser, movable part. With channel locks, the top part of the pliers is the fixed part, and should be positioned so it is actually causing the turn. Meaning, it should be on top. When it is positioned like this, the force of the turn naturally causes you to grip the pliers tighter. Try it both ways. If it feels like it just isn't working for you, flip it over and try again. Really. Same exact thing goes for an adjustable wrench. (Did you know "Crescent" is a brand and that these are actually just called adjustable wrenches?) Make sure you are applying the most force with the larger, fixed part of

the wrench, not with the slidey adjustable part. That part can wiggle and has a little play, so if it feels like the wrench keeps slipping, flip it over and try again. Cool!

Push or pull? This is a good question. Look at where your body is positioned and decide which will give you the most force. When I am standing over a bike and need to loosen a real tight bottom bracket locknut, I put my arm through the triangle on the bike so I can get the wrench in a position where I can get a long PUSH down. I am over the part so I get more arm strength by pushing down. Or, when you need to unlock some tight axle nuts to adjust an axle, set the wheel upright on its rim and position the wrenches so the one you need to loosen and turn counter clockwise is being pushed down. Try it. Under a car, one often gets more force by pushing up… You can sometimes do this with a bike if you are stuck and a part is stuck and maybe the longest stroke or the most unobstructed path would be easiest if you got below the part and pushed up. Try this when you get in a bind. It will help.

Find a clear path. If you have to really rail on a part to get it loose, try to find a path where you aren't going to hit yer knuckles or other body part real hard. For one, this will help you not to hurt yourself or bust a knuckle. But it will also give you the confidence to push real, real hard. I mean, I know that if I think I'm gonna bust a knuckle on something, I won't use all the force I can. So find a place you feel safe to use all your strength.

Force! Sometimes force just takes plain and simple strength: a stronger arm. Sometimes force just means really getting it without holding back. A little hitting with the hammer can also help, if it is safe and you're not gonna ruin a part. My boss once wrote a facetious letter to the editor of some bike magazine that had written about how no shop should ever even have a hammer. He wrote about all the sizes of sledgehammers we had and the specific use for each size. Funny thing is, while he was exaggerating, he

wasn't going too far. I mean, we worked on some crazy crappy bikes, with some incredible amounts of rust. Sometimes a hammer whacking down on a wrench stuck over a bolt was all we could rely on.

In general, with leverage, it is good to think of your hands as an extension of your tools. They are, in fact, tools them-selves, as are your arms, and, at times, so are your legs and torso. You can use their strength in that way to make your tools work better for you.

3. Patience

Take things apart slowly. Memorize how it looks PUT TOGETHER before you take it apart! Take your time and pay attention. This will really help you with reassembly. Keep small or rolling parts together. It's nice to have a rag laid out where you can set things in the order you took them off in. This also helps to keep bearings from rolling away. Label things if you need to. Use individual boxes or cans to keep stuff together. Keep each repair simple and organized. And hey, have a good repair manual lying around in case you get stuck! And if you get really frustrated, take a step back. Go out for a while, or work on a different part of the bike. Working when you are stressed and frustrated isn't fun and usually doesn't work. Having to listen to someone in a shop curse and yell really takes the fun out of work. Don't do it. Don't throw your tools either.

4. Lube: not meant to be nasty, kids

Use the right lube! (Yes, to avoid stripping when you are screwing. Geez.) Use chain lube on chains. (I like Tri-Flow, but everyone has a favorite, and there are different ones for different conditions. Ask at your local shop.) NEVER use WD-40 or motor oil on chains! (pic. 82)

Never! These attract dirt and wear parts down. You can use this Tri-Flow (or other brand) lube on things like brake pivot points, derailleur pivot points, and other moving parts as well. Use dry lube (waxy style) on cables inside the housing for brakes and gears. Liquid wrench and WD-40 are for stuck parts only! These are for loosening up stuck, or very stuck parts, not for lubing. Good bearing grease for bottom brackets, axles, headsets. There is Tri-Flow brand, Park Tools brand, the kind you can get at auto parts stores. Whatever you like. Phil Wood green grease is great, or good old white lithium grease is fine. Phil oil is great for lubing spoke nipples and for dropping down the holes in those funky old three speed hubs. Once our friend Buddha came into French Quarter Bikes with a bottom bracket that sounded like it was possessed by banshees because Mitchell had gotten all drunk and told him to overhaul it with Vaseline. Don't do that.

General Troubleshooting

Auto repair manuals make trouble shooting lists. This makes sense for something with all that gasoline and electricity, but for a bike, all you need for good troubleshooting is your eyes and ears. Be logical. If you hear a funny noise, or some grinding, try to find its origin. Is the chain rubbing on your derailleur? Crank hitting a kickstand? Does the noise happen once per crank revolution, or is it real random? Look for clues. Think critically. Be logical. Here are a few hints:

Funny creaks? Check for cracks in the bike frame. Tighten pedals, seat, and those little bolts that hold our front chain rings onto the crank. Check the crank bolt! Tight tight!

Random knocking and grinding? Check your axles and bottom bracket. Check for saggy kickstand. (Hmmm, a knock once per revolution? What could do that? Pedal hitting the kickstand.) Real random knocking more than likely means some messed up bearings somewhere. Be logical.

Rubbing? See if you can hear where it is coming from. Check derailleur high and low adjustments causing the chain to rub on a derailleur, loose chains, brake pad clearance. See if your frame is broken anywhere, like the chainstays causing your wheel to rub only when you are sitting on it and riding it but not on a stand (especially if it is an aluminum frame from the eighties!). Roll up pant leg, check for a bag strap hitting a wheel.

Bike sluggish? Look for low tire pressure, brakes or wheels rubbing, tight axles or bottom bracket, loose chain or spokes.

The important thing here is to be in tune with your bicycle! Listen to it, feel it, and notice things that are a little wrong before they get a lot wrong. A good life rule in general I think. Don't leave it up to people like me and my friends who chronically, manically, insanely dissect the workings and unworkings of every bike that passes us as we chat on the street corner, yelling shit like, "Hey! Tighten your chain!" or whatever. Don't ignore problems. Think about it.

Extending the life of your bike

Keep your bike inside.

Keep your bike clean. Especially your drive train!

Keep your bike tuned up! Make a time, like spring, that you do this every year. Every 6 months is even better!

Inspect your bike now and then for worn or broken parts. Don't neglect things that will lead to bigger repairs later.

Adjust! Adjust! Adjust!

Once your bike is in order and tuned up great, don't quit there! Keep things adjusted when they start to loosen up again. They will. It is the law of nature, of physics.… So keep the moving parts on your bike, especially the bearing systems (axles, bottom brackets, and headsets), adjusted well. Adjustments are WAY simpler than overhauls and keep your parts in good shape. When things are adjusted well there is no space for dirt and grime to get into your grease and this will keep all your moving parts wear-free and rolling smooth. Keeping things adjusted will always save you time and money in the long run, and make your day-to-day riding safer and more enjoyable.

Finally! Now that you have done all this work and your ride is as sweet as it's going to get, do yourself a favor, and don't get your bike ripped off! Here are some tips on what to do:

Locking your bicycle

Every time someone came into French Quarter Bicycles, crying that their bike had just been stolen, I asked if they had locked it. Sadly, most people said no. In a town where bikes disappear as quickly as they do, I have a hard time feeling sympathy for these folks, especially because the only two bikes I have lost have been due to friends borrowing them and leaving them unlocked (sorry guys). Don't do it, not for a half hour, not for a minute. Not in a backyard, not in front of a busy shop. It may seem paranoid or negative to think one can't do this in any city, any neighborhood, but you can't. If you choose to be this openminded, consider your stolen bike a gift to the universe and don't cry to me about it. No offense. If you don't want to lose your bike, lock it right and lock it every time!! Dammit! I mean it!!! Here are my suggestions:

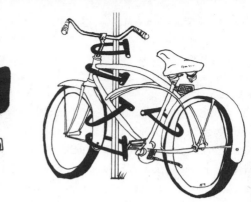

Always use a U-lock, or something stronger, like the huge and heavy "New York Lock" (but if you do this, don't keep bragging about how light your bike is, because if it takes 20 pounds of metal to lock it up cause it is so fancy, what's the point, huh?). Here in New Orleans, I have only heard of one U-lock ever being cut. It is a deterrent here in a city where people don't lock up, or use crappy little chains (even dog collar chains!) or teeny cables that are easier targets as they can be cut with strong hands using a pair of pliers. If you live in a city where U-locks do get cut, use something better, or get the highest quality U-lock you can get.

Editors note: It was discovered in New York City that a Volvo carjack would easily pop a standard U-lock. This led to a rash of theft and is why companies now make smaller U-locks, where the jack cannot fit inside the lock. I have had numerous locks cut and bikes stolen. A cheap U-lock one time; a thick cable lock another time. The unfortunate reality is that a person with enough determination can really cut any lock. This is not to say we should be paranoid all the time. I use a small U-lock now that has served me well ever since. Making your bike appear unappealing to thieves doesn't hurt either.

Lock your bike well. This means: lock it to something solid in the ground that can't be pulled up (like a street sign in a grassy median). Make sure the top of whatever you lock to is tight too, like the sign on the post, or the top of the parking meter. Here in New Orleans, there is only about a 50 percent chance

that either a stop sign or a parking meter is actually cemented into the ground. Don't lock to anything loose or wobbly. If you think someone will stop someone from pulling a bike up over a ten foot post, think again. Worse things have gone on, unstopped in the middle of a crowd or in broad daylight. Lock in a well lit, public place. Despite what I just said, it is better there than in some dark alley.

Check the lock twice! Especially if you've been drinking— sorry, has to be said. I had more than one person come into the shop I worked at perplexed as to how their bike was gone but the lock was locked and untouched attached to the thing they had locked to! I would ask, "Were you drunk?" The answer was almost always "yes.". Well, guess what? You locked the lock but missed the bike! I've seen 'em like this myself and just hoped nobody but me stares at every bike so much that they would notice. Oh, and if you ARE drunk, make sure you didn't accidentally lock to someone else's bike (never, NEVER lock to a strangers bike!) or to a pole through someone else's bike frame or cables! Duh! Check your lock. Enough said.

Lastly, lock as much as you can. If you have quick release wheels lock them both, or at least the most expensive one. A good rear wheel with the cluster and the tire and tube can cost you half the value of a bike. I usually still lock just the frame and the front wheel. Why? I guess, psychologically, the front looks easier to steal to me—so I lock there. So far, so good. If your wheels are quickies and you don't want to take them off every time you lock up, you can do a few things. One is to hose clamp the quick release lever to the frame. Good, but a little inconvenient if you take the wheels off a lot. Another option is using a little luggage lock and locking the lever down to the frame. I think that looks pretty cool, but again, slightly annoying. Or, you can just get locking skewers, or anti-scam cams, which use a torx wrench or other gadget to loosen the skewers. More expensive, but easy enough. Or, get a cable to thread onto your U-lock and through your wheels. I've seen cables get cut for a whole bike before, but not just for wheels. Again, though, you never know....

Safety tips for riding

In theory, bicycles have the same rights as other vehicles on the road and should, therefore, follow the same rules. Neither seems to actually be the case. Most vehicles (cars, trucks, and the ridiculous SUVs) think they have domain over the road and will treat it as such, leaving bicycles at their mercy. Many rules of the road actually put the cyclist in a more dangerous position and really should be broken. It is a very fine line.

In any case, there are two important things to remember:

ONE: Each and every bicycler should remember— YOU HAVE THE RIGHT TO BE ON THE ROAD! Do not feel bad or apologize to a driver for being on the road! Not only do you have a legal right to be there, in many cases you are legally obligated to be there instead of on the sidewalk. Because you are clearly doing a respectable thing by cycling for

transportation, you have MORE of a right to be on the road! Don't forget it! Ride proud! Know that you deserve your space. Use it and enjoy it! Be determined and decisive and feel good knowing that you are the most efficient and socially responsible for your transportation!

but...

TWO: Know when to give in! There are drivers that you will be up against that, sadly, have no respect at all for the cyclist. These are the people that we need to be afraid of. Cars are bigger and, in a fight, they will more than likely win. Don't get into a situation over pride that will get you hurt or killed. The biking community needs you!

So! Remembering these two most important things, here are some basic safety rules to help you get by:

LOOK. Keep your eyes moving. Pay attention. Watch for cars wanting to cross your path, for reverse lights, for turn signals, for the evil car door opening into your path! These are your enemies! Watch for them! Keep your eyes out and looking for distracted drivers, especially with texters and callers on the road. These drivers are not paying attention to you! So watch out for them!

LISTEN. Listen for cars coming up behind you. Are they speeding? Are they slowing down to make that totally lame right turn right into your path? Pay special attention for quieter electric and hybrid cars that you may not be used to not hearing. Know what is around you, with all the senses you have.

COMMUNICATE. Whenever possible. Look the driver in the eye, make sure they recognize you, and communicate with them about where you are going. Eye contact is great for awareness. Hand signals for turning or intersection stand-offs. And be sure to communicate to the bad driver. Your voice (yelling!) can save you from bad situations (like a car door or a pedestrian walking aimlessly into your path). Your voice can also let a driver know when s/he really fucked up. Cursing or shaking your fist works great. Flipping the bird (your middle finger) may seem great, but might make matters worse. Be careful.

RIDE WHERE DRIVERS EXPECT YOU TO BE. Meaning, ride with traffic on the right side of the road and not all over the place (especially for new bikers or in a new town). Drivers are taught where to look for a bicycle, and most will not go out of their way to look in the place where they won't expect you to be. (For example, they will not look to the right when making a right turn out of a driveway, if you're going up the street the wrong way, you're likely to get hit.) It is not just safer for you to be where you legally should be, but if you get into an accident, more than likely their insurance will pay for your hospital bills. If you were at fault, they won't. I got hit riding my bike in a crosswalk. Not only did I get the bill, but I got a traffic ticket too, while I was lying on the asphalt with a broken leg. Lame.

BE COURTEOUS. Let a driver know you appreciate it when they give you the right of way, or the space you need on the road. Smile, give them a thanks.

BE PREPARED TO STOP. Always have your hands on the brakes and be ready to stop. Have an out, or a plan to get out of the way if you can't stop (driveways, sidewalks, etc.) hit the thing that will hurt the least.

ALWAYS ASSUME THE WORST. I know this sounds pessimistic, but remember that it is up to you to keep yourself alive. Assume there is a car speeding down the road you want to cross, assume that behind the truck stopped in the lane ahead of you is another car riding past. If you can't see past an obstacle, slow down or stop until you can. Never trust that a driver sees you. Assume that they don't, or that if they do they might just not care if they kill you. And don't assume that you know what a driver will do next. Four out of five bicycle accidents are caused by a motorist breaking a rule.

TAKE A SAFE POSITION ON THE ROAD. Ride safely enough away from parked cars to keep you safe from their doors. I prefer to be a bit in the lane. Cars having

to swing out a little alert the ones behind them to my existence and also alerts them to slow down. If I am really in the lane and causing a delay, I give the drivers a sign to let them know I'll be out of the way as soon as I can.

BREAK THE RULES WHEN IT FEELS SAFE. Finally a fun rule! Now, I am not saying to ride crazy. Ride to your comfort level and your experience. Ride safe. But if you come to a stop light and the coast is clear, by all means, cross the road! It puts you ahead of traffic and in a safer position. Cross the road safely only when it's not gonna freak out anyone coming on a green— use your common sense.

MAINTAIN YOUR BIKE. Make sure your brakes are good! And that your bike generally runs well. Have good tires for fewer flats. Have lights, or, at least, reflectors, for riding at night. Be as visible as you can, dress up crazy, dress your bike up crazy, the more of a spectacle you are the better.

BEWARE OF the deaf and blind, music-blaring window-tinted cruisers, cab drivers during festival time in New Orleans or other big cities, the ever present car door opening in your path (r.i.p Lucas Cox), streetcar tracks that grab your wheels and throw you off your bike, dogs chasing you through neighborhoods kicking and screaming, paranoid speeding cops, cars hurrying to make the yellow light, drunk tourists wandering into the street, the cell phone driver, etc, etc, etc.

A couple more things. . .

Group riding

As antisocial as this sounds, I secretly avoid group riding at all costs. While here in New Orleans it may seem safer to ride with others late at night, I find it a little distracting. If it is late at night, or other riders have been drinking, I feel more afraid for them and don't watch out for myself. Or there will be one hot shot up ahead, running lights and making other people risk themselves to keep up. If you ride together, everyone should be extra cautious; watch out for each other but for yourself, too! Take it slow, take up more space, but don't block traffic. Ride to the ability of the LEAST experienced rider, or the crappiest bike.

Helmets

One day I was biking and I ran into a friend I hadn't seen in a while. She said, "I saw you from up the street, but I didn't think anyone I knew would be dorky enough to wear a helmet."

You know what, though? I don't give a shit. I've been in two wrecks in the last year, both times I just suddenly hit something and flipped. Once I wasn't wearing a helmet, and I ended up in the hospital, with a broken collarbone, a concussion, and some stitches to the head. The second time I was wearing a helmet. I landed on my head. When I came to, I couldn't remember a lot of things. The helmet was smashed, but my head wasn't. That's all.

Ok! I think that's it! I hope we haven't made biking seem rigid or boring. Biking is fun! Despite the cars. And even with all these rules, I know which streets I can haul ass on in the middle of the night, which ones I can ride down with a cup of coffee in my hand blaring my own radio. But I know that in traffic it is up to me to stay safe. I have been in a few accidents, all typical; an obstructed view of the road and me trusting the driver who actually waved me INTO oncoming traffic; a car right hand turning in front of me, stereo blaring in the dark; even a car door in the face. I hope I have learned all of my biking lessons because of those accidents and the loss of a couple of friends to their own, I am more careful. I hope you will be, too.

Bike extras

Getting parts

If you need to get new parts, put some thought into your purchase and choose a nice place to give your business to. Be creative! Independent bike shops are great. If you have a community bike project in your town, try it! They are usually great places to go to get weird sizes, old parts, cheap wheels, or things that you need only one of that are only sold in pairs. These places are fun to rummage through and a good place to meet other bike geeks. Ask around your town to see if there is a great old bike wizard who stores old bikes and parts that might be fun to check out. And there is always the computer, that internet thing, where you can find lots of stuff for sale. But I think you all probably know more about that than us.

Throughout this book we discuss replacing worn parts. Again, if it has not already been said, always try to save your old parts. It is good because if there is any confusion about what size part you need, what thread, length, whatever, you will have your old part for comparison. Bring it down to the place you go to for parts and say, "I need one of these." It can never hurt.

Accessories

By accessories I mean extra stuff, maybe upgrades too. There is a lot of stuff out there to put on your bike for convenience and to alter your ride, from old school dove bars on a road bike for fun to baskets or a rack to make your bike a more utilitarian machine. Whatever you do though, try to get good quality stuff. A good seat may cost 20 bucks more but will last you longer and make every day on your bike a little nicer. Think about what you want your bike to do for you and then build it so it can. Not all shops have a great accessory selection. If they don't, ask to look through a catalog. You'd be surprised at the stuff in there that you may never have even seen before. It's fun to look at and get to dreaming. Customize your ride! It can become an obsession though, so be careful.

Need vs. want—when each counts

Need is easy. We need to get to work, we need a way to get there, maybe what we need is a bike. But is it all that easy? When we need new tires for our bike, do we get cheap ones or quality ones? Do we buy flashy ones with red stripes down the sides or whitewalls? When does fashion beat function? When is that okay, and when is it just frivolous? I guess the answer depends on the person, his or her needs, desires, and means. Whatever the case is, get your stuff and be satisfied. Try not to be too much of a show off about all your rad gear, though it is nice to show people the bike parts that have made life a little easier for you. Like, I love my little chain tensioner that allowed me to switch my little Bridgestone road bike into a single speed. People ask me about it and I explain why it was a good purchase for me but how one could get away with a cheaper single

speed conversion. "The tensioner is great, but the company that makes it uses crappy installation instructions and if I hadn't had a wholesale ordering hook up, it would have cost me an obscene 50 dollars and I could have done the same conversion with a cheap little derailleur." That kind of thing, just so people don't feel like they have to get hyped up on the fancy shit. Unless they want to, of course.

Fancy stuff

Working at the shop and at Plan B in New Orleans, using lots of old parts and trying to get bikes working on the cheap, it often felt like we were trying to build Frankenstein monsters. Yes, hopefully they were fairly efficient, graceful Frankenstein monsters, but still they were all pieced together from resurrected parts. Once I got a job in a shop in Asheville working on fancy newer bikes, it was a totally different thing—more like assembling space craft out of new fancy spacecraft parts. BORING! I even got hassled by my boss (a nineteen year old jock) for working on

SOME PEOPLE WILL CONVERT THEIR BIKES TO SINGLE SPEED OR FIXED GEAR TO CUT DOWN ON THE WEIGHT OF THE BIKE.

the floor. Jeez, whatever! I missed the grease and the grit and the serious head scratching sessions to solve a problem as quickly and affordably as we could. (Though I didn't miss all the baskets I had to assemble in NOLA, that's for sure.)A lot of the fancy stuff just seemed so ridiculous to me, like most carbon fiber components. You'd only need them if you are some completely over the top pro-racer type. On the street, who cares about a couple of grams? Once you have crusty punk dudes putting all this crazy stuff on their bikes, you've got to stop to wonder why, if they're so concerned with weight, are they still wearing Carhartt over-alls and a million little metal things hanging off their belts? Whenever people were doling out their paychecks at the shop for some fancy-shmancy new technology, I just thought about how Shimano pushed biopace so hard in the eighties, spending millions on marketing, and how people flipped out over this revolutionary "new" design (it had actually been done before—in the 1890s) and now it's discontinued and all that biopace stuff is getting dumped in the scrapyard (not to dis the stuff, there are people who still swear by it out there).

That said, there is some fancy stuff, or not even fancy but new stuff, that I think is actually just better than the old stuff. Lots of punk-type mechanics (and even older framebuilders I've met) immediately scoff at any type of new technology, writing it all off as marketing schemes to get dollars out of yuppie's spandex pockets. Some of that stuff is just legitimately superior, and some of it, while not superior, certainly has its place. Here are a few examples:

Fancy Stuff I'm Into:

Cassettes. I am completely convinced that the cassette is superior to the older freewheel. Here's why: On freewheel hubs, the axle is threaded into the hub and the freewheel is threaded onto the hub, over the axle. This means that the bearings are more than an inch away from where the axle is supported by the bearings. Therefore, every time you hit a bump, your dropout is basically going

to try and bend your axle way back there where the cone is rolling on the bearings.

The cassette, however, has a free-hub body, which is attached to the hub and has bearings in two places—at the hub and further out towards the end of the axle. If you think about leverage for a sec, you can see why this would be better. And I'm not saying it as a mechanic, I'm saying it as someone who used to ride around New Orleans with a freewheel and snap axles like crazy, especially if I was carrying anything. Since having a cassette I have yet to break or bend an axle, even riding on a trip through mountains with like sixty pounds of crap on my bike.

Freewheels certainly do work fine for most people, but if you have problems with bent or broken axles, that could be why.

Threadless headsets. I don't actually have one of these, but I appreciate them. I think they make sense, and are easy to adjust (see "threadless headsets" section). I mean, if you think about it, the old quill-stem system, with that big chunk of cast steel in the middle of it, is kind of weird. I apologize in advance to my friend Johnny, who builds beautiful hand-brazed quill stems.

Sealed bottom brackets. I understand why people think that these things are just another piece of disposable crap, destined for the landfill when it wears out (see "bottom brackets"), but I've used both and, weighing the options, I feel like these are worth it. It's not like a coffee cup or something; you're not breezing through three a day. They last a good long time, especially if you're just tooling around town. It seems worth it to not have it loosening up all the time.

Things I'm Not So Into:

Track bikes. Now, I have a track bike. I actually built the frame at United Bicycle Institute's chromoly brazing course. I like it. I'm proud of it. But I don't ever ride the thing since moving to the mountains. I had one scary incident where my chain popped off (I'd skimped on parts and my chainline was off by a few millimeters) when I was flying down this busy road at about 30mph. Luckily, I'd thought about what to do in such a situation, so I calmly put my foot back on the top of the rear wheel, slowed down and pulled into the parking lot of a diner. My wheel actually burned through my shoelaces, which were now reduced to smoking scraps that I had to tie back together to keep my shoe on.

I can hear macho track bike enthusiasts saying, "Well, that's your own fault, don't knock track bikes for it." and that's true. The real reason I'm not into track bikes is because I was just up in New York and every hipster in Bedford seems to be shitting their tight pants over track bikes, and it just doesn't make sense to me. In ten years you'll have made pudding out of your knees, or worse, your skull, if you don't get some brakes.

Clipless pedals. Not so into them. I've used them, and, if you're touring or racing or even training and going out on thirty mile rides, I can understand it. In town, though? When you're having to unclip at each red- light or every time some jerk on a cell-phone cuts you off? No thanks. What's wrong with toe clips? I've never heard of anyone getting a broken ankle (or even falling down) because of toe clips, but have heard some horror stories about clipless.

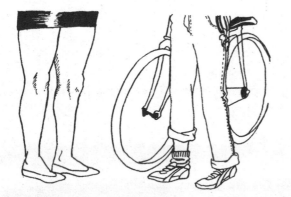

Bike aesthetics and fashion

I really like a pretty bike. Whether that means a conventional, clean type of beautiful, simple little single speed road frame, or rough-edgy and scratchy like a heavy old, antique cruiser. For me it is worth putting the effort in to make it pretty. It is worth the extra effort to me to find even the practical items that I use that are in some way beautiful. Like the little plate I eat toast on every morning. It's a utilitarian little plate, but it's really pretty! It makes me happy in the morning. And just tonight, my friend Tony told me that while having a conversation on the phone, he saw beauty in his bicycle he had never noticed before. Like how straight the fork was and how large the wheels seemed to him all of a sudden. It's great to like the way something looks! But, as with anything, never sacrifice beauty for functionality, or do it just for fashion. I've seen some people make some pretty dangerous conversions to their bikes that they weren't ready for, just to make them look a little hipper. Like cutting and flipping bars to make bullhorns and then putting really crap old brakes on a fast single speed road frame just so it looks like a coolie track bike. Not smart. Your brakes should always work as well as your bike is fast. Duh. Be smart and do things right. Function first and beauty can be a close second. Just like choosing a friend or a partner, they may look pretty, but if they're no fun to hang out with, things get old pretty fast, you know?

Same goes for fashion. These days, fashion seems to be key, and there are some pretty heavy looks going on with biking. From racer style spandex mania, to the uber bike punk messenger bag, one pant leg rolled up, little lock in your back pocket style. It's all fine, but not when it gets competitive or out of hand, when the fashion outweighs the simple radness of biking around cause it's fun. We don't need a uniform to do it, you know? I mean, we could do one of those silly drawings here with a bunch of little arrows pointing out all the things one needs for real bike style, but do we really need to? I mean, come on. Isn't it better when people break the rules? Like a girl in a little mini skirt and high heels (like my friend Rose!) on a bike. A boy in a mini skirt on a bike, even better! People who REALLY break the rules and look just totally regular. Like my friend Wink who bikes to his job at City Hall in a suit. Or like my friend Jacques, who cycled from New Orleans to San Francisco on a Schwinn three speed wearing cut off shorts and flip flops with his gear in a plastic chainsaw case bungeed to a back rack! Holy Crap! Now that's style! Don't think you gotta look a certain way to cycle. Be comfortable, be yourself.

Community bike programs

In past editions of *Chainbreaker*, we have had long lists of awesome bicycle projects that are running all over the world. But with so many additions (yay!) and so much moving and changing of the facilities, having a written directory is really just not very practical. And nowadays, the internet can tell you a lot of what you need to know about these kind of things. So, you can look up bike projects in your town, or if you are traveling look up a site like www.bikecollectives.org for a list and a map of bike projects all over the world, as well as information on the annual bicycle conference known as Bike!Bike! (which was started in New Orleans by the way!). If you are visiting a town and looking for a place to work on your bike or find parts, ask other bikers or at local bike shops. Someone will likely lead you to a bike project or bike recycling center, or just some bike tinkerer who may be hoarding bike parts for fun! Good luck!

Closing statements

Well, hopefully, if you have made it this far you have a great running bike to show for it. Thanks so much for reading and trying and for making a stronger connection with your bicycle and for adding another dimension to the way you are engaging in your world!

You may think you simply did a little tune up on your bicycle, but if you think about it, you did a whole lot more than just that. Mechanics are a way to explore the workings of the physical world around you and to think about how to apply what you see to other parts of life that may seem unrelated. For me, mechanics are stability in a world of variables where there is so much to negotiate, navigate, blah blah blah. Machines are stable and solid, there are rules to follow, and they are made of metal that only changes under the most extreme conditions. With bikes, as with most machines, each part has a job. I always know what to expect from a bottom bracket, or headset, down to how it will break. The bearings aren't going to decide to melt just to freak me out or otherwise ruin my day. They will simply do their job day after day until they wear out, and I've learned to expect that,. too. Things break and there is nothing else to say but simply, "broken!" There is no fault to be found anywhere but in the simple truth of impermanence. It is comforting for me to know that in a world where dealing with things like humans, jobs, and money, which all can be so trying, that there is some aspect of my life that is dependable. It gives me a little inspiration to think that if I practice and someday master problem solving skills with my bicycle that, with some effort, the knowledge might just spill over a little into other parts of my life. I hope so, at least.

So everyone, have faith in your bicycle and learn what you can do to improve your relationship with it. Love your bike with all of your heart and know that someday, when you feel like the rest of your life is slipping through your little fingers, that your bike will always be there for you, waiting to be included in each day of your life. Don't give up on it!!!

Reprints from the original Chainbreaker *bicycle zines!*

For those of you not familiar with zines, or with the Chainbreaker Bicycle Zine, let me explain. Zines are small, self-published, copied and pasted, homemade magazines. Zines come in all shapes and sizes, and can range from being personal stories and artwork to being ways of sharing information and skills. "Chainbreaker" was a zine all about bicycles that had some personal stories and a lot of skill sharing. From 2001 - 2005, I (Shelley) printed just four issues of "Chainbreaker", all of which had roughly 44 pages of gathered information, stories, artwork, comics, repair information, and so much more. Some of it was written by me, but much was also written by friends and also strangers who wrote to me with their additions, which I would lay out and print in the upcoming issue. People wrote in from all over the world with their contributions and ideas, and it was so fun hearing from everyone! We talked and wrote about everything, from bike history and culture, to gender issues in the bike shop, to city planning, to how biking was part of different countries' cultures. So many things!

The zines were printed over that period of 5 special years, when I lived in New Orleans in my favorite tiny apartment, working at the best bike shop in the world (French Quarter BIkes!). I biked everywhere during that time and had a simple life that consisted of work, all of the perks of life in the incredible city of New Orleans, and yearly travel to India for Buddhist studies. Life felt perfect. But alas, impermanence stuck, French Quarter Bikes lost their lease and closed, and then, after just returning from India, Hurricane Katrina arrived and the flooding broke the levees and everything abruptly ended.The city was in ruins, all of our lives changed forever.

As for the zine, I had lost my apartment to the flooding, my typewriter, desk, bikes, supplies. The shop that kept all of my zine masters flooded and closed and I never got the masters back. We didn't get mail delivered for nearly 8 months and by then I had been forced to move and lost contact with all my contributors and supporters. So, after all that I stopped writing the Chainbreaker Bicycle Zine. Ethan and I had talked about writing a bike repair manual for some time when Joe at Microcosm suggested we combine it with reprints of the old zine. And thus the idea for the Chainbreaker Bicycle Book and Repair Manual was born! So here are the the zines. I hope they can fill in the backstory of our enthusiasm for bikes and bike culture. There are so many funny stories and great ideas in here, and I am so happy they are still around to share. Thank you to all the old contributors and sorry for the sometimes low printing quality due to the loss of the masters copies. There is still a lot of fun in these pages... ENJOY!

chainbreaker.

your favorite bicycle zine

♡ for the love of a bicycle ♡

It is hard for me to quantify just how much i love bicycles, for me to tell you how much joy they bring me, how much meaning they have given my life. I can tell you this... I ride my bike most everywhere i go, i have a job mechanic-ing at a bike shop, i volunteer at the non-profit bicycle project here in new orleans. When i go to the coffee shop the girl behind the counter askes me for bike advice, when i go to the market somebody inevitably says, "hey, it's the bike girl," i have bicycle grease under my nails constantly, and i can't stop diagnosing every bike that passes me on the street, thinking to myself "loose bottom bracket... brakes aren't toed in..." and the like. i am not alone, friends who all ride bikes, work on bikes, love bikes, do this as well.

What is it about the bicycle that can bring a person so much joy? Why are there so many songs written about bikes? How do they become so much of who we are? It is not just their beauty, their geometry, or that they bring freedom and fun to the most average chore. It isn't just their fabulous history or the way they help open minds. It is all this and more. It is that the bicycle shows a person that their are options, that there are other ways of living, new horizons undiscovered. For me, the bicycle showed me how to live more simply, and that life could be less complicated, that i could slow down, have less obligations and therefor see the world with fresher eyes. The bicycle taught me to enjoy my alone time more, to enjoy moving my body, being more a part of the environment around me. It has made me feel more socially responsible, made me more aware of excess, privilege, of the tiny bubbles that people create for themselves to live in. It has made me feel more vulnerable and therefor MORE AWARE.

The bicycle has caused an evolution in myself. it has helped me to change and expand my values. i have a hope that if this happened for enough of us there would be a revolution, as kropotkin says, "a time of accelerated evolution," where cooperation, simple mechanics and fresh air could work against the capitalism, technology and fear that threatens to wreck this world.

In essence i believe a simple bicycle ride could save us all.

bicycle Revolution

"Throughout the world, bicycles offer people a means of self-empowerment. As transport, human powered vehicles are clean, quiet, healthy, safe, quick, economical, space-saving, and self-sufficient. When compared to automobiles, bicycles represent the most logical, sustainable means of daily travel. With growing issues such as overpopulation, land use, economic viability, energy efficiency, and environmental degradation, the bicycle enters the twenty first century as the vehicle for the future." (David B. Perry)

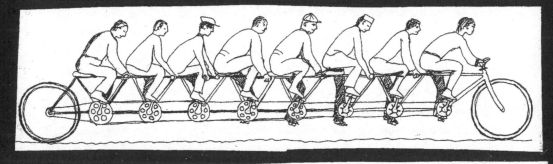

Besides the most obvious qualities of the bicycle, that it is the most efficient and fun form of transportation, that it is a source of immense freedom and leisure, that it is economical and has utilitarian beauty, the bicycle has an even more interesting and admirable role in history, economics, politics and society. The bicycle has served as a great emancipator, a social equalizer, and people liberator all over the world. The depth of the importance of the bicycle is... well... DEEP.

Bicycles played a huge role in womens' liberation. Women fought for the right to ride along with and without men, and continued to fight into realms of dress and other aspects of social life. Bicycling also gave America its first nationally recognized and acclaimed black athelete (and role modle), Marshall Taylor. His fight for equality in bicycle racing and the struggles he was put through shined the spotlight on negative race relations that plagued our country. Though blacks fought oppression long after his stardom which peaked in 1900, he helped force Americans to question their feeling toward the black community by being a person who they couldn't help but love and trust and look up to for his amazing abilities in their most beloved sport.

Bicycles also helped to break down barriers between classes, when in 1884, bicycles began being mass produced, making them both available and affordable to both the rich and the poor. Bikes were much cheaper than the upkeep of a team of horses and people from all levels of society began riding side by side and fighting for their shared rights as cyclers. Bicycles even drew people out of churches and saloons alike and into the countryside, where they learned to appreciate leisure and adventure, life and the fresh air.

These radical changes happened in American society during the last decades of the 1900's. The economic effect of the bicyles was profound. Watchmakers, piano builders, horse and even candy salesman lost money and work due to the great sucess of the bicycle, and due to the way the bike changed the priorities of the American people. Many of these changes would still be felt today had a newer and shinier toy not come along to woo the upper classes. The automobile.

The automobile. Where the bicycle had a leveling influence, the automobile unleveled it. The auto re-introduced extremes on the social scale, it brought back a division between humans and nature, it brought noise and pollution where the bicycle brought peace and health, mechanical difficulties where bicycles brought simplicity in design and repair. The automobile undid what the bicycle had done so well with so much ease and in so little time.

Though the automobile has become such an all encompassing part of American life, and of life in almost anyplace and with most any culture in the world, it is important for us to remember the positive effects of the bicycle are still visible and that it is still more than worthwhile and rewarding to ride a bike. Bicycles are still easily affordable to all. Prices range from free to more expensive than some cars. Yet all those bicycles in that range have the same positive effect on the world around us and on the individual that rides it. The bicycle is the most free-ing vehicle. As biker / writer richard ballentine says, " the bicycle is an Anarchistic machine; it confers independent mobility at minimum expense or bother to anyone else. bikes do not need licensing or regulation. people can just use them. this is exactly what drives bureaucrats, government agencies, politicians, and profiteers crazy." well said richard.

They heyday of the bicycle is now. Let us not be discouraged by the car centered lifestyle that we watch most Americans buying into. Globally, bicycles are still far outnumbering the automobile. An estimated one billion were in exsistence in 1994, compared to a mere 500 million cars and 150 million other motorized vehicles. Three times more bicycles were produced than cars that year. And more importantly still, the effect bicycles are having on the world is growing as well. Cities are starting to plan the bicycle into their models, adding cycling lanes and paths, laws to protect the biker. Critical mass bike rides are popping up in cities all over the world, showing that bikes and politics still go hand in hand, whether it means signing a petition for safer streets or using the more hands on approach of taking over the city streets. There is more equality among cyclists here in America. In fact women make up 55 percent of our cycling population! There are more free bike projects like the Yellow Bikes in Austin, Texas, or Plan Velo in France. Bikes not Bombs and other groups like Bikes for Cuba are building and delivering free bicycles to underprivileged people in other parts of the world. Bikes are used for many types of jobs, such as delivery, messengering, postal workers, pedicabs, rickshaws, ambulances, and other transport. And, despite the seeming perfection of the bicycles original manufacturing, the bicycle is making huge technological advances, giving us lighter bikes, stronger frames and wheels, and simply more crap for us bike geeks to talk about.

YOUR FRIENDLY BIKE STORE

BICYCLES DONT POLLUTE

BIKE ROUTE

BIKE POLO

"Few articles ever used by man (sic) have created so great a revolution in social conditions as the bicycle."

Marshall "Major" Taylor

(1878 - 1932)

Marshall Taylor was born in the outskirts of Indianapolis, the grandson of freed slaves, during a period in American history where racism was upheld by the "seperate but equal" code. As a young boy he delivered newspapers by bicycle and at age 13 was hired by a local bicycle shop to do odd jobs and publicity work, which consisted of him performing bicycle tricks while wearing a military uniform. This is how he got his nickname Major. He was later coerced by the shop to race. Unexpectedly, he won. He was stuck on racing from that moment on.

He started a bicycle club called the see-saw cycling club, consisting of all black members. This club joined with others to form the Colored Wheelman's Association. They had been excluded from the country's largest cycling association, "The League of American Wheelman" when, due to their ambiguous race laws, many blacks began joining the group, causing a huge uproar among its white members. The group had a vote and passed a ban on non-white members, though they conceeded to allow blacks to race in L.A.W. events.

Taylor moved to Massachusets in 1895, looking for a place where he could ride a train more, finding too much opposition to his color in Indiana. He found the east coast to be much more open. He raced and won more and more. By 1897 he rose to the top ten in the american sprint champion series, winning in cities all over the country and raising tensions from the white riders were becomming more apparent. The hostility reached its peak in Taunton, Massachusetts where a losing racer grabbed Taylor at the finish line and choked him into unconsciousness. From that point on race promoters began to ban him and white riders refused to race with him. He recieved letters threatening his life, but continued racing and setting records, becomming the fastest man in the world, at a 1 minute 45 2/5 second mile.

From then until 1902 he experienced a peak in his career, with consistent wins, huge prizes, and spectacular press coverage he grew from being not just a world champion but to the status of a world wide hero. Thousands came to see him in cities all over the world, and loved him for his charm and humor, because he was intelligent and down to earth. He would always be remembered after his retirement and after his death in 1928 as the first athelete of African-American heritage to establish world records, the first to be a member of an integrated professional team, and the first to have commercial sponsorships. He remains the finest black cyclist of all time and one of the greatest of cyclings heros.

"The bicycle makers accomplished more for dress reform in two years than the preachers of that cult accomplished since clothes began to be the fashion." Puck Magazine 1895

Bicycles and Women's Fashion

When sarah got home from her trip this summer, we sat having coffee together and she started telling me about the book she was reading about transgender and sexuality. she said to me, "shelley, the way you dress, according to definition, you would be considered transgender." it was interesting to hear it that way. i had just been doing all this reading about women's clothing changes due to the bicycle, just writing about my own issues with being taken seriously as a woman doing work like i do, mechanics, construction, and even as a teenager selling tools. it dawned on me that for me, getting the respect i feel i deserve from men often means ridding myself of my sexuality and sex appeal all together. and is that why some men i know like to put on a skirt now and then? not because it is more comfortable, as they say, but it is because it is the only way they feel a woman will respect them for their emotions, and their softness, the things that are normally only attributed to the female sex?

Even as i write that now, i think, "is that why i have grown up to dress like i do?" all in boys clothing. i always say i wear army clothes all the time because it is the most practical for hard work and to hide all the damn grease on my clothes. is that really it? or am i trying to tone down my woman-ness so i can get taken seriously by men, so i get fewer hollars on my bike. i get enough as it is just being female, but man, it multiplies exponentially when i put on a skirt or dress.

It is an interesting question. Then i came across this quote, "Photographs and pictures show a tendency of women's cycling costumes to adopt masculine lines, collars, ties, coats, vests, hats." all of these changes in clothing were happening during a time when women were not just fighting for ration dress, but for rights, for the vote, fighting to be done with being thought of as "the weaker sex." were women at this time really wearing the

CELEBRATE PEOPLES' HISTORY
Gyda Stephenson

In June 1895, Miss Gyda Stephenson, a schoolteacher at Humbolt School in Chicago rode her bicycle to school, and seeing no reason why she could not wear her cycling clothing to teach class in, showed up in her knickers, causing a heated debate. Though some colleagues attacked her knickers as improper, the majority of the teachers reportedly applauded.

Miss Stephenson stated that she did not belong to any special dress reform movement. She said she wore the bloomers simply because they were the most sensible attire for one who cycled.

Without knowing it, she opened a new debate for rational dress that had been being fought by the likes of Amelia Bloomer, the creator of the bloomer herself. This helped the bicycle to make its most lasting impression on American culture yet - the liberation of women from oppressive clothing styles such as the corset, multiple petticoats and yards of heavy fabrics women had been fighting against for over 50 years. Thanks Gyda Stephenson!!!

BIKE TUBE BELT

ALRIGHT AFTER I MADE THIS REALLY DURABLE
BELT OF COURSE I FOUND OUT IT'S BEEN
DONE OVER & OVER AGAIN! THEN I FOUND
OUT THEY CAN GO FOR 30 BUCKS A POP AT
SOME "OOH, WE RECYCLE AND RIP YOU OFF"
FANCY STORES! SO MAKE ONE AND SHOVE
IT IN THEIR FACE AND SHOW THEM WHAT
AN AWESOME JOB YOU DID!

① MEASURE TUBE AROUND WAIST &
ADD 5" (TO TUCK THROUGH 1ST BELT LOOP) CUT.
② FIT TUBE THROUGH BUCKLE, POUND A HOLE
THROUGH TUBE WITH A NAIL FOR THE BUCKLE
PRONG TO FIT THROUGH. SNIP CORNERS #
TO CURVE & SEW DOWN. SEE FIGURE 1
③ MEASURE WHERE YOU WANT TO FASTEN
BELT POUND *EYELETS IN WHERE YOU
WANT THE PRONG TO GO THROUGH.

*EYELETS - YOU CAN BUY THEM FOR A
COUPLE OF BUCKS AT A FABRIC STORE.
OR
YOU COULD SNIP A SMALL HOLE AND HAND
SEW WASHERS TO FRONT AND BACK OF
BELT, TO PREVENT RIPPING IN THE TUBE.
YOU CAN GO CRAZY WITH DIFFERENT SIZE EYELETS.

FIGURE #1

YOU CAN SEW A SEAM DOWN EACH
SIDE TO MAKE THE BELT MORE FLAT.

*TIP - PUT A PEICE! OF NEWSPAPER
ON EACH SIDE TO HELP GLIDE
EASIER THROUGH YOU SEWING
MACHINE.

reprinted from:

SPITSHINE THE EYE a
sewing lovers zine
by
JEN 918 e. gonzalez street
pensacola fl 32501

113

THE THINGS THEY CARRY...

people and cultures all over the world use the bicycle for transport. in china, the world's largest bike using population, bicycles are used for transporting anything from the daily mail, to geese, to huge stacks of furniture. when i lived in india, i would watch construction workers load 25 feet of rebar and bags of cement on loading bikes and weave them through the narrow alleys of new delhi. i saw the thinnest of indian men load as many westerners and their bags onto a rickshaw and pedal them through the most dangerous intersections, dodging cars, scooters, huge trucks and cows for mere rupees, hardly enough to survive on. apparantly, as many of them slept curled in tiny positions on those rickshaws at night. in america, bikes are used in many large cities for messenger services. did you know that ups was even a bike delivery service in its beginning in 1907, with six teenagers and two bicycles? here in new orleans the oil refineries use heavyduty worksman bicycles to transport their employees around the huge grounds. and in the french quarter the bicycle deliverer is more than just part of the eclectic scenery, she or he is the life blood of the quarter, carrying anything from beer to po-boys, to whole chicken dinners, pizza, 50 lb bags of cat litter and even sushi and fancy coffee drinks. the bike delivery job is pretty coveted in this town, a deliverer makes decent tips gets to ride a bike outdoors, trades shifts and gets vacations covered fairly easily, and is offered a view of the city never seen by the simple tourist. it's not all fun though, dealing with traffic, hoards of people during mardi gras; side jobs like washing dishes and prepping shrimp, and some really lame bosses. i have never had a delivery job,

DELIVERY!

delivering food to every overpriced hotel, every dishroom, every nightclub, every back door, to stripclubs, gaybars, and excessively landscaped courtyards, to health spas, swingers clubs, chain stores & the dill store. Bored teenagers at the voodoo shop, drag-queens at the daiquiri stand, junkies in their apartments, bartenders on Decatur. Garbage alleys, street corners, balconies. Tarot readers & horse cabbies. Given: kisses, attitude, marijuana, cocaine, shit, alcohol, coffee, tips. A useless job designed for wasteful people, but I like it.

i have never been a deliverer. i only know these things because
i fix their bikes, some of the sorriest wrecks of machines you
have ever seen, all with huge front baskets, jumbles of bungee
cords, various squeaks and usually dried chunks of gravy (or
something) stuck to the fenders. some of this cities best musc-
ians deliver on bikes, most of my friends do, lots of women too.
it wasn't always that way though. back when i first moved here
about seven years ago now, there was only one woman delivery

person. she worked for the quartermaster (the
nelly deli) and i always thought she was tough
as hell. there are some deliverers who i have
watched ride through the quarter at top speeds
to deliver a hot oyster po-boy for years now.
i am amazed at their dedication to the job.
i am amazed when i sit with a group of friends
who all deliver and think of this strange cult
they are a part of, that cannot be understood
by a simpleton like myself, how saying a number address can stir
up hisses, how a single low tip (like 19 cents!) can be enough
to ruin a persons hope for humanity. i listen and i learn. while
writing this it made me think of a long term friend and now neig-
bor of mine. his name is steve and he has delivered at various
places since he moved here, about the time i did. he is the most
dedicated bicycle delivery person i know, he works hard, he loves
his job, even travelling to other cities around this country to
start bike delivery, because he knows it is a beautiful addition
to any city, offering less traffic, decent jobs, and food for the
masses. he used to write me letters when i would travel away from
new orleans, entertaining me with a cartoon series he called
Johnny Bicycleseed, the story of a travelling bike deliverer (not
unlike himself!) i will leave you with one of his tales:

"JOHNNY BICYCLESEED"

Well, old Johnny Bicycleseed had created a safer, cleaner
industry for America, which benefitted greatly the poor huddled
urban masses, as well as some rural ones (although it wasn't
as easy in the beautiful outer regions - those areas didn't need
much "improvement" anyway). But spreading his gospel all over
the U.S.A. was physically taxing of course, bein' on a bike, but what
was even more tiresome was the dizzying, unsettled pace. He did much
good for others, and he had some fun with all the great places he saw, 5

but he didn't feel like he had the whole picture. His great
influence was subtle, so he was a total stranger in one
town after another, after another, and the anonymity freed
him, in an odd way. The experiences were richer & more
valuable than most people have in a course of a lifetime (x2),
but in the midst of all that wonderful noise, he was soon
energy-drained to the core. He got to a point where he
would've traded everything he got out of these journeys
for stability & warmth. But that always eluded him, so he
had to continue on the road to outrun his failings. THE END

Don't get Hit!

In theory, bicycles have the same rights as other vehicles on the road and therefore should follow the same rules. Neither seems to actually be the case. Most vehicles (cars, trucks, and the ridiculous suv) think they have domaine over the road and will treat it as such, leaving the bicyclers at their mercy. Many rules of the road actually put the cycler in a more dangerouse position and should actually be broken. It is a very fine line.

In any case, there are two impoatant things to remember.

ONE: Each and every bicycler must remember - you have a right to be on the road! do not feel bad or apologize to the driver for being on the road! Not only do you have the legal right to be there, but because you are clearly doing a better and more respectable thing by cycling for transportaion, you have more right to be on the raod! Don't forget it! ride proud, know that you deserve your space and use it and enjoy it, be determined and decisive and feel good knowing that you are using the most efficient and socially responsible form of transportation! but...

TWO: Know when to give in! There are drivers that you will be up against that sadly have no respect at all for the cycler. these are the people that we need to be afraid of. cars are bigger and in a fight, they will more than likely win. Don't get in a situation over pride that will get you hurt or killed. The biking community needs you!

SO! remembering those two most important things, here are some basic safetly rules to help you get by...

1. LOOK. Keep those eyes moving. pay attention. watch for cars wanting to cross your path, for reverse lights, for turn signals, for the evil car door opening in you path! these are your enemies... watch for them!

2. LISTEN. listen to cars coming up behind you, are they speeding? are they slowing down to turn right in front of you? know what is around you, with all the senses you have

3. COMMUNICATE: whenever possible, look the driver in the eye, make sure they recognize you, communicate with them about where, you are going. eye contact is great for awareness. and be sure to communicate to a bad driver, your voice can save you from bad situations, or at least let the driver know when they really messed up. cursing or shaking your fist usually works fine.

4. RIDE WHERE THE DRIVERS EXPECT YOU TO BE: meaning, ride with traffic on the right side of the road and not all over the place. drivers are taught where to look for a bicycle, and most will not go out of there way to look in the place they won't expect you to be. it is safer for you.

5. BE COURTEOUS: let a driver know you appreciate it when they give you the right of way, or the space you need on the road. smile, give them a thumbs up.

6. BE PREPARED TO STOP: always have your hands on the brakes and be ready to stop. Have an out, or a plan to get out of the way if you can't stop (driveways, sidewalks, etc.).

7. **ALWAYS ASSUME THE WORST:** i know this sounds crazy and pessimistic, but remember that it is up to you to keep yourself safe. assume there is a car speeding down the road you want to cross, assume that behind the truck stopped in the lane ahead of you there is another car speeding past it. if you cannot see past an obstacle, slow down or stop until you can. Never trust that a driver sees you. assume they don't or that even if they do they might not care if they kill you. and don't assume that you know what they will do next either. 4 out of 5 bicycle accidents are caused by a motorist breaking a rule.

8. **TAKE A SAFE POSITION ON THE ROAD:** ride safely enough away from parked cars to keep you safe of their doors. i prefer to be a bit in the lane. cars having to swing out a little alerts the driver behing them to my exsistence and makes them slow down. if i am really in the lane and causing a delay, i give the drivers a sign to let them know i will be out of the way as soon as i can.

9. **BREAK THE RULES WHEN IT FEELS SAFER:** now, i don't mean to tell you to ride crazy. ride safe, but if you come to a stop light and the road is clear, by all means, cross the road! it puts you ahead of the traffic and in a safer position. cross the road safe, use your common sense.

Ten little bike riders,
In a single line,
One swerved out to pass,
Now there are nine.

Nine little bike riders,
Not inclined to wait,
One ignored a stop sign,
Now there are eight.

Eight little bike riders,
Out until eleven,
One went without a light,
Now she's in heaven.

Seven little bike riders,
Cutting up for kicks,
One got too "fancy,"
Now there are six.

Six little bike riders,
Eager and alive,
One didn't signal,
Now there are five.

Five little bike riders,
Hurrying to the store,
One dashed out the driveway,
Now there are four.

Four little bike riders,
Carefree as could be,
One didn't check his brakes,
Now there are three.

Three little bike riders,
Distracted by the view,
One hit a parked truck,
Now there are two.

Two little bike riders,
Having lots of fun,
One rode against traffic,
Now there is one.

One little bike rider,
Who's still alive today,
By following the safety rules,
He hopes to stay that way.

10. BEWARE OF... the distracted stiffnecked cell phone talker, the the deaf and blind music-blaring-window-tinted cruisers, cab drivers during festival time in new orleans with nothing but dollar signs in their eyes, as i say, the ever present car door opening in your path (R.I.P lucas (ox), street car tracks that grab your wheels and throw you off your bike, dogs that will chase you through a dark neighborhood kicking and screaming, speeding cops near the projects, cars speeding to make the yellow light, drunk tourists mistaking the french quarter for disneyland, starry eyed looking for mickey mouse, not for your bicycle...

11. ..MAINTAIN YOUR BIKE!: make sure your brakes are good, that your bike in general runs well. have good tires for fewer flats. have lights or at the very least reflectors for riding at night. be as visible as you can. dress up crazy, dress your bike up crazy, the more of a spectacle you are the better...

i think that is all. i hope i haven't made biking sound rigid or boring. biking is fun! despite the cars. i know what streets i can haul ass on in the middle of the night, which ones i can ride down with a cup of coffee in my hand blaring my own radio. but i know that in traffic it is up to me to stay safe. i have been in a few accidents in this city, all typical... an obstructed road (leaving me with a broken leg, a hundred dollar ticket from the lovely NOPD, a hospital bill that didn't get paid because i was breaking the damn rules), a car right hand turning in front of me - stereo blaring in the dark, even one car door in the face. i hope i have learned all of my biking lessons. beacuse of those accidents and the loss of a couple friends from their own, i am more careful now. i hope you will be too...

PLAN 9

Years ago, when I lived in San Jose, we had a basement full of bikes and not much else, as far as tools or knowledge or anything like that. Scott was a tinkering wizard who would drunkenly repair electronics and not remember how he did it in the morning, and Alan would get drunk and enthusiastic about making chopper bikes. I had no idea how to do any of it - I desperately wanted to be able to fix bikes, but I was intimidated. I hadn't yet figured out how I would learn how.

Then again, maybe it's best that I didn't start then - Scott claimed the only bike tool he needed was a hammer. To his credit, he was the only one of us who built any bikes from that pile under our house.

Bikes. Yeah, I know, what's new? Everywhere you go, everyone loves bikes. There's always some bike-obsessed groups of folks. Working on bikes, building them, making tall bikes, working as couriers. But it's exciting to me, right now, to be learning to fix them. For so long I was intimidated by tools and mechanics. My dad was often exasperated at what a pansy I was, growing up. I didn't ever know how to check the oil on a car, much less change it. I couldn't change a flat on my bike, and I could never put that poor little worm on the hook when we went fishing. I would just cast and reel in, over and over, with no hook and only a weight on the line. Or I'd lay on my back in the boat and look at the clouds.

My dad took me to the hardware store before I moved away and bought me a toolbox and some wrenches, insistent that I'd need them someday. I've still got that stuff, and these days I do actually use it. It took a while, though.

It's been a long time, overcoming all the bullshit and not being embarassed to make easy mistakes and ask a lot of questions and look dumb and fuck up a lot. I've known for a long time that I was a skinny pansy cry at the movies can't play sports what's a lug nut? kind of boy. But the voices are still deep in there, the voices that say I should be good at tools and grease and not have to ask directions or ask questions or get help.

With anything new, we have to start from the ground up, as Merrydeath said to me once. We have to be confident, but not arrogant. We have to remind ourselves to start over, no matter how good or experienced we are at other things. The first part of learning is figuring out how we learn, in a given situation. It's good to remind myself of this.

Bikes is one thing I'm learning. I work on bikes for fun and I ride my bike for my job and for transportation. I work on bikes in a context that complements my community ideals, the things I most strive for. I dream about bikes (also, dishwashing, flying, monsters, mundane conversations, sex). I ogle bikes, I recognize my friends' bikes parked places or wonder who owns a particular bike that I see around. I cruise bikes the way I don't cruise people, all lascivious stares and lingering glances. I feel like I'm going to get slapped one of these days, nonetheless. I notice work people need, I cringe at the sound of a dry chain or squeaky brakes. I'll ride by someone and ask why they haven't been back to Plan B to true that wheel or adjust that bottom bracket, before realizing what an intrusion into their privacy it feels like to do that.

Of course, it's not nearly as bad as Ethan and Shelley at the bar, yelling at some guy who seemed to be cheating on his girlfriend. "You can't do that! Look, we're your bike mechanics!"

Plan B is the New Orleans Community Bike Project. It's a DIY bike shop located in a huge warehouse near the French Quarter that also has shows, Recycle for the Arts, trapeze practice, Food Not Bombs, yoga, art shows, and other stuff. We're all volunteers, and have all kinds of tools and resources for people to use, as well as piles of parts and old frames and bikes. People can come in to fix their bike, get a little help, patch a flat, or build a bike.

This has been an ideal environment for me to learn in, because of the concerns kept in mind and the challenges that arise. I used to be really intimidated to come to Plan B, because of my lack of knowledge. Even though it's always been friends involved in the project, I lacked confidence and didn't want to look dumb. I was unsure of how best to learn. I learn best, I've found, by being shown how to do something, and then messing up a lot until I get it right, and asking lots of questions.

It's exciting learning how to learn, while also learning how to share these newfound skills. We don't fix your bike at Plan B - we're there to help you learn how to do it yourself. So as I figure out how I learn best, it's complementary to be seeing how other people learn, and how to figure that out with them. How to present information in an accessible manner.

It can be an intimidating space - messy, dusty, not well-lit, in a big funky warehouse. Lots of guys in there sometimes, in various states of dude-ness. Issues of gender have been raised and addressed in a variety of ways; right now we have a women-only day twice a month, and it's great that we have a good mix of people involved in general, all the time. Still, there is no denying that it can be intimidating to walk into a place like that, for anyone, especially if you don't know anyone else there and/or don't know much about bikes. Gender is a good point to focus on, as it addresses concerns that can then be expanded on into all aspects of how we operate - that is, how to make it the most welcoming and accessible space for everyone.

A broad mix of people does come in, and that is exciting to me. It's a measure of success in any community project that gets beyond it's own specific community - in this case, for the most part, scrappy young white people. Sarah says she learns best by getting outside of our community, interacting with other people. I'm proud that, while it is rooted in the ideals that are formed within my specific community, Plan B does interact with a broad cross-section of New Orleans. Yuppies, college kids, European tourists, homeless folks and street performers, clowns and circus freaks, neighborhood kids. Really, people of all ages and walks of life come in.

The kids are my favorite to work with. It can be kind of over-whelming when the shop is already full of people, and six kids show up. Kids can demand a lot of attention, and it's hard work to make sure that they are engaged and learning. For awhile I think that people were worried about kids being unruly or stealing things. But the kids who do come in have been overwhelmingly respectful. Most are really good learners who then teach their friends - some of our best mechanics are between the ages of thirteen and seventeen.

Timothy comes in a lot, he's thirteen and small for his age, but confident in his abilities. Every person who walks in, he'll ask, "What do you need?". They usually look at me, with a look that says, hey, don't you work here? Who's this kid? I tell them, "He probably knows more than I do." He struggles with getting their bike upside down, but he can almost always fix the problem. As Ethan put it, "I love seeing these macho dudes who act like they know everything come in here and just get schooled by a little black kid. The look on their faces is priceless."

The other day, a man asked me a question I get asked pretty often. "So why do you do this? What do you get out of this place?" I answered him this; "First and foremost, I'm learning a lot about bikes. I don't have a car, so not only are bicycles interesting to me, and I think people should ride them and drive less, but it's necessary that I know how to fix mine. In a larger sense, this place is a working example of how I think things could be different. It's a place where people can share resources and skills and knowledge, and not have to pay for every single thing. I think people can help each other out more than we're lead to believe, and it feels good to also learn so much while I'm doing it."

He told me, "Yeah, I was just curious. I think this is great - I just got out of jail, and my friend gave me this bike so I could find a job. I sure don't have money to fix it. This is great."
That's why I do it.

Come to PLAN B!
Side door of the ARK, at 511 Marigny, at Marigny and Decatur.
Mondays: 4 - 10pm
Thursdays: 2 - 8pm
Women only on the first and third Friday of every month:
4 - 8pm

REVOLUTIONARY
it something's broke
don't wait fix it
>code of ethics#6<

MECHANICS

One of the greatest things about the bicycle is that it is very simple to repair. all of the parts are there moving right before your eyes just the way they should according to simple physics. it is all pretty logical and most repairs require the most simple tools. finding bicycle repair manuals isn't too hard either, many can be found cheap in used book stores. and never be afraid to ask a friend or even a shop mechanic how to do a repair, most people who know mechanics are totally obsessed with bikes and are more than willing to show anyone who has interest. The important thing is to try not to be intimidated. and to have patience, pay attention, and put your hands on the bike and the tools. once you do a repair yourself, doing it a second time is super easy.

Ethan and i recently taught a class at the bike project on how to do a simple tune up on a bicycle. teaching is hard, for me, i think it is even harder than learning. i started working at a bike shop a couple years ago. though my boss did show me some things, he made a point to leave me alone to figure many repairs out. i was never really instruced, so i think instructing is pretty difficult for me. i have a tendency to show things, but have a hard time taking my hands off the tools. ethan was much better at it, a better explainer, and broke down bike repairs into a few basic lessons. watching him taught me a lot, and watching natalia at ladies night at the bike project has too. she is so patient, always teaches by words, allowing the person to do all the reapirs and tool handling herself. The lesson here is that when you are learning, make sure you DO the repair, be forward about picking up those wrenches!

Bike mechanics is empowering. i hate to use such a cliche term, but really it is! For me it helped me feel more confident, i was more willing to ride far, to depend on my bike as my only form of transportati on. especially the simple knowledge of how to fix a flat. it makes you free, and it won't cost you any thing either. Remember that mechanics are a process of trial and error. don't be afraid to mess some-thing up, most things on a bike are pretty difficult to break beyond repair. start looking more closely at your bike, use an old bike to take apart so you

can see the insides, be amazed at the beauty of the
bearing! touch them! look at your bike and appreciate the simplicity of it. handle your tools and know
they give you the power to be less dependent.

   Bicycle mechanics really WILL change your life,
your perspective on things. Learning simple repairs
will soon spark your desire to learn more complicated
repairs. it is an evolution, from repairing, to building, to creating! You will learn to make your dreams
come true, simple breakdowns will become opportuni-
ties to learn! you will become a fixer, a problem
solver in all aspects of your life! You will learn
how much you can control things in your life, to
change, to create, to simply make things in your
life run a little smoother. try it, i gaurantee
learning to fix your bicycle will improve your life!

Hey Ladies!

   A special note to women: i have this dream that women
bike mechanics will take over the industry. i love to
see ladies working on bikes. i love being a lady working
on a bike. I can't tell you the kind of looks and com-
ments i get from men who come into the shop i work at.
from total amazement that a girl can fix anything, which
somehow manifests itself as men talking to me as if i
am a child, calling me sweetie, even thinking that telling me that mechanicing makes me sexy is a compliment.
ya - whatever, just tell me what's wrong with your bike
buddy. jeez. i especially love when a woman comes in and
i shocked by a girl working at a shop, i love the way
they watch in interest, taking mental notes, maybe being
awakened to the mechanic in themselves. i hope anyhow.
ladies, don't be discouraged if you have never fixed any
thing before, don't be afraid or ashamed. mechanics are
not on the top of the list of things to teach young
women in this world we live in. it sucks! it's like we're
living in the fucking dark ages! just get in there! don't
be shy, get greasy, be assertive, ask questions, go home
and practice, get some other ladies together to try with
you! mechanicing with other women changes everything, you
will feel more secure, more supported. and let the boys
know when they are leaving you out, when they aren't
teaching but doing the repairs for you (like i do). i
understand it is hard not to be intimidated, especially
when you are new at something, a little clumsy, and i
understand that this is compounded by often being the
only girl working in a room full of boys. it is difficult, but very worth it!

How i learned to fix things

i feel very lucky. mechanics have been a part of my
life since i can remember. my dad was an auto mechanic.
i remember as a little girl, the smell of the car grease
on his hands, the junked out cars that would come up the
driveway for him to repair and sell. the first photo i
have of myself with him, he is wearing the blue mechanic
style shirt with the name patch (chris) on the right pocket. i love those shirts. When i was in highschool my step
dad taught me to work on my first car, a volkswagon, bug.
he wanted to be sure i could tune it up myself and change
a tire if i needed to. that man was all about self relia-
nce, i respected him for it. he taught me that a little
work and a little grease would prevent a lot of work in
the end. he was damn right.

Around that time i get my first real job,working at a hardware store selling tools. i swear this was my first real experience of true, blatant sexism. this was in east county in san
diego and believe it or not, there were straight up country boys
who came in, saying to my face, "get me a guy, girls don't know
anything about tools." some would just laugh and walk away when i
asked if i could help them. i tried dressing more like a boy, dressing more like a girl. i always got the same treatment. but i
stuck with it, i worked there all through highschool. the boys
i worked with learned to work the situations with me. when a man
would walk up with a question, looking my male co-worker in the
eye and ignoring me all together, my comrades would play dumb, say
"i dunno ask her..." and force the sexist jerkfaces to be belitt-
led when i would teach THEM how a router worked, or show them
the best tool they needed for a job. i secretely learned to love
it.

my next experience with mechanics was an accident. i
finally decided to leave my home city for good when i finished college, bought a van and went driving. i got it cheap
for a reason, and in new mexico the thing started throwing spark plugs all over the place. i was sent to a guy
named bob in silver city, a vw genius, a madman with a
sawmill he created out of a v8 engine, a homemade house
and his very own junkyard (dream). he looked at my van and
told me to come back for dinner. we made a deal that i
would stay there and work trade for a rebuilt engine, no
money at all. my friend and i did it, and after tearing
down many engines, cleaning parts, (and building walls out
of glass bottles, chopping wood, cooking dinners, organizing rooms full of junk and more...)we undid my engine down
to the smallest bolt, put her back together, popped it in
and drove off. i have never felt so proud. that engine
took me across the country relatively trouble free about
six times.

Now life has simplified itself to bicycle mechanics, and an occasional oil change on a vehicle. i got the job at the shop i work at by going there one day, and as the boss was fixing my brake cable, i said half joking to my friend, "if this guy would give me a job, i could quit." as i was complaining about my lame job at the time. a couple months later at a decatur street bar i ran into the guy. i had never spoken to him and hardly remember saying that i wanted him to hire me, but he says to come in if i still wanted the job, I was so so so excited, finally a JOB doing mechanics! could it be real? i hardly new how to change a flat on my bike. i was so intimidated when i got in there, only calmed down a bit because at least the tools were familiar to me. i have worked there on and off since the winter of 1999, and have learned a lot. remember that: everyone starts out new, time and effort can help you to learn anything. it is as simple as that. it is a life lesson.

as i said before, mechanics is an evolution. i started with cars, evolved (yes evolved) to bicycles, and through learning these things i learned to be more confident in my abilities to fix things and figure things out. i moved into a collective warehouse and learned to use power tools, to build my own room, to fix things around the house. i got jobs working construction, painting hanging sheetrock, repairing walls, building floors, a little plumbing a little electric. i realize now that the mechanical aspects of life are the simplest. man, compared to holding down a simple relationship, not getting freaked out when my life gets a little complicated, house mettings, jobs, ect... compared to those things, rebuilding an engine or changing a bottom bracket on a bike are CAKE. its just moving around some nuts and bolts. you can do that.

my dad

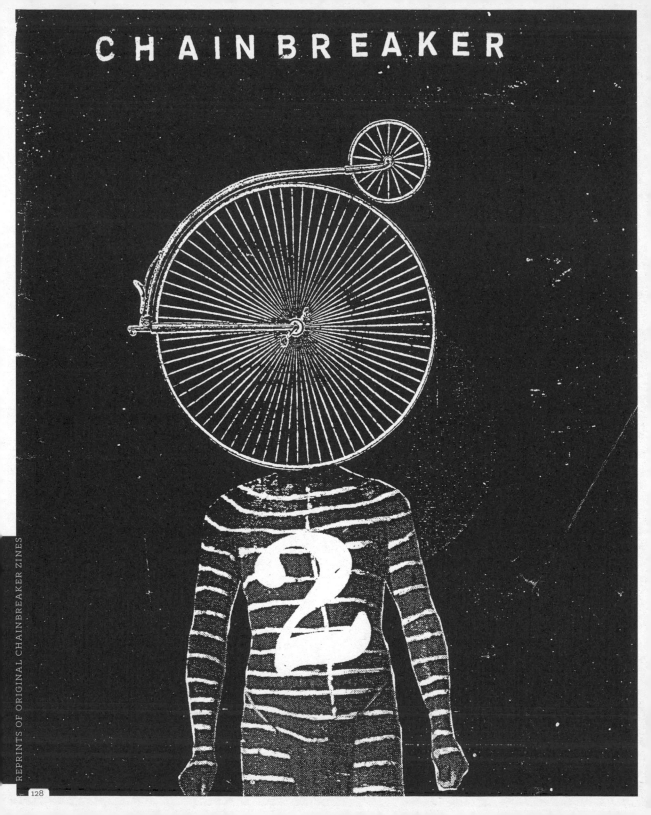

it's another hot night here in new orleans. summer is coming on and the termites are swarming. nights like these i can hardly stay home, i want to go out and ride my bike around in the dark heat, visit friends, sit on the streets, talk a little...

but not yet!

first i'd like to welcome you to issue two of chainbreaker!

i just returned from a trip to india and ireland. i've been looking forward to getting home and working on this project. i got so many ideas while i was away, about how differently bikes are used and viewed in other parts of the world. last issue had me gushing about bikes, about what a special part of my life biking has become, preaching about what i see as a major lack of bike love and respect in america, and about how i think that bikes can change the world. it's true - bikes can change the world, but this here is to show you how the world can also change bikes.

paying closer attention to the bike scene in india this trip, i became aware of how indian culture has shaped bicycle culture to fit its needs. how bikes are created out of necessity there to serve special purposes, from building really great rear racks that can make one bicycle easily acc-modate a family of three, to making a bike that both functions as a bike and a pedal powered knife sharpener, thereby becoming both a job and a mode of transport. it made me realize how narrow the perspective of biking that i have written about has been. in the west, and in more developed countries, bikes are used for sport and for leisure more than for transportation or transport. bikes here become expensive, fashionable objects to show off and ride on the weekends. it becomes who has the best mountain bike, the most stylie cruiser, or the lightest track bike. all for a simple ride down the road.

but in other more developing countries, (and in poorer parts of america), Biking is a nec-essary form of transportation, riding is not a political statement or a competition, but simply a way to get from one place to another and bikes are as respected and accepted on the streets as any other vehicle. bikes of all kinds travel the streets and serve many more purposes than they do here in america, mov-ing things and bodies, becoming tools for labor and for jobs. this necessity also calls for creativity and innovations, allowing peo-ple to look at the bike as a tool, to examine its mechanics and see how they may be applied elsewhere. This leaves me to wonder why, here in the west, we think of ourselves as more technologically advanced for making the same machine perform the same function, only changing it up by making it lighter, shinier and more expensive. and why with all our other technological adv-ances and our glorification of sport and leisure, have we not changed some-thing as simple as city planning to include bike lanes to create a safer biking environment and promote more biking for the health of people and the environment?

COST OF BICYCLES IN SELECTED CITIES, 1985-1992			
CITY, COUNTRY	CURRENCY	COST OF BIKE	DAYS WAGES
Havana, Cuba	Peso	65–150	3–12 days
Copenhagen, Denmark	Kroner	2,000	10 days
Estonia	EEK	800–2600	90–275 days
Ethiopia	Dollar	390	1,100 days
Guangzhou, China	Yuan	1000	60 days
Amsterdam, Holland	Guilder	200–6,000	2–30 days
Shanghai, China	Yuan	200–400	30–60 days
Tianjin, China	Rmby	300–600	30–60 days
London, England	Pound	150–3,000	2–30 days
Chicago, U.S.	Dollar	150–4,000	2–30 days
Zanzibar, Tanzania	Shilling	15,000–20,000	350 days
Zambia, Kasama	Dollar	160–180	110 days

this got me even looking at how biking is viewed in america in a different way. because of western privilege and prosperity, biking becomes a choice, not a necessity for most people. because it is a CHOICE, it becomes a political statement to ride a bike for transportation. it is a political statement because it is viewed as some kind of sacrifice to bike, because it is seemingly more difficult than maintaining and aquiring a vehicle like a car. (in the same way that choosing a vegan diet is political because one is chosing to do a harder thing than just simply diving into fast food cult-ure). let us not forget that it is a matter of privilege to have that choice. the 65 year old man riding past me in one of new orleans' poorer

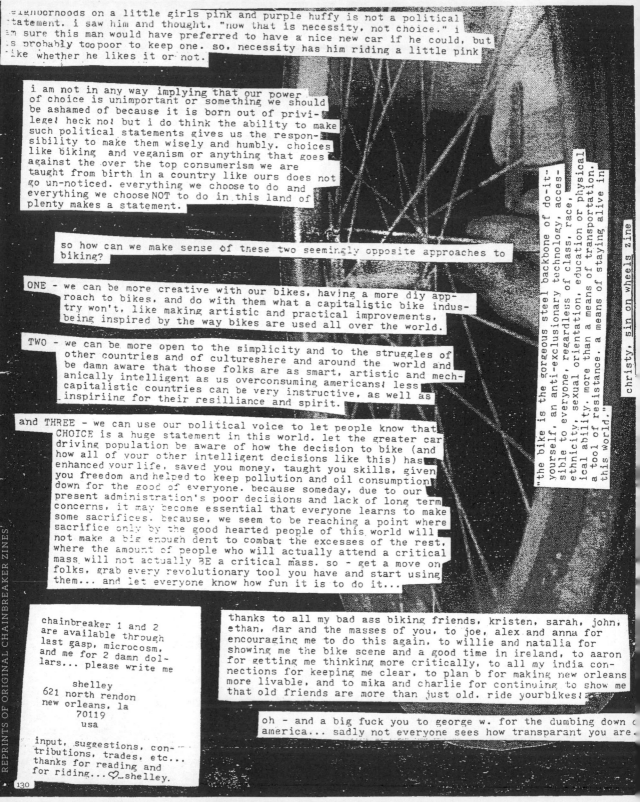

neighborhoods on a little girls pink and purple huffy is not a political statement. i saw him and thought, "now that is necessity, not choice." i am sure this man would have preferred to have a nice new car if he could, but is probably too poor to keep one. so, necessity has him riding a little pink bike whether he likes it or not.

i am not in any way implying that our power of choice is unimportant or something we should be ashamed of because it is born out of privi-lege! heck no! but i do think the ability to make such political statements gives us the respon-sibility to make them wisely and humbly. choices like biking and veganism or anything that goes against the over the top consumerism we are taught from birth in a country like ours does not go un-noticed. everything we choose to do and everything we choose NOT to do in this land of plenty makes a statement.

so how can we make sense of these two seemingly opposite approaches to biking?

ONE - we can be more creative with our bikes, having a more diy app-roach to bikes, and do with them what a capitalistic bike indus-try won't, like making artistic and practical improvements, being inspired by the way bikes are used all over the world.

TWO - we can be more open to the simplicity and to the struggles of other countries and of cultures here and around the world and be damn aware that those folks are as smart, artistic and mech-anically intelligent as us overconsuming americans! less capitalistic countries can be very instructive, as well as inspiring for their resilliance and spirit.

and THREE - we can use our political voice to let people know that CHOICE is a huge statement in this world. let the greater car driving population be aware of how the decision to bike (and how all of your other intelligent decisions like this) has enhanced your life, saved you money, taught you skills, given you freedom and helped to keep pollution and oil consumption down for the good of everyone. because someday, due to our present administration's poor decisions and lack of long term concerns, it may become essential that everyone learns to make some sacrifices. because, we seem to be reaching a point where sacrifice only by the good hearted people of this world will not make a big enough dent to combat the excesses of the rest. where the amount of people who will actually attend a critical mass will not actually BE a critical mass. so - get a move on folks, grab every revolutionary tool you have and start using them... and let everyone know how fun it is to do it...

"the bike is the gorgeous steel backbone of do-it-yourself, an anti-exclusionary technology, acces-sible to everyone, regardless of class, race, ethnicity, sexual orientation, education or physi-cal ability. more than a means of transportation, a tool of resistance, a means of staying alive in this world."

christy, sin on wheels zine

chainbreaker 1 and 2 are available through last gasp, microcosm, and me for 2 damn dol-lars... please write me

shelley
621 north rendon
new orleans, la
70119
usa

input, suggestions, con-tributions, trades, etc... thanks for reading and for riding... ♡ shelley.

thanks to all my bad ass biking friends, kristen, sarah, john, ethan, dar and the masses of you, to joe, alex and anna for encouraging me to do this again. to willie and natalia for showing me the bike scene and a good time in ireland, to aaron for getting me thinking more critically, to all my india con-nections for keeping me clear, to plan b for making new orleans more livable, and to mika and charlie for continuing to show me that old friends are more than just old. ride your bikes!

oh - and a big fuck you to george w. for the dumbing down of america... sadly not everyone sees how transparant you are.

chainbreaker is a zine focused primarily on biking, bike culture, history, bike creativity, mechanics and do it yourself bike ethics. but, it is also edited and partially written by me, shelley, a female biker and bike mechanic, and i try as much as possible to discuss how many things in the biking world that we take for granted apply differently for women. things that may not be so obvious and therefore are important to discuss. biking IS different for us women, from trying to get respect as a mechanic or even as a customer in a bike shop, to being taken seriously when we apply for jobs as messengers, deliverers, or in shops as mechanics. and even (surprisingly in this day and age), to how we dress on a bike and how it effects how often we get hit on while riding.

it is nice for me to hear from other women bikers, both for support and for new perspectives, and to get letters from male bikers as well about how they see our experiences, and about experiences of their own. i am pleased to know that as many guys as girls seem to be reading this, and even happier to hear that it has gotten many of them thinking about ladies in the bike world for the first time! i too forget how exclusionary the biking world can be sometimes. i have been working in the same shop for more than three years now, and am surrounded by some amazingly supportive and evolved men who i work with at the bike project (plan b!) here in new orleans. we hang out and fix bikes together and talk bike stuff and i never feel inferior or excluded. we all share openly and equally and this makes my love for bike and bike culture even deeper. i wish it could be this way for all women! but i still hear stories about ladies feeling left out, feeling like they aren't given the proper instruction in mechanics, women who have a difficult time getting the same jobs the guys get in bike work, things like this. it makes me feel frustrated, but thats why i am writing this. we still have a way to go yet ladies!

so this is my space to give you all a pep talk! alright ladies, and you guys too!... i want again to encourage you to get out there, read about bikes, find more biking zines and write your own, be strong, ride your bikes, mechanic! talk to boys and girls about bikes, and about why you love them! try not to get discouraged when you feel left out - stay in! listen and learn and do it with your mind and heart open! share what you learn with others with humility and compassion. approaching a subject which is new to you openly as a beginner will get you a long way. pretending to know everything won't. as my boss at the bike shop once told me, "i'd rather hire a woman who knows she knows nothing about bikes than a guy who thinks he knows everything." that is how i got hired, and that is how i learned what i know about bikes!

other great bike zines by ladies.
(please write and tell me about more. or send me yours!

spin on wheels - by christy (this one is so good)
    408 w. 130th apt 51 ny ny 10027

saddlesore - by lisa anne auerbach
    p.o. box 938 south pasadena ca 91031

political mass - by andelusia (out soon!)
    3807 melwood ave pitts. pa 15213

is yr bike for the apocalypse - by kailey & misha

fix yr bike for - by kailey and misha (boy!)
the apocalypse   4514 thackeray pl seattle wa 98105

i haven't met a woman yet who was not happy to learn how to fix her bike. and i don't know many women who would be unwilling to teach what they know. so get together and teach each other and learn from each other. ok? and ride yer bikes to

PEDALES GIRANDO

by AndALUSia

One day a little idea popped into my head that I should avoid the harsh Pittsburgh winter and head to the southern land of Guatemala. What I would do there was unbeknownst to me until my sweetie visited *Bikes not Bombs* in Boston. Two years ago BNB collected 400 bikes, parts, and funky costumes, which had been forgotten by the American people, and shipped them off in a container. The recipient of this container was Maya Pedal, the bike shop of our dreams set deep in the Guatemalan mountainside. Maya Pedal is a bicycle-recycling center that both repairs bicycles and also converts them into pedal powered machinery.

The project is located close to Guatemala City in the small town of San Andres Itzapa, which is home to Maximon- the patron saint of drunkards, prostitutes, gamblers, queers, and all other oppressed people.

With two weeks of snow on the ground we busted out of Pittsburgh and made our way south of the border, while visiting bike projects on the way. When we reached Guadahoochie (a trucker once called it such) we got our Spanish on at the super awesome language school- *Proyecto Linguistico*. San Andres Itzapa then gave us a call and we rolled up to town on a chicken bus crazily packed with color, chickens, and people. The bus dropped us in the town square, a congregation place for all townsfolk, something all Us.cities seem to lack yet all Latin American cities seem to have. The songs of tone-deaf evangelical ministers echoed throughout the valley as we started to walk towards a billowing cloud of smoke. This smoke was rising out of the ravine where garbage was burning in the towns' fresh water supply. Just before we reached this rubbish inferno we stumbled upon Maya pedal. Greeting us at the door were mangy dogs licking the pinchazo (tube puncture) water and the usual crew of young boys who gather at every recycled bike shop around the globe.

It was a seemingly normal repair shop until you ventured upstairs to see the flying sparks, welding flashes and inhale the aroma of burning metal. Scrap metal lies everywhere waiting to be united with "caja centrals (bottom brackets) and multiplicadors (chain rings) and then constructed into bomb diggety bike machines. The scrap metal has a whole list of machines that it can choose to be turned into including the *bicimolino*- which grinds corn, coffee, etc., the *biciteja/vibrador* which makes ceiling tiles, *bicigenerador* which generates electricity, a corn dehusker and the coolest of the all- the *bicibomba* which pumps water.

Guatemala is currently recovering from a 25 yr old civil war in which thousands of indigenous people were massacred. There is incredible inequity and a large percentage of the population subsists off of $2 a day that they earn picking 100 pounds of coffee on a finca. To escape the coffee exploitation many people are banding together and forming various cooperatives that include different Mayan cultures, women and campesinos. Pedal powered technology is a super important tool for these fledgling cooperatives One cooperative uses the bicimolino to grind corn, fish and soybeans to make chicken feed, which they feed their egg producing chickies. Another cooperative *Technologia Para Salud*, sold roof tiles made on their *biciteja* to support their center which has solar ovens, composting latrines, medicinal herb gardens.

As Maya Pedal volunteers we got to tear apart bikes and put them back together to make the machines for these cooperatives. We also got to help develop new technology including a *bicilicuadora*- bike powered blender that made smoothies galore and a *bicilavadora* - bike powered washing machine since Laundromats exist only for tourists. Other folks were working on a *bicisierra* – wood saw and a bike apowered grinder. The power of the pedal is endless!!!!

My time at Maya pedal was super great and I even became a workaholic never wanting to leave the shop. It was kinda crazy to go from working at *Free Ride* our Pittsburgh recycled bike program to working at *Maya Pedal* and feeling like things weren't all that different. Bikes seem to have that wonderful cross-cultural effect and can help bring anybody together. It was interesting to see men's surprise at the abundance of female bike mechanics since it's rare to see female bike riders. *Maya Pedal* was quite different from *Free Ride* with that whole different language thing. I felt dumb when people would come in for repairs and I wouldn't know what the hell they were talking about. But then again it felt totally awesome to be able to repair people's bikes, especially knowing that their livelihoods were dependent on it. Maya Pedal is such a super awesome empowering project that I recommend any bike lovers to go volunteer at. You even get free grub and housing for dirtying those fingernails.

Here we are at a bicibomba

you start pedalling the res stance builds up and out a poring comes the water from 60 feet down

go to www.pedalpower.org for info or you can email me baglady@graffiti.net

im doing a zine Zolitical mass about ladies and bikes. send 2 smackers to 3807 melwood ave pgh pa I52I3 for a copy

here is a windmill made from an old wheel with a dynamo hub

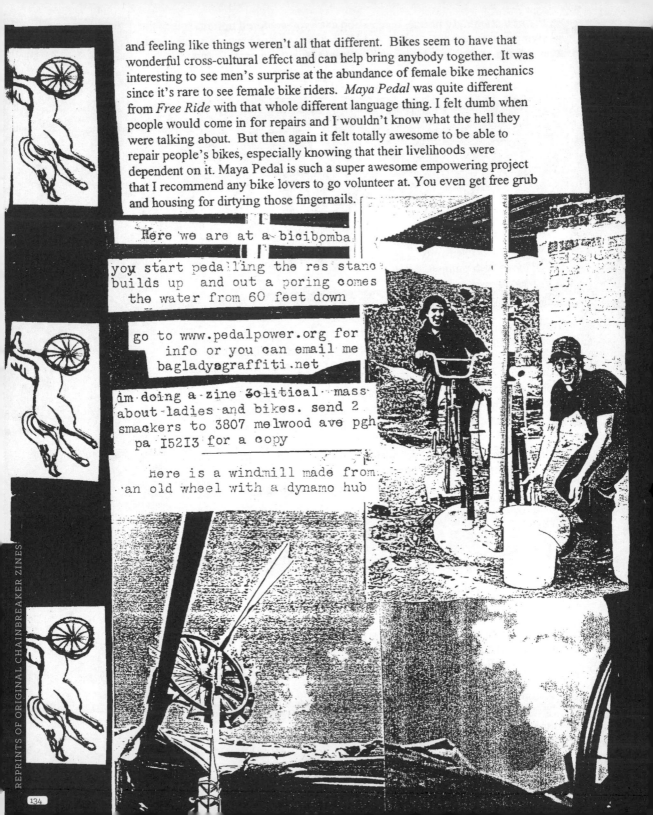

rickshaw madam?

this winter i spent two months in Bodh Gaya, a small dusty little town in the state of Bihar in northern India. during the season, tibetans from all over the country, as well as from bhutan and nepal and tibet, come to hang out under the tree where the buddha was enlightened, making prayers for peace for hours, days and weeks at a time. it is quite a sight, with around 7,000 monks and nuns in their maroon colored robes walking the streets and mingling with the indians and the few westerners who are there. tibetans

in all kinds of regional dress, indian women in colorful saries, beggars and children , cows and cars, and bicycles and rickshaws all sharing the roads. though i didn't visit india to do an intensive study on bikes in india, my obsession with bikes kept my attention to how bikes fit into society there. i stopped to take photos often, and always kept an eye out for differences and similarities to bike life here in america.

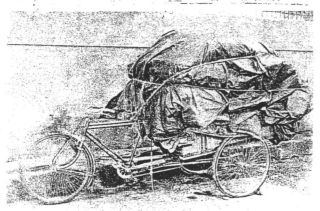

"Cooly" trishaw, 1883, migrated from England to India with the British East India Company.

one of the most seen bicycles in india is the cycle rickshaw. rickshaws are like pedicabs that we have in the west, where the driver sits up front, pedaling the passenger who   sits on a bench in the rear to wherever she or he needs to go. rickshaws in India are beautiful when new, but are most often seen covered in dust and passengers, with untrue wheels and torn seatcovers. many are equipped with canopies that pull up over the passenger, which depite their usual state of disrepair are quite beautiful when put up. in Bodh Gaya, rickshaw drivers come from all over the state with their cycles to accomodate all the tourists visiting for the winter festivals. they line up in long lines fighting for the attention of each person walking by. "rickshaw madam?" is heard so often it begins to blend with the onslaught of noises that make up any indian street. responding to each driver with a polite "no thank you" becomes an unfortunate impossibility, and one begins the task of dodging the bikes as they ride into your path, hoping to persuade you to take the ride.

when one does require a ride, the driver helps you onto the bench, arranges your belongings and off you go. i have seen rickshaws carry loads of people, people and five heavy trunks full of merchandise to sell, rickshaws with monks hanging from all over the bike laughing and playing. strangely, the price per trip never seems to vary due to excessive weight, though the price can vary greatly due to festival times, or the nationality of the passenger. as a tourist, the rate for a trip is easily double or quadruple the proper rate, especially during festival times. a kind local, strangely enough, a 50-ish westerner from los angeles who had been living in bodh gaya for many years hopped into my rickshaw one night and taught me the rules of the road. "never discuss price, " he said, "find it out ahead of time and just get in and pay when he stops." he rode along with me for a couple miles, yelling jokes in hindi and french (and english to me) shaking his stick and cursing and laughing with the driver when we got caught in a little indian traffic jam. at the end of the ride he insisted on splitting the ten rupee fare.

Handlebar decorations and hood ornament on Dhaka rickshaws.

from a local newspaper →

the rickshaw drivers are almost always very sweet. they always seem so small and thin compared to the huge rickshaws, whose frames seem too large for anyone to ride, making it seem a struggle for the drivers feet to reach the pedals. the drivers ride loads, big and small, all day, eating and sleeping on their rickshaws. i am not sure if this is because the driver is in from other towns, or if this is simply the life of a rickshaw driver. they all seem quite poor, especially in bodh gaya where everyone makes all their money during the tourist season in the winter, saving all they can to make it through the summers, when it gets too hot for tourists or business of any kind. the drivers do seem to love their cycles though, one can often see them washing them down, or wiping off the layers of dust, sometimes even painting them with bright colors and symbols, decorating them a bit... but perhaps this is not so much out of love for the bicycle as for the desire to attract more business. i'd like to imaging it is the former.

rickshaws are not the only bikes found on the streets of india though, many many people use bikes as their transportation. there is an estimated 45 million bicycles in india compared to only 1.5 million vehicles! (170,000 of those are rickshaws) bikes are everywhere, weaving through all kinds of traffic and obstructions, gliding down polluted streets, some loan riders, some loaded down with 10 foot high plies of hay, some with the wife and kids riding on the back, some with jugs of milk or jugs of kerosene. sadly, men do the nearly all the pedaling in india. it wasn't until i arrived in bodh gaya that i saw a woman on a bike, and the ones i did see were western buddhist nuns! i don't think i have seen yet an indian woman on the frontof a bike (nor behind the wheel of a car). i'd like to think it is because those beautiful saris are just to difficult to ride in, but as we saw in american history, oppressive clothing on women is another way women are controlled and limited. india is still very oppressive to women in general, and a woman riding a bike would be an outrage to men and women alike. instead, women gracefull sit side saddle on amazingly strong racks that most bikes are equipped with, their saris blowing in the wind are some of the only bits of color and beauty seen in indian traffic. the women look so calm with the cars darting around them, seeming to nearly miss smashing both pedaler & passenger. sometimes the racks are loaded with children being taken to school. the "school bus" for many small kids, kindergarten age, is a bike with a huge cage on the rear which holds 10 to 15 small kids, the side painted with the name of the school or daycare, and always steered by the most cheerful looking of all cycle riders i have seen in india.

(except for one small boy i stopped who was riding himself and three friends (one on the seat and two on the
rack) down the road by hanging off the left side of the
bike and reaching his right leg through the triangle of
the frame to pedal! amazing!
i gave him some cookies and
complimented him on his style
and he just smiled and told
me he loved the bicycle.
cute...

another type of bike one sees
quite often in india is the
three wheeler, built to be
pedaled by hand. it has a wide
bench seat for one or two
people, with two wheels in the
rear and one up front. the
driver sits on the bench and
pedals by hand the crank which
is at arm level near the steerer. these are made for people
without the use of their legs, and are popular it seems due
to polio being a semi-common disease in india. there are
remarkable machines, allowing the user mobility and freedom
that one doesn't get with a wheel chair, where one is dep-
endant on being pushed around. they seem to be as respected a form of transportation as any and are seen cruising
even the busiest streets of india.
      for having so many bicycles, india has very few large
bicycle shops. most are small shacks on the road with a few
tools and the equipment to patch a tube. most don't have
parts and accessories to sell as shops in the west do, and a
are there for repair purposes only. the shack near my room
in bodh gaya served as a bike and motorcyle repair shop, but
was tiny and empty inside. repairs are done on the dusty
path outside. there was no table or chair or bench to work
on, all the work was done on the ground, while squatting.
i found the shop owner one day truing a wheel in his suit
with a nice little truing stand. i asked if i might take a
photo of him and he said yes, posing with the wheel on the
stand looking straight into the camera most seriously.
      there was one larger shop in town that did sell some
accesories and parts. i priced the amazing rear racks there
(55 rupees!) and bought some bells for friends back home to
the amusement of the staff who all gathered around to watch
the weird western girl at the counter asking to see this

and that (in india, one does not browse at a shop, but stands behind the counter asking for each item which is brought out seperately by the shop keeper). i took some photos of their sign out front as the owner stood proudly by.

while in delhi, i did manage to hunt down the "bicycle market", walking for what seemed like miles through busy streets in places that apparently westerners never go. it was difficult to ask directions out of the tourist area, difficult to get the attention of a rickshaw driver or any- one for that matter (though everyone seemed to be staring!) . i was even stopped by a police officer who asked what i was doing out of the tourist area. "pahar gang is that way" he said pointing in the direction i had just come from. i finally found the market, a huge warehouse building filled with smaller bike shops, selling all new bikes and parts here, no repairs. it was the only place i had seen bikes which varied from the standard black and chrome bike i saw everywhere (as in this ad). in this place there were small childrens bikes with banana seats, and mountain bike styles like we have in the west (though they didn't look very strong, just showey). there were thick spoked rims for rick- shaws, wooden wheels for cargo bikes, bells, and tires and all sorts of hindu symbols and mantras in bright colors one could add onto their bike for decoration and for protect- ion. outside was a huge pile of rickshaw and three wheeler frames ready to be painted and assemebled.

अगर इससे बेहतर साइकिल मिले, तो खरीद लीजिए!

HERO ROY.

bikes in india seem more practi- cal than bikes here in america. they are built to be strong, and because labor there is so cheap, they are made to be easily repair ed, instead of replaced. many parts of the frame are replace- able, unlike bikes here. many of the frames are double tubed for strength. bike theft doesn't seem to be a worry. most bike locks can be easily removed with a scr- ewdriver, but aren't.(it seems more people in america carry guns than indians carry screwdrivers. sad.) bikes also seem so much a part of the road there. here in america, i feel like many driv- ers look at the cycler as a person

who is out on the road for fun, with no priorities of their own,
we are honked at and pushed aside. in india, where traffic itself is much crazier, with so many more obstacles to dodge, the
bike seems to fit in somehow with the flow,i often see them
given the right of way. they seem to be treated with the same
respect as a car or tuck or cow, all have equality on the road,
all somehow find their place in the mess. even in delhi, where
the traffic is something we can hardly comrehend here in the
west, i feel safe on a rickshaw, weaving between the traffic.

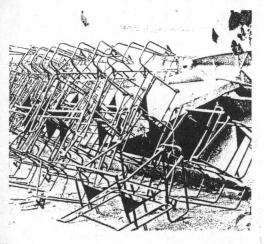

    i wish biking in america was more like biking in india. no,
i don't want traffic here like they have there, but it seems
that bikes are more accepted there. is it due to the population being so large there that it seems like anything goes?
is it because there is a higher level of poverty there, making
the poor bike rider seem less of an anomaly as it is here? i
can't imagine in india, seeing enormous vehicles honking in
anger as they swerve around a biker on the road as they do here.
(as happened to me THREE times coming home just today - leaving me to wonder where these impatient drivers expect me to go
in order to get out of their damn way). in india, everyone honks
all the time, but nobody seems to think they have more of a
right to the road than anyone else. is it the unity of the struggle in traffic that they have, somehow bringing them all together in the midst of that chaos to compromise and look out for
one another? it is strange to me that in a land where the caste
system is alive and well that there is co-operation, and here,
in the land of opportunity the more weight you carry the more
you get to throw it around and shove people out of the way. yes,
i realize that i am being extreme, i know the poverty in india
is something i am idealizing at this moment, yet still, in traffic, on a bike, being surrounded by people who are with you in
the struggle seems to make things a little better, power in numbers i guess. maybe what we need here is more bikes, or just
more competition for the cars. maybe we should have critical
mass with cows and elephants and motorbikes and carts and wagons
too... now that would be a real critical mass...

Make a Kid seat!

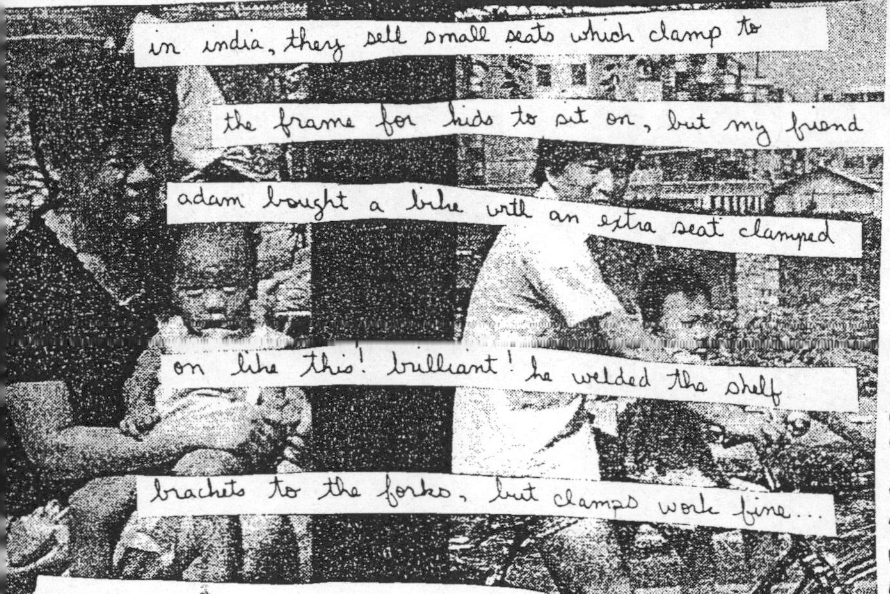

in india, they sell small seats which clamp to the frame for kids to sit on, but my friend adam bought a bike with an extra seat clamped on like this! brilliant! he welded the shelf brackets to the forks, but clamps work fine...

141

Parts you'll need...

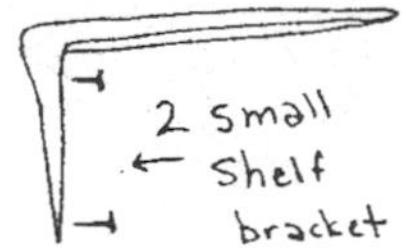

← 2 small shelf bracket

← 4 hose clamps

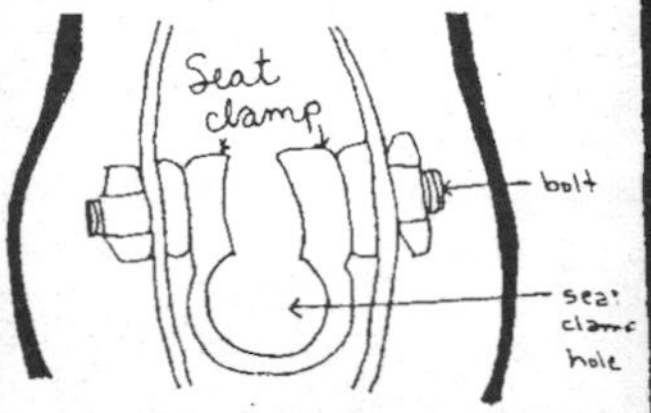

Seat clamp — bolt — seat clamp hole

it looks like this:

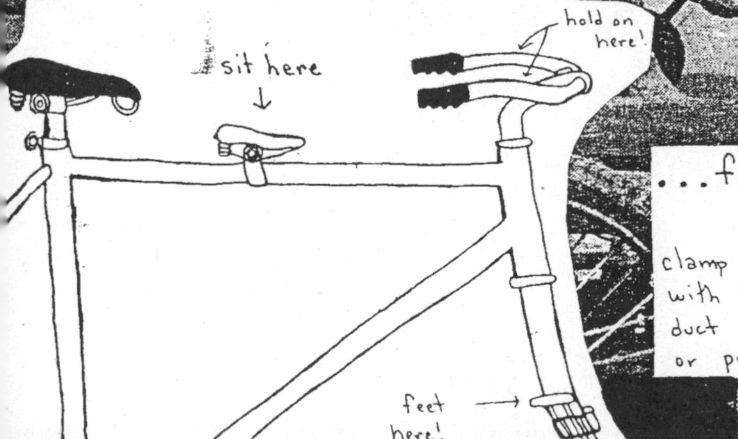

↑ sit here ↓

hold on here!

feet here!

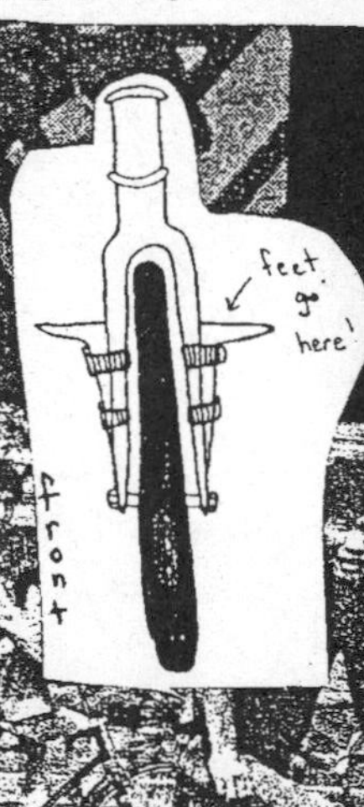

...for the seat:

just turn the seat clamp so the hole is parallel to the top tube of the bike & clamp it on! (you may need a longer or thinner bolt as you may need to widen the clamp- a thin tubed boy's frame bike works best).

...for the feet:

clamp shelf brackets to forks with hose clamps! you can duct tape padding onto them, or push on some old grips.

feet go here!

front

← without cool seat ↑

My Life at the Square Wheel

DUBLIN-IRELAND

OR HOW I SPENT MY SUMMER, UM, VACATION

BY ETHAN

FROM 17 RAILWAY ROAD, DALKEY, IT'S AN EIGHT MILE RIDE INTO DUBLIN CITY CENTRE, TO TEMPLE BAR, TO SQUARE WHEEL CYCLEWORKS. YOU CAN JUST HOP THE FENCE AT THE D.A.R.T. STATION PRETTY EASILY, SURE, BUT I'D STILL FORCE MYSELF TO MAKE THE LONG BIKE RIDE.

I'D COME TO DUBLIN TO GET PERSPECTIVE. AFTER BREAKING UP WITH MY LONG-TIME GIRLFRIEND, LOSING MY NICE HOUSE WHERE WE HAD ROCK SHOWS AND GETTING FIRED FROM MY JOB FIXING UP FUCKED-UP BIKES FOR NEW ORLEANS LOW-LIFES.

I'D PACKED UP MY BATTERED OLD ROAD BIKE AND HOPPED ON OVER TO DUBLIN TO STAY WITH MY FRIENDS WILLIE AND NATALIA. MY PLAN HAD BEEN TO CYCLE AROUND EUROPE, TRY TO CYCLE OFF ALL MY EMOTIONAL BULLSHIT. PRETTY GREAT PLAN, HUH? YEAH, GREAT, UNTIL MARDI GRAS NIGHT, RIGHT BEFORE MY TRIP, A SWIFT KICK TO A CAR THAT NEARLY HIT ME LANDED ME A DAY IN JAIL AND A BIG, FAT FINE. SO WHEN I ARRIVED ON THE EMERALD ISLE, I WAS NEARLY BROKE. SO THUS, INSTEAD OF LONG, TEARFUL DAYS BIKING AROUND EXOTIC LANDS, I GOT LONG, TEARFUL DAYS FIXING FUCKED-UP BIKES FOR DUBLIN LOW-LIFES.

SENSING MY APPREHENSION, NATALIA ADDED "YOU'LL PROBABLY LIKE IT, THOUGH." UM, OKAY... I WASN'T REAL SURE WHAT THAT SAID ABOUT ME, BUT I DECIDED TO CHECK IT OUT. I DIDN'T HAVE MANY OPTIONS.

NATALIA GUIDED ME TO SQUARE WHEEL CYCLEWORKS ON MY THIRD DAY IN IRELAND. MY BRAIN HADN'T CLEARED FROM THE JET-LAG AND ALREADY I WAS PURSUING EMPLOYMENT. BAH! SOME VACATION. WE WALKED INTO "TEMPLE BAR", KIND OF THE SOHO OF DUBLIN: OVER THE LAST TEN YEARS, I'M TOLD, THE AREA HAS BLOWN UP FROM A RUN-DOWN ARTIST GHETTO TO A CHIC AND TRENDY PLAYGROUND FOR BRITISH TOURISTS. WHERE THERE USED TO BE ARTISTS' STUDIOS AND DERELICT LOTS, THERE ARE NOW ART GALLERIES, CHI-CHI CAFES AND ANNOYING DANCE CLUBS. ONCE, WILLIE POINTED OUT A BUILDING TO ME AS "THE FIRST PLACE I WAS EVER INTERVIEWED ABOUT MY BAND." THEN IT HAD BEEN A CRUMBLING ABANDONED BUILDING. NOW IT'S A FIVE-STAR ITALIAN RESTAURANT.

NATALIA STEERED ME ONTO TEMPLE LANE, A TINY COBBLESTONE ROAD LINED WITH FOOFY BISTROS AND RECORD STORES.

"IT'S RIGHT THERE," SHE SAID, GESTURING. "I'LL BE AT THE END OF THE BLOCK," AND SHE SHUFFLED OFF TO HIDE FROM A POSSIBLE RUN-IN WITH HER EX-EMPLOYER. I TURNED TO WHERE SHE'D POINTED BUT FOUND NO BIKE SHOP. JUST A RESTAURANT THAT WAS CLOSED. "UM... WHERE?"

NATALIA HAD FIRST TOLD ME ABOUT THE SQUARE WHEEL. SHE'D WORKED THERE BRIEFLY AND THEN QUIT BECAUSE, AS SHE PUT IT, "IT'S FUCKED-UP IN THERE. THAT DIDN'T SOUND LIKE ANYTHING NEW. I WAS USED TO FUCKED-UP. AFTER ALL, AT THE SHOP IN NEW ORLEANS THE JOB APPLICATION HAD QUESTIONS LIKE, "ARE YOU A SMART ASS?" AND "ARE YOU A SPACE CADET?" THERE AN AVERAGE TRIP TO THE TOOL BOX WAS MORE LIKELY TO SURFACE A NEAR-EMPTY BOTTLE OF ROBITUSSIN THAN A FIFTEEN MILIMETER WRENCH. THAT'S KIND OF FUCKED-UP, RIGHT? BUT WHEN I ASKED NATALIA IF THE PLACES WERE AT ALL SIMILAR, SHE SHRUGGED AND SAID "WELL... NOT REALLY."

"OKAY," I PRESSED, "IS IT FUCKED-UP LIKE PLAN 'B'? THE NEW ORLEANS COMMUNITY BIKE PROJECT, WHERE NATALIA AND I HAD BOTH LOGGED HUNDREDS OF HOURS OF VOLUNTEER TIME, COULD EASILY BE DESCRIBED AS "FUCKED-UP." AFTER ALL, WE'D HAD TO DEAL WITH CONIVING CLOWNS, HAMMER-WIELDING CHRISTIANS AND AN ENDLESS PARADE OF DRUNKS, PUNKS AND WINGNUTS IN NEED OF TRANSPORTATION TO THE BARS OR FOOD STAMP OFFICE AND WHATNOT. THAT'S FUCKED-UP, YEAH?

BUT WHEN I ASKED ABOUT A PARELLEL, NATALIA ONCE AGAIN SAID SOMETHING LIKE, "NO, IT'S DIFFERENT. IT'S JUST, WELL... FUCKED-UP."

IT WAS MAKING ME A TAD EDGY THAT WHETHER OR NOT I WOULD BE EATING FOR TWO MONTHS RELIED ON GOING TO WORK FOR A PLACE THAT A FORMEREMPLOYEE COULD ONLY DESCRIBE AS "FUCKED-UP."

I CALLED TO THE FLEEING NATALIA, "LOOK DOWN!" SHE YELLED. I LOWERED MY GAZE TO TWO WOODEN DOORS THAT OPENED INTO THE RESTAURANT BASEMENT. THERE WAS NO SIGN, JUST SOME FADED YELLOW LETTERS ON ONE DOOR, LIKE THIS:

I STEPPED INTO THE CAVE-LIKE DOORWAY AND WAS HIT IMMEDIATELY BY THIS THOUGH; "MAN! THIS PLACE IS... REALLY FUCKED-UP!" THERE WAS A STEEP STAIR-WELL IN FRONT OF ME. IT WAS LINED ON THE RIGHT BY A RAMP FOR WHEELING BIKES DOWN AND ON THE LEFT BY AN AMAZING PILE OF BIKE-JUNK SO PRECARIOUSLY-HEAPED THAT I DIDN'T EVEN WANT TO WALK BY IT.

SQUARE WHEEL CYCLEWORKS
HOURS: MON-FRI: 10:30-6:30

DOWNSTAIRS WAS NO LESS-FUCKED-UP. WHEN MY EYES ADJUSTED TO THE DINGY, FLUORESCENT-LIT ROOM, MY FIRST INSTINCT WAS TO, WELL... **RUN.** NATALIA'S SPEECHLESSNESS WAS SUDDENLY UNDERSTANDABLE: IF YOU'D TAKEN EVERY SHITTY CRUISER FRAME, BENT RIM, GUTLESS COASTER-WHEEL AND USELESS WORN-OUT TIRE OUT OF PLAN "B", THEN JAMMED THEM ALL INTO FRENCH-QUARTER BIKES (MY OLD PLACE OF EMPLOY), THEN SET OFF A FRAGMENTATION GRENADE IN THE MIDDLE OF IT ALL, YOU **MIGHT** GET AN IDEA OF THE SQUARE WHEEL'S FUCKED-UP-NESS.

I WAS APPROACHED BY A MAN WHO WAS EITHER THE CURATOR OF THAT CHAOTIC CYCLERY OR HAD JUST BEEN DIGGING FOR OIL. HIS BLACKENED, GRIMY CLOTHES AND SKIN MATCHED HIS SHOP.

HE WAS KIERAN, PROPRIETOR AND (UNTIL THE FATEFUL DAY I STUMBLED-IN) SOLE MECHANIC OF THE SHOP. HE HAD THE NERVOUS LOOK IN HIS EYES AND AWKWARD DEMEANOR THAT COMES FROM YEARS IN THE COMPANY OF WRENCHES, SCREWDRIVERS AND GREASE.

I INTRODUCED MYSELF AND ASKED IF HE NEEDED A MECHANIC. HE NODDED AND, WITH A VERY HEAVY STUTTER (THAT I WON'T TRY TO REPLICATE, USE YOUR IMAGINATION), SAID "YEAH, I COULD USE SOMEONE. CAN YOU WORK THIS AFTERNOON?"

UH, WHOAH. I WASN'T QUITE THAT ANXIOUS TO RE-JOIN THE RANKS OF THE WORKING CLASS. I EXPLAINED THAT SOMEONE WAS WAITING ON ME, BUT AGREED TO RETURN IN THE MORNING. WHICH I DID. IT WAS ROUGH, WAKING EARLY IN MY COLD TENT ON THE PATIO AND RIDING EIGHT MILES ON THE LEFT SIDE OF THE ROAD, THROUGH DUBLIN'S ANCIENT, CHAOTIC CITY-PLANNING. EVENTUALLY I MADE IT, LATE.

KIERAN, WHO HAD OBVIOUSLY JUST SHOWED UP (AN HOUR AFTER THE DOOR CLAIMED HE WOULD), ASSURED ME NOT TO WORRY ABOUT THE TIME. IN THE BACK OF THE 'SHOP WE HAD TEA. I'M NOT A BIG TEA DRINKER, BUT

I TAKE IT WHEN OFFERED BECAUSE, SHE EXPLAINED, "IT'LL MAKE HIM HAPPY." OVER THE TEA AND SOME CAKES, WE MADE CHIT-CHAT. HE GAVE ME SOME MAPS OF DUBLIN AND HI-LIGHTED PLACES OF INTEREST. DRINKING TEA AND LOOKING AT MAPS, I WOULD LEARN, WAS OF MORE INTEREST TO HIM THAN DO-ING SOMETHING LIKE, SAY, FIXING BIKES.

EVENTUALLY, THOUGH, TEA FINISHED, CAKES EATEN, WE DID WORK. "I USUALLY DO A BIT OF CLEANING BEFORE WORK-ING ON THE BIKES." KIERAN SAID. THEY WERE SOME OF THE MOST HORRIFYING WORDS I'D EVER HEARD. LOOK-ING AROUND THE SHOP, EVERY POSSIBLE SURFACE THAT COULD BE COVERED WITH CRAP, WAS. THE TOOLS AND PARTS WERE THROWN INTO FILTHY BUCKETS. WHEELS AND FRAMES WERE HEAPED UP EVERYWHERE. UNLESS "BIT OF CLEANING" ACTUALLY MEANT "TAKING A BLOWTORCH TO ALL THIS SHIT", I WASN'T SURE THAT I WANTED ANY PART OF IT. BUT, ALAS, HE WAS SERIOUS, SO TEN MINUTES OR SO WE'RE SPENT FETCHING ESCAPED WRENCHES (I MEAN, "SPANNERS") AND WHATNOT AND DEPOSITING THEM IN BUCKETS. THE PLACE WASN'T EXACTLY SPARKLING LIKE A STAR WHEN WE WERE "DONE", BUT KIERAN ANNOUNCED THAT IT WAS TIME TO FIX STUFF. O.K., FIXING STUFF, LET'S ROCK! THERE WAS NO STAND, NO CATALOG SYSTEM OF WHO'S BIKE WAS WHICH OR WHAT THEY NEEDED; THE TRUING STAND WAS HOMEMADE AND MISSING ONE OF THE LITTLE ARMS. I ASKED KIERAN ABOUT THE A.W.O.L.

APPENDAGE. HE COCKED AN EYEBROW AND DARTED HIS EYES BACK AND FORTH AS THOUGH LISTENING FOR THE PIECE, THEN TOLD ME, "IT WAS UNDER THAT PILE OF WHEELS AT THE END OF LAST YEAR, BUT I HAVEN'T SEEN IT LATELY." HE ACTED LIKE THAT ABOUT ALL OF HIS EQUIPMENT. IT WAS NEVER, "I PUT IT... BUT "I SAW IT..." AS THOUGH THE TOOLS MOVED ON THEIR OWN OR POSSIBLY WERE HIDDEN AND RE-ARRANGED BY _EPRECHAUNS WHO VISITED THE SHOP AT NIGHT.

WATCHING KIERAN WORK EXPLAINED THE STATE OF THE SHOP: HE'D BOUNCE FROM BIKE TO BIKE, TINK-ERING, LEAVING TOOLS EVERYWHERE HE STEPPED AND NEVER QUITE COMPLETING ANYTHING. "WE'L LEAVE THAT ONE FOR LATER IN THE WEEK. "HE'D SAY. I COULD NEVER TELL HOW KIERAN PRI-ORITIZED THE REPAIRS, EVEN. IT SEEMED THAT QUICKER SERVICE WAS GIVEN DEPENDING ON HOW SHORT A TEMPER THE CUSTOMER SEEMED TO HAVE. MORE PATIENT CUSTOMERS' BIKES, I SAW, WERE PUT OFF FOR "LATER IN THE WEEK" FOR THE WHOLE MONTH I WORKED THERE.

AFTER THAT FIRST DAY, I DIDN'T THINK I COULD POSSIBLY MAKE IT A MONTH. "BOSS, LOOK AT THE STATE OF YOU!" WILLIE SAID WHEN I WALKED INTO THE HOUSE AT 17 RAILWAY ROAD. ALREADY MY CLOTHES AND SKIN MATCHED THE GRIMY HUE OF THE SQUARE WHEEL.

People struggled together the weird bicycle shop out. Kieran fought in court and clung to his business. The co-op dissolved somehow (that he didn't seem to want to go into), and the building was re-built around him. The mural was done away with, but he stayed open, despite the chaotic state the place was left in.

He told me also about the Dublin cycling campaign, his long trips on recumbent bikes, and even showed me newsclippings about how he got even with illegally parked cars on Temple Lane by wrapping them in packing tape so drivers can't open their doors! "One roll of tape," he said in the article, "will go around a car eight or nine times." Good to know!

Between Kieran's stories and the parade of cyclists in the shop: from rushed couriers with broken rims to eccentric millionaire painters with busted baskets, I got to see not only the bike-culture of Dublin, but also a pretty unique perspective of the city as a whole, especially the sordid politics of Temple Bar. I didn't go to Belfast, didn't kiss the Blarney Stone or even tour the Guinness Brewery. But, I saw Ireland. I saw it from behind a work bench and bucket of spanners. Though the work hurt my knuckles and wrecked my back, it was a pretty-damn okay vacation.

SEND!

But I did make it a month. As a job, it was ideal for my tastes: since everything from what needed to be done to the prices of parts and labor were in Kieran's head, there was no way for me to deal with customers (which is how I like it. I just sat in the back, fixing the bikes.

It starts to wear on you, though, kneeling all day in a grimy, windowless room, twisting bolts. My salvation came from two sources: RTE 1 (Radio/Television Eire, I think) radio was the first. It was my window to Ireland for that month: I kept up with the war, grateful to be in a country with pretty unbiased reporting. I heard about the "Good Friday Agreement" and the endless Northern-Ireland struggle. I heard arts shows and sappy Irish ballads that made me pine for my ex-girlfriend. I learned that while the reporting, talk radio and music was generally better than in the U.S., radio advertisements are just as fucking annoying.

The second was my conversations and tea breaks with Kieran. He doesn't talk much, but when he did it was always interesting. He told me about Dublin and Temple Bar history. He'd been in the shop for twenty years. It had originally been a co-op, with a huge, funky, pro-bike mural on the front, when urban renewal hit Temple Bar.

Vice-Grips*: Enemy of Bike-Kind!

ALLRIGHT, KIDDIES, LISTEN UP! I DON'T KNOW IF ALL PLACES ARE LIKE THIS, BUT, SOMEHOW THE GENERAL CYCLING POPULATION OF NEW ORLEANS HAS GOTTEN THE IDEA THAT THE ONLY TOOL THAT YOU EVER NEED TO FIX YOUR BIKE IS A PAIR OF VICE-GRIPS. THESE MIS-INFORMED D.I.Y. MECHANICS SOME-TIMES EVEN RIDE AROUND WITH A PAIR OF VICE-GRIPS CLAMPED ONTO TO SEATPOSTS. GOOD SURE, BUT, THERE'S

GRRR!! I KILL YOU BIKE! I MANGLE YOUR AXLE NUTS!! AARRRR!!!!

THEIR STYLE, A PROBLEM, SEE:

9 TIMES ARE THE VICE GRIPS STRIPPED, STUCK REASON PLACE ON

CROSS-NUTS & NUTS ARE IS FROM THEM. THEY NAME. AT THE IT GOT TO THE ING THEM UP.

OUT OF TEN, THEY WRONG TOOL!!! ARE MEANT FOR REMOVING THREADED, OR OTHER-WISE BOLTS. **PERIOD!!** OFTEN THE STRIPPED IN THE FIRST PEOPLE USING VICE GRIPS CRUSH STUFF. HENCE THE COMMUNITY BIKE PROJECT POINT WHERE WE WERE LOCK- **USE A WRENCH!!!** IDEALLY A

NON-ADJUSTABLE ONE THE SAME SIZE AS YOUR NUT/BOLT. **OKAY, WORD!** -ETHAN 04/03

*OR, AS THEY ARE KNOWN IN NEW ORLEANS, "GRIP-PLIERS".

...On Bicycle Delivery

by happy   ... new orleans style.

A certain co-worker of mine, who is also a minor local celebrity, was interviewed by the local monthly music magazine where he said something I didn't believe. Like me, he works for this restaurant, delivering food around the French Quarter on his bicycle, and he was telling this story about how he once delivered food to a stripper who was on stage when he got to the club, and she stopped dancing to beckon him over and pay for her fried chicken. he made it sound very dashing and alluring, like, "Oh, I'm this underground musical genius with this fascinating lower strata day job, look at the suave things that happen to me every day while you are sitting in your office, chump."

And that's all very well and good, and I didn't grudge him his little fib, but I was like, come on, dude. what stripper would be all dancing naked in these spotlights and everything in front of a crowd of people, and then pause to stroll over to the edge of the stage to get her greasy paper bag from this dirty sweaty person, and then just walk back and keep dancing? None of the strippers i deliver to, apparently.

So naturally I assumed it was just some glamorous story to propagate the bizarre mythology of the delivery boy, but then since I read that interview it has happened to me twice! Once this lady was actually all up with her leg wrapped around the pole when she spotted me, and when she hopped down to get her food she gave me a wad of ones out of her garter even. It was a truly surreal experience. but that's not even the weirdest thing that has happened when I've delivered to a strip club. The really weird thing is when somebody goes and gets the stripper out of a VIP room to collect her food. Then, naked, the woman brings her food back into the VIP room. So, I've been wondering, does she share her liver and onions with the guy in there? Or is there some weird Naked Girl Eating Fried Chicken fetish amongst the denizens of strip clubs that no one knows about because it is too shameful? Some kind of banana pudding dance, perhaps? I mean, I guess I could just ask someone, its not as if I don't know any strippers or anything, there are almost as many strippers as there are delivery girls amongst the people I know, but it is kind of more fun just to speculate. Imagine the seedy underbelly of New Orleans being a place where men paid to see a woman eat fried chicken and mashed potatoes in the nude, gorging herself on lucious proteins and starches, grease dripping off her chin. It totally boggles my mind.

editor's note: though this is not a story about bikes in some other country, it does reflect cultural things specific to the south in america. food delivery is to the french quarter what messenger-ing is to nyc. delivery is as much it's own sub-culture, with its own language and bike styles. like rickshaw drivers, chinese mail deliverers, and nyc messengers, the n.o. bike delivery person is attached to their machine, and has a secret world of their own.

Almost all the strip clubs I deliver to are on Bourbon St., which means every time someone orders to there, I have to ride my bike down a parallel street to the block they are on and then get off my bike and walk it through screaming hoards of drunk people, all of whom are getting their years worth of pent up aggression and lewdity out on their trip to the big easy. It is like a college town on a Saturday night times a million, but there are actually old people there too, and every man jack of them is behaving in the same aggressively festive manner. Skin-blisteringly bad karaoke pours out of the patio bars, wrinkled old men accost people and try to sell them roses,

and on the street corners the living statues are being hassled by the cops. The alpha pi omegas from Nebraska and the housewives from Oklahoma, all of whom are wearing Mardi Gras beads, feather boas and carrying drinks, splash through the puddles of urine and vomit and revel in this mad debauchery that they would never find at home.

All these same people clog the entrances to the strip club. And they are very loud and pushy, as one might expect, and they are sweaty, and one has to squeeze through them. Once inside the club, though, the waitresses and dancers are for the most part very accommodating and nice, offering to watch my bike and find the person who ordered the food, which is sometimes a huge ordeal. I have had door girls, thinking they had'nt left enough money for me, throw down some of their own money to add to my tip.

Of course there are total assholes and lunatics working at these places as well. Once I delivered to this strip club in the daytime before they were open, and this janitor, who seemed to be speaking in tongues to imaginary people, led me back past the snake tank to the offices, where there was a huge sign saying "any dancer caught leaving through this exit will be fired on the spot". The manager (or whoever he was) who's food it was, ignored my presence as thoroughly as he could, leaving me with a dollar tip and never taking his eyes off of the Saints game on the tiny TV on his desk. "that crazy motherfucker will show you the way out" he said, and slammed the door in my face.

I had never been in a strip club before I started delivering, and I mean, sure, I've seen my share of rotisserie chicken fucking ravers and naked clowns and what have you, its not like I'm totally sheltered, but this whole naked lady lookin' sexy on a stage scene is just mystifying to me. I have never had friends, even, who would head out to the titty bar for a good time, which maybe explains why its appeal escapes me so. I mean, a naked girl is just a naked girl, right? She's not doing magic tricks or playing harmonica or anything, she is just shaking her booty, which is something you can see outside for free all year long on Bourbon St., and its not as if she cares about her audience beyond how much money they tuck in her undies. these ladies, while they may be several heads taller than me, shinied up with makeup and wrapped around a brass pole, are still just trying to get their living out of the tourists pockets, just like me and nearly everyone else in this city, so why is stripping such a big hornking deal? maybe this whole ritual where people pay money to have naked people be nice to them is just an answer to the depression and disconnectedness in our society. Maybe there is something about being surrounded by assholes in a crowded and smoky dimly lit room that makes nudity so special. Or maybe it is, just maybe, and I might be over emphasizing my importance in this whole scheme of things, but maybe it is actually just the fried chicken.

THE
END.

I want bike lanes!

when scott wrote to me and asked me how the biking
is in new orleans, i thought to myself, well, not so
great. sure, we have virtually no hills to climb, and
a beautiful city to admire, but we also have lots of
drunk drivers and sadly some of the worst roads in america. and we have no bike lanes. then kristen called me
a couple days ago and said she had been hit by a car
while riding her bike. ya, she got hit, so did don,
karen, philip, yoni, lucas, shana, dante the magic-
ian, and all those folks who came into the shop or the
bike project with folded up wheels. the amount of peop
le in my immediate community on crutches has me feeling like i live in a war zone. in a way, i guess i do.
i know it is not just new orleans, it is portland, philly, it is everywhere the cyclist is, riding amidst
distracted drivers, unaware folks trapped in the bubbles of their vehicles. drivers here in new orleans are
not yet taught how to drive cooperatively with bikes,
and the lack of our own space on the road puts us at
even a greater disadvantage. here in new orleans, not
only do we not have bike lanes, we kind of have what one
might consider the opposite-of-bike-lanes. it seems the
road pavers, in their mad rush to fill the 60,000 pot
holes in the city (really), pave down the center of the
streets, leaving this weird drop off onto the "bike area
(i.e. where the cars park) leaving the pavement there in
its original state of bumpiness, where garbage, glass
and gravel then easily collects, making riding in this
space nearly impossible. if there is a hole here, it gets
skipped all together (like the two HUGE ones on magazine street, big enough to grab one's entire front wheel.)
and, if the street does somehow get entirely paved, the
pavers leave the sides all gloppy with asphault, cre-

ating a succession of
little bumps and cur-
ves the biker must then
ride over. these are
most apparent on st.
claude and camp st.
(where lucas was kil-
led) where the line
painters even painted
the white dividing line
over these little bumps
leaving a waving and
curving line all the
way down these long
streets. it looks crazy,
accentuating every little fun hill and bump, leaving the
biker painfully (literally) aware of the impossibility of traversing them. all of this trouble in a city where
25 percent of the people don't even own a vehicle, and
where 25 times the national average of people ride their
bikes to work each day. geez.

SO THE BIKE
LANE WILL BE
NEXT TO THAT
NARROW
WHITE LINE?

BIKE
LANE

THE BIKE LANE
IS THAT NARROW
WHITE LINE...

so bikers! be careful. pay attention. and let's start
fighting for our place on the road!! we need you all!

dar says: want bike lanes? ASK FOR THEM. a place to lock your bike?
ASK FOR THEM. racks on your buses? ASK FOR THEM. laws to protect
your pedalin' ass? ASK FOR THEM. ASK!!! = knock on your elected
official's door, make a phone call, attend a meeting, paint a stripe,
flyer, be verbal on your bike "behind you! on left!", ring a bell,
paint a notice on your helmet (i commute and don't pollute), wave
at kids, smile at frustrated rush hour drivers as you move past them,
teach your friends how to change a flat, explain to everyone why you
like riding instead of driving, ask your co-workers how much they
spend on gas and parking, ask your mayor to ride a bike with you, join
your local bike activism group, in other words -

FIX YOUR REALITY.

campaign for sustainable
transit
504.945.2835

for information on bike lane
meetings in new orleans
green.rox.com/transit

New Orleans Community Bike Project

PLAN B

NEW HOURS:

Monday 4 - 8pm
Thursday 2 - 6pm
Saturday 4 - 8pm

Located in the ARK at 511 Marigny
at Marigny and Decatur
Plan B is at side door on Decatur

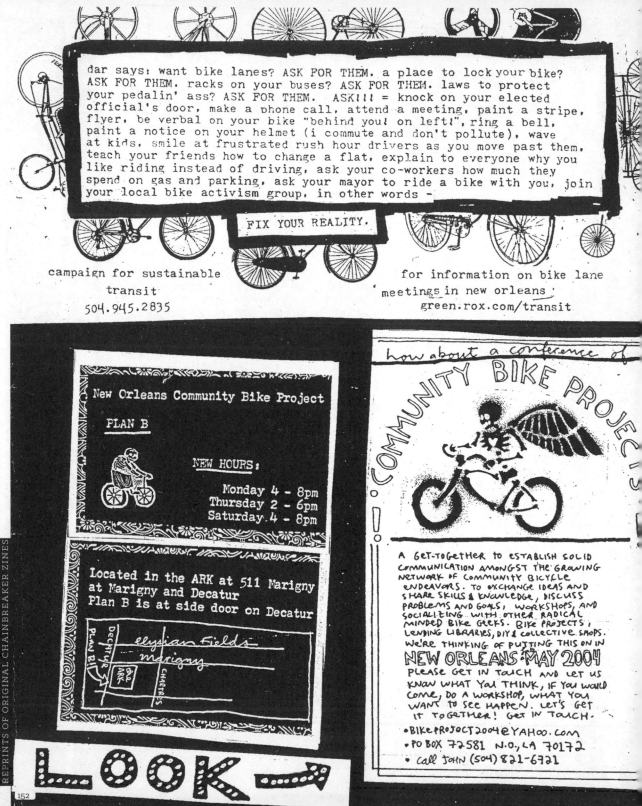

L OOK →

how about a conference of

COMMUNITY BIKE PROJECTS

A GET-TOGETHER TO ESTABLISH SOLID
COMMUNICATION AMONGST THE GROWING
NETWORK OF COMMUNITY BICYCLE
ENDEAVORS. TO EXCHANGE IDEAS AND
SHARE SKILLS & KNOWLEDGE, DISCUSS
PROBLEMS AND GOALS, WORKSHOPS, AND
SOCIALIZING WITH OTHER RADICAL
MINDED BIKE GEEKS. BIKE PROJECTS,
LENDING LIBRARIES, DIY & COLLECTIVE SHOPS.
WE'RE THINKING OF PUTTING THIS ON IN
NEW ORLEANS MAY 2004
PLEASE GET IN TOUCH AND LET US
KNOW WHAT YOU THINK, IF YOU WOULD
COME, DO A WORKSHOP, WHAT YOU
WANT TO SEE HAPPEN. LET'S GET
IT TOGETHER! GET IN TOUCH.

• BIKEPROJECT2004@YAHOO.COM
• PO BOX 72581 N.O., LA 70172
• CALL JOHN (504) 821-6721

CHAINBREAKER 3

print by andalusia

MOTION

The other night, riding my bike home drunk from the south-side, I passed out. I half fell onto the side of a car and regained consciousness in time to pull out and away before I ran into the side mirror of the car. When I told this to my friends everyone expressed concern with my drinking, but no one seemed all that impressed that I could pass-out and still remain mostly upright on my bike. I made it home safe.

My life is half spent on a bike, dreams, plans, frustrations, moments of clarity and confusion. Pure physical exhilaration or fear. Time to myself. The tedium of established routes and the finding the new way. Biking with friends and strangers. My belief in beautiful simple machines, the potential for technology to be liberatory. The bicycle, for me, is a hight of human achievement. I'm a big man on a three speed who's been riding on city streets since I was a young lad.

DESTRUCTION

Luke and I used to get drunk and go out kicking rear-view mirrors off cars. One night we were a little drunker then usual, so we took off for an evening of mayhem. We started on upper Clinton St. and used the downhill to our advantage. Like many destructive acts, there was a pure joy in the physical sensation; gathering up speed, sticking your leg out, and then the snap as the mirror flew off. It was a successful night as far as that goes, we got maybe 20 mirrors?

We turned at 24th or something, I eyeballed my target, sped up, put my foot out... DOOSH! The fucking mirror was reinforced. My foot hit it, which (not budging) pushed me off the back of my bike; my body hit the concrete, my bike careened off into another car and set off an alarm.

Injured (but drunk and scared), I jumped up, grabbed my bike and Luke and I sped off around the corner. Unfortunately, around the corner was a cop cruiser, stopped in the middle of the street, with its spotlight aimed right at us. We both stopped. Luke said "fuck". I agreed. Then the cop turned off its spotlight, kicked into high speed reverse, backed back around the opposing corner, and then sped off. I love this story, told it too many times probably! But I haven't told the rest of the story very much.

The next week was the 2nd critical Mass in Portland. Lots of people showed up, it was fun. After it was over about 10 of us biked up to City Bikes, got 40's and drank in the back-yard.

Luke and I met this older punk girl there, she was nice and very excited about this new kind of bicycle protest. She was the only non-drinker there, we thought maybe she was broke so we offered her some beer. But no, she wasn't drinking because she had to drive later that day. She was sad because she had to go to the junk-yard, a drunk driver had knocked off almost every rear view mirror on her block, she said. "Oh", Luke asked, "where do you live?" Clinton St. Luke and I gave each other guilty looks, ~~a really ugly guilt~~ commiserated with her, and otherwise kept our mouths shut.

CRITICAL MASS

I've been running my head around in circles all morning trying to figure out how to write about why I think critical mass is dumb without sounding like a prick. If it's just people, bike riders, getting together to have fun together, fine why do I have to be so uptight about it? Maybe I shouldn't take the rhetoric of the relovtion so seriously.

But if I do take it seriously, it gets on my nerves, cause I don't like to ride slow in big clumps, with police "escorts", obeying the lights. I don't like that it feels like it makes no difference except to the people riding. That it feels like a waste as far as activism goes. I believe american drivers are agents of oppression, shit I've been in lots of cars, we are agents of this giant system when we drive. And I appreciate confronting our fellow citizen drivers, saying you are part of this, but it seems that we confuse more than we confront. Though not as mean-spirited or destructive, it feels like me and Luke's mirror-breaking kick: muddled and random, fun but not accomplishing anything.

Bike riding, recycling, composting, stealing, dumpstering are ways we disinvest from capitalism — lifestyle choices, ways in which we can feel better about our impact. But even with thousands of folks dropping out, getting off the grid or whatever it doesn't slow down the giant waste, destructiveness and violence of our government/corporate state. If we have the energy, we need to couple these lifestyle choices with attacking the system. I think maybe everyone knows this, most critical massers I know work on many levels; bike projects, protesting freeway expansions, painting DIY bike lanes, etc...

So if we're gonna have a monthly celebration that we belong on these streets too, if we're gonna be muddled random and confusing, I'd rather it be more like when 10 of us would ride through the CBD and the French Quarter in New Orleans. Faster then the artery-clogged cars and taxis, being loud, scary and superior. Running lights, breaking laws. Critical Mess.

LAST RANDOM THOUGHT

Bike lanes are nice, here in Chicago. This city sucks to ride in sometimes and they definately make things a little more safe. But America's got a problem with laws. Those bike lanes and routes in Oregon have come coupled with light and helmet laws, enforceable by large fines. A direct attack on poor bike culture. Beware of bicycle advocacy groups, the laws hammer swings both ways.

— ICKY

(My dirty little secret)

i have said it before and i will say it again, bikes are simple. the design is simple, barely having changed at all since its inception in the late 1800's. biking creates a simpler way of life that spills over into other parts of ones life. bikers spend less money on simple transporation. life has less overhead, fewer bills, keys, worries. no parking hassles! insurance hassles! none of it! and if the darn thing breaks down, the cause and repair are both easy to navigate. cheap too.

having said that, i am now going to say something that might cause gasps from a lot of you in the bike industry, even from a lot of you diy punkers out there!gasps like one would hear from republicans if george w. said he were pro-choice, or, gasp! anti war! i may be risking readership, causing upheaval within the community of bike punks and messengers... but the hell with it! here it goes....

(i hate track bikes.)

ok! i said it! it is not the bike itself that i hate mind you. it is difficult to hate any bike, especially one that is so darn simple, and often built with such care and craftsmanship. what it is that i hate about track bikes is the jock mentality that often comes hand in hand with them. the attitude,of, my bike is lighter faster, more crazy. people talking shop about their components till the rest of us in the room are bored to tears. all that says to me is that the person put a lot of money into their bike, or that, having a bike with such great shit on it makes them feel more superior, like they are more "in" than the rest of us. it is egotistical, wasteful, and for the most part, it leaves many people feeling left behind and alienated by the bike scenes in many places. track bikes are wonderful for those skilled to ride them, but riding them should be treated with care and caution. most don't come with brakes (too heavy, right?), and i see so many young punk kids get lured by the scene, the uber track bike dudes (and sometimes women) who talk up their bike, their stuff, i see those kids want to join in and hop on one and ride off. (one woman came into the shop i work at and saw my roadbike with cut off bull horn bars and thought she could jock-talk me about track bikes, when i asked if she had ever ridden one of the beasts she so desperately wanted she said,"ya, for like a block.") these kids are putting themselves in danger over peer pressure, or fashion. is some track bike friend going to teach them to stop properly, or is this person going to ride out into the streets, hills, traffic, maniac drivers without the skill of how to save their own ass? i wonder.

i don't mean to rail on all you out there who happily ride your
fixed gears, with skill and ease, and especially those of you who
do it quietly, out of the joy of your swift and beautiful machine.
i do mean to rail on all of you out there who use these machines to
jock out with each other, talk up high end shit, leave out the little
people who simply want to get a bike to make it around town, who
are too broke, to buy such a machine, or just too uninterested to
want one. chill out kids, remember the joy of the ride, the joy
of the simplicity a little. share about your bike, teach, and also
listen and learn. sometimes the functionality of a balloon tired
cruiser with a 50 pound metal basket on the front will beat out
your 20 pound high end little machine. and anyone on any kind of
bike should be welcomed as a comrade for their effort in making life
simpler, quieter and more beautiful for themselves and the rest
of the world. a'ight?

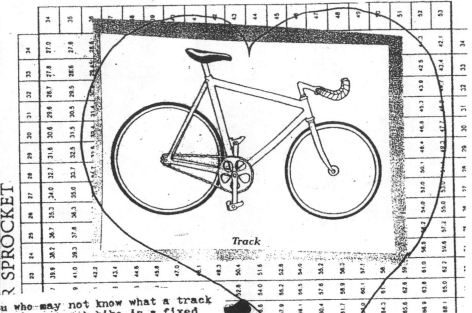

Track

for those of you who may not know what a track
bike is (bless you), a track bike is a fixed
gear bicycle, that means it is a single speed
and the rear cog does not freewheel (so you
move backwards if you pedal backwards), - the
front and rear cogs always move in unison -
you are always pedaling if the bike is moving.
they are built with no gears, brakes, cables,
anything with weight. in order to keep them
light (as they are built to race on wooden
tracks, not in traffic). so in order to stop,
the rider hops the rear of the bike up and back
pedals quickly causing the bike to skid to a
stop. they are preferred among bike messengers for their quickness, superior control, and
maneuverability, and loved by many for their
lightness and simplicity, and for how they make
one feel "more connected to their bike."

SPROCKET

CHAINWHEEL (FRONT SPROCKET)

p.s. if one of you track advocates would care to enlighten me out of
this opinion, please write. and if you could tell me why having
a break for emergencies on a track bike is so silly, i would
really love to hear that too. really.

A NIGHT AT THE RACES.

by Ethan

I was looking at pictures of a New York Alley Cat race with a friend when the idea began to form. In the magazine spread a gaggle of couriers on fancy road bikes shot down an alley crowded with rowdy, drunken spectators. "Hey..." We began to think, "Our friends ride bikes...and our friends are rowdy and drunk, why dab-nabbit, we should do that in New Orleans!" Later, though, I realized that there were a couple of hitches with our impulsive plan.

Hitch #1:

I'm not really sure why this is, but the Crescent City isn't equipped with any alleys. Didn't the whole French Quarter burn down at one point? You'd think that little bit of space between buildings would be helpful, but apparently New Orleans city planners see things differently. Thus, all dubious dealings: drug sales, execution-style slayings, drunken acts of public sex and illicit, late-night bike races, must be played out in the streets. No one really seems to have a problem with this.

Hitch#2:

No one really rides racing bikes here, besides myself, a few friends, some uptown yuppies, and the four or five couriers there are in town, who, despite their minimum wage jobs and the eternal struggle of keeping their bikes intact, still manage to take themselves really, really seriously.

See, the city of New Orleans, geographically, shouldn't be here. Down here in the swamp it's quite the triumph of human perseverance that there are so many roads buildings built on ground that is, pretty much, the consistency of tofu. Originally, the sidewalks here were just logs that were laid down in the mud. When the logs would sink, which they inevitably did, whatever poor sucker was in charge of that sort of thing would come out and lay more logs down. So it's pretty amazing that the streets here did go on to be made of gravel, oyster shells, and, eventually asphalt. It isn't as simple as in some cities because the streets (and, for that matter, buildings) here are pretty hell-bent on returning to the swampy earth. A stretch of road that looks like a topographical map of the moon, or has a tree growing out of it isn't even worth looking at twice here. When I first moved to this city, in fact, the newspapers were just announcing that New Orleans had tied with Detroit for having the worst roads in the country.

Point being that there aren't a ton of New Orleans cyclists around who are willing to go flying 'round on skinny racer tires in the gravel pits that pass for roads here. What they do want to fly around on are cruisers, big old balloon-tired cruisers, the heavier duty the better. Old Schwinn "Truck Bikes" or the tank-like Worksmans, the bikes used by oil refineries to haul fifty-five gallon drums around.

The reason that there aren't too many spandex-clad couriers whizzing around and fucking up everyone's floors with their cleats is because there isn't really that much white-collar wheeling and dealing going on, at least compared to other cities. The money here is in tourist dollars, and it's all in the French Quarter. Thankfully, a handfull of macho courier dudes is enough to handle all of the corporate gophering of the Central Business District. The real need for wheeled errand-running revolves around the tourists and the businesses catering to the tourists. And what those businesses and tourists want delivered isn't paychecks or whatever it is couriers spend all day couriing, it's po-boy sandwiches, pizza, fried chicken, sushi, beer, cigarettes, gumbo, seafood platters and anything else that the hotels, bars, art galleries, jewelry stores, strip clubs and boutiques of the french quarter's workers could possibly want to put into their mouths.

Practically every corner deli or greasy fish place in town has delivery, and all you need to get into one of these jobs is a bike, a basket (or just a milk crate strapped to your handlebars), and a few days to spend going around asking for a job. Eventually you're sure to find a place that's just fired their deliverer for showing up drunk or something, and voila, you've joined the ranks of the food delivery army. Congratulations.

As with any trade, the delivery folk of the French Quarter have developed a sense (though be it a loose one) of community. Lots of deliverers have a sense of pride about their deliverin' skills, their own silly lingo, and even rivalries against other riders. You'll see them around all the time, groups of riders hanging around in the street when work is slow, leaning on handlebars and talking shop, saying shit like: "...You've got a delivery to Jax Brewery, then three to the Marigny. The Brewery order came in first, so do you take it, haul the other three deliveries all the way upstairs, or do you go to the Marigny then hit the Brewery on the way back?", "...Fuck Cherish, she's the only stripper that's ever stiffed me. We won't even deliver to her anymore.", or "...There goes the new guy at Mona's that never says hi. Dick."

With all of these deliverers hanging out on bikes all of the time and talking shit anyway, a competition seemed natural. A race seemed natural. Loads of people have talked about having one, or even a delivery olympics with different competitions like the "Leaky bowl of scalding gumbo dasho" or "Delivery person vs. Asshole customer Greco-Roman style wrestling", maybe. SOmehow, though, it never really came together. Last Janu ary, though, bored and unemployed, about to leave the country for a while, I decided to do it. A whole olympics was a little more than i cared to take on, but a race wasn't. I was up for putting on a simple, straightforward race between all of the getting drunk and packing that I had to get done.

First I picked the course. The city had recently repaired a street in my neighborhood called Press Street. The repairs had (for reasons that remain a mystery) transformed this unused, muddy, gravel road by the tracks into the smoothest road in the metropolitan area (though still unused). It was perfect. The race would begin on the corner of Press and Burgundy and go to the end of Press, two blocks down. A straight dash wouldn't have been too fun, So, at the parking lot of the art school by the end of Press, everyone would dismount, leave their bike, dash across the lot, retrieve a flag, run back to their bikes then loop around up Montegut Street and back over to Press. I figured the threat of being hit by either a freight train or car or both would add some excitement to the event.

A date was chosen and word began to spread. I pust up posters around town and Happy drew up "invitations" for me to pass out, informing delivery-job workers that their attendance at the race was, of course, required.The invitations even had a blank space where I could write in people's names. I rode around town filling them out and dropping them into baskets or tucking them under brake cables. If I didn't know the name of the bike's owner personally (which I often did -thanks to my own time delivering sushi and fixing delivery bikes at the cheap local bike shop) I would write in things like "Verti Marte Girl" or "Moon Wok Dude" and hope tht it was in fact that peron's bike. A couple of times i just flagged down deliverers on the street, barking, "What's your name!?" at them and scribbling it in on the invitation. I scrapped thta method, though, after spending five minutes convincing a sketched-out deli employee that i wasn't a cop.

Excitement grew about the race. Loads of random people came up to me to say how stoked they were, but also I started having people telling me just how the race was going to "HAVE TO BE".

"Everyone HAS to be on the same kind of bike". "The course HAS to go through the French Quarter." "There HAS to be real food involved". People I'd never interacted with (or even seen) before in my life were coming up and telling me just how it all HAD to go down. And I told them all the exact same thing: "That's a good idea. Maybe the race that YOU organize can be like that."

The worst thing, though, was that lots of these super-competitive delivery dudes became hell-bent on bringing money into the race somehow. An entry fee and monetary award, some said, or a betting pool (I'll admit the idea of figuring out every riders' odds struck me as pretty fun sounding; we could get someone to go around inspecting their gums and feet.). I couldn't believe that all these riders who spend so much time busting their asses to get tips from asshole bartenders, art dealers and bouncers were so hell-bent on trying to take money from one another. Fuck that!

Also a big cloud of testosterone-filled competition formed around the race. As with pretty much all hyper-physical occupations, bicycle delivery is, unfortunately, over run with really macho, aggro dudes who jumped at the chance to get all, well, macho and aggro. I tried my best not just to quell all of that but also to get people involved who weren't super-competitive guys. There are lots of women delivery riders, whom I made sure to get invitations to, as well as the older deliverers, like the middle-aged chinese guys who work on Canal Street and the older guy that works at the Cuban restaurant and cruises around all day reeeeaaally slowly, smoking weed.

"HAPPY'S INVITATION" TO THE RACE.

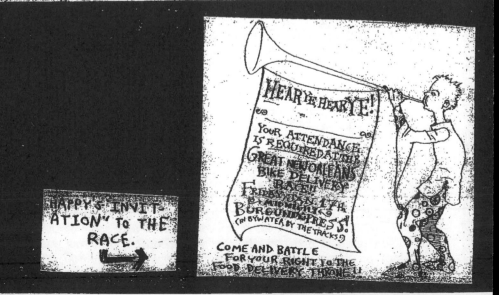

HEAR YE HEAR YE!

YOUR ATTENDANCE IS REQUIRED AT THE GREAT NEW ORLEANS BIKE DELIVERY RACE!! FRIDAY JAN 17TH @ MIDNIGHT BURGUNDY PRESS (IN BYWATER BY THE TRACKS)

COME AND BATTLE FOR YOUR RIGHT TO THE FOOD DELIVERY THRONE!!

Despite my efforts, though, the only riders getting really stoked about the race were the ones who were taking it all way too seriously. It got so bad that I was considering calling the damned thing off. Then one night, as I passed out invites at the bar, Jeff Shyman approached me. I cringed when he got in my face and turned the drunken conversation to the race. Jeff is the self-declared "King of Delivery", the kind of guy who'll see other people making deliveries and say shit like, "I have, in the last thirty seconds, made note of exactly nine things you've

done wrong." After one day delivering half an ocean's worth of fish in one shift, Jeff had decided that he was no longer a lowly delivery boy, but that he'd now graduated to the prestigious level of "Delivery Man". To celebrate his evolution he'd had business cards made up and gone to work for a week wearing suit and tie. I was sure the man was going to have a basket-full of gripes for me about the race but, actually, he just wanted to tell me that didn't actually care who won the race. I asked him why, a little surprised, and he yelled, "Because I'm number two, baby...I'M NUMBER TWO!!" Thanks to Jeff I decided to stay the course. The race was a go!

Everyone else continued to complain, but I ignored it all until the day of the race finally rolled around. When I woke up that morning there was already a slew of messages on machine. Daniel had to work and was wondering if someone could order food to the race so that he could be there. John had heard you had to have a basket to enter the race and he wanted the rule expunged because the shitty bar he delivered for was so slow that when the rare food delivery did come up he just held it in his hand. Buddha had gotten out of bed that morning to find both the wheels stolen off of his cruiser and was calling to let me that he "Suspected sabotage", Jamie, who'd agreed to be the flag-liaizon in the art-school parking lot, called a couple of times panicking because the temperature was supposed to drop like forty degrees right at midnight, same time as the race. "It's going to snow!" He screamed into the phone, and suggested cancelling the race.

I looked in the paper. The weather report was calling for the coldest night of the year, but snow, in New Orleans, is completely fucking unheard of. I think it snowed once, like two hundred years ago, and everyone just wrote that off to voodoo. I reminded Jamie's answering machine of this. I also reminded it that he had grown up in the arctic-tundra known as Iowa, and that if born-and-bred Southerners could go out and deliver that night, he could stand in an art-school parking lot and hand out scraps of fabric.

I spent the day running around making last minute preparations. By nightfall it really was starting to get cold. Very, very cold. So I figured I'd better make a morale-boosting visit to the big punk house in mid-city, where lots of deliverers and would-be race contenders lived. As I'd suspected, a gaggle of kids were sitting around in the kitchen and debating whether or not to show up at the corner of Press and Burgundy at midnight. When I entered the room, proudly holding up the trophy for the race, Yoni threw his hands down on the table and said, "Okay I'm going." Several other fence-straddlers agreed. It wasn't money. I'd spent all day constructing a silver and gold crown out of oyster buckets and bolts, topped with a pair of shiny gold vice-grips. It wasn't too shabby.

I kicked it at the warehouse for a while, had a couple of beers and more than a couple homemade donuts, then Ski and I left to get more beers and head down to the race. When we got into my van and took off, we heard a strange "Thunk." I didn't think much of it, though, The van was a twelve year old minivan that I wouldn't hold coolant. I hadn't added oil (or made any other sort of maintenance efforts) to the thing in ages. It shouldn't have even been running. When your mini-van is the automotive equivalent of the undead, you don't question strange "Thunk" noises.

When I swung by my house to pick up some supplies and my dog, I realized that the crown was nowhere to be fund. We dug through the garbage-filled cab of the van. Nope. We hurried back over to the warehouse. Nope. "Uh-Oh." I thought, "Maybe that "Thunk" wasn't just the long expected death-pang of my shitty car. Either some warehouse-dweller (possibly the same saboteur who'd made off with poor Buddha's wheels) had absconded with the coveted crown, or I'd absent-mindedly set the thing on top of the van and taken off. Short on time, but hating to put on the race crown-less, Ski and I scooped back up Banks street with the brights on, Ski hanging half-way out the window, despite freezing wind, searching. SOmething gleamed in the headlight and Ski yelled "There!" leaping out before I'd even stopped. There it was, wedged under the tire of an SUV, still intacted, just a little scuffed up. "Onward!" I yelled and we hauled ass down to the race.

When we arrived at Press Street, I started to get nervous. Things were pretty quiet. THere were a couple of vague acquaintances of mine milling around on their bikes, puffing air into their cupped hands. Jamie was there, bundled up like he was oging on a dog-sled expedition. Buddha was there, bikeless and so wasted that Squirrel was having to brace him up on her shoulder. And it was fucking cold. I stated getting nervous. For all I knew all of the delivery community could've skipped town to the warmth of sunny Florida; it would've been time better spent than coming to some stupid race on the coldest night anyone could remember New Orleans ever having. I was trying to figure out how I could laugh off such a miserable failure of an event and extricate myself from the situation. Then...they started to appear.

At first just a couple of the warehouse residents from mid-city rolled up, greeting the other patient attendees. After that a couple more kids from the Bywater showed up, then from all sides came squeaking, baskated bicycles, ridden by frost-bitten folks who, though red-faced and grumbling, were ready for a race.

Jeff Shyman, Delivery Man, lumbered up with two very drunk but very enthusiastic cheerleaders clad in puff-paint covered shirts reading, "GO JEFF/ YOU'RE #2!!!!" and the like. John Philth, possibly New Orleans' newest delivery guy, who'd left the message on my machine about not having a basket, had squeezed through the rul rulesvy modifying a road bike so that a basket would fit on it. Suzanna showed up even though she wasn't a deliverer, but she'd borrowed a bike off someone who was. A pack of excited crusties had even shown up to scream and cheer and get drunk and let their pitbulls try to kill one another and us.

When the crowd seemed to peak at about twenty people, I climbed up a tree and, despite heavy heckling, announced the course the race would take and the rules. The rules basically boiled down to not riding your bike in the art school parking lot, getting a flag and not getting killed by traffic or trains. Easy enough. When I'd finished screaming instructions, the first heat of racers lined up at the starting point. I remember that among the four racers were Jeff "I'm number two!" Shyman, and JOhn on his rule-bending racer. Through already quitting vocal chords I screamed, "On your marks...Get set...Go!" ANd they all took off down Press Street. Well, all of them, that is, but SHyman, who forced his little maroon Murray about three feet before slamming down his shoes on the pavement and coming to a dead stop. "Jeff!" I yelled, "What in the fuck are you doing?!" He looked at me and shrugged. "Eh, I wasn't really feeling that one." He said. "Whatever, Jeff." I said, rolling my eyes, then rushing over to the pack of crusties. I grabbed two of them and blurted, "Make yourself useful.", shoving a roll of toilet paper at them. I stationed them at the finish line, with the roll of paper spread across the street. As I was getting them into place, Buddha stumbled over to us. He put his bulky hand on my shoulder and gestured with his other one, "Man," he said, "This...is awesome." I began to agree with him and tell him I was sorry about his wheels, but before I could finish the first racer rounded the corner onto Burgundy Street. Not surprisingly, it was John Philth on his fancy road bike, the useless basket he'd attached clattering away as he sped across the uneven pavement. He crossed the railroad tracks and busted through the T.P. ribbon a good ten seconds ahead of the other racers.

The next heat lined up. Shyman was warned that if he didn't go when instructed to I would wrap his little Murray girl's frame around his head. He seemed to understand. Before I could yell the command to go, though, we saw a lanky figure in puffy garb loafing up Press Street. It was Jamie, coming around from his post in the art school parking lot.

"What's up?" I yelled as he approached.

"There's a security guard down here..." He called, then closed the space between us, panting the rest of his sentence. "And...he's a little freaked out...at...all these freaks...running through....his parking lot. I told him we were just...having...a race, and that...we'd make it...quick."

"Okay...." I said, "Let's make it quick."

"Okay...." He said.

"Okay." I said.

He left a puff of steam out of his lungs then turned and jogged back to his post. As we were giving Jamie time to get back and have a few more words with the guard, I passed out the flags that the first heat had brought with them, so that they could be returned to Jamie in the second heat. The second heat lined up and I was about to send them off when Daniel rode up, looking more winded than the folks who'd just raced. Apparently Jamie had used his cell phone, as Dan had requested, to order a bunch of food to the race. But Dan's last delivery had been to a crowded strip club across town, and he had several more deliveries waiting for him back at work. He'd hauled ass down to the race (which was well outside of the radius he'd normally ride at work), but was way too tired to race.

"I...have...this...chicken, though." he said, dejectedly holding up a greasy

paper bag. "Chicken?" I said, "Jamie doesn't even eat chicken. Plus he's down at the art school parking lot arguing with a security guard." Dan looked exasperated. He explained that somehow his manager had caught wind of the race and warned him not to try and come while working. He was stressing out about getting back to work so he made quick work of auctioning off th eunwanted bag of chicken to a happy crusty, for, like, two bucks or something, then he trotted slowly off to pick up his waiting deliveries. Poor guy.

In the second heat, Shyman was feeling it, apparently, and he raced against Brice, Suzanna, and some guy from out of town. Had Shyman's bike been powered by puff- paint t-shirts and big talk, than he would've smoked everyone, but as soon as I yelled "Go" it became obvious that even #2 was a delusion of grandeur for the King of Delivery. He was the last to round the corner, by a long way. As he did, I started rallying riders for the next heat. As soon as I called out, though, my voice was drowned out by a loud bellow. I turned around to see a freight train slowly rolling towards us, right through the middle of our race track. It was going so slowly that I thought surely the racers would make it back before it cut them off. They rounded the corner, and we could see them, but the train kept whistling and kept going, then stopped Directly between the racers and the finish.

The twenty-odd spectators on my side of the train just stood there, for a moment, wondering what would happen. The train didn't do anything. It hissed and clunked and rattled, but it wasn't moving. Then, suddenly, a big bulky, heavy as shit Worksman bicycle crahsed to the ground, thrown from the train. On the other end of the same car, another WOrksman smacked against the gravel. Both Brice and the guy from out of town had been riding the huge industrial cruisers, which, with basket, must weigh over forty pounds, and now both Brice and the guy from out of town were racing each other over the train. They both hopped down form between the cars and hurried to mount their bikes. I twas pretty close, but guy from out of town made it through the ribbon of toilet paper first. After they both dropped their bikes and started gasping for air, the train let out a crash and rolled away.

There was a third heat, then we were one rider short of a fourth. I screamed and shouted and heckled and tried to shake another rider out of the crowd, to no avail, Then Brice, holding out his own bike, said, "Why don't you race, Ethan?" Hmmm. I clutched my belly and felt the homemade donuts wrestling around with the four or five Schlitz tall-boys I'd had. But what choice did I have? The beer and donuts gurgled in protest, but I took Brice's Worksman.

Brice shouted off the command to go. I took off as fast as I could on the heavy loaner bike, quickly leaving Mitchell, Stella and Yoni behind me. "Hey, this is gonna be easy!" I thought. As I rounded the corner and careened up onto the sidewalk beside the art school, everyone else was still behind me, even Mitchell, who has a fancy bike and legs almost as long as I am tall. When I jumped off of the bike and tried to run, though, everything went to shit for me. My knees just buckled and I hit the ground. I remember thinking, "This isn't so bad...lying here, on this parking lot. Maybe I'll just stay." I heard Mitchell's bike clatter to the pavement. I just lay there staring up as, a second later, a pair of infinitely long, Wrangler-clad legs appeared above me, blocking out the sky. Mitchell leapt right over me and cleared the whole parking lot in just a few gaping steps. He

slapped the flag he was carrying into Jamie's hand and looped back towards his bike. I hadn't even regained control of my limbs yet. Stella and Yoni both passed me, making it back to the finish line a half block ahead of me. When I finally did get back, I barely made it into the grassy lot beside Press Street before the donuts and beer were in full revolt against me, demanding their freedom, which they got. I puked more than I thought possible. When it ended, Dempsey came over to comfort me. He'd raced in the heat before me, and had also puked in the field. He pointed over to a spot in the grass that the crusties' dogs were taking a keen interest in. Then we heard a third person wretching and heaving. We looked over to the source of the noise. Dempsey and I then both felt a little better about our weak stomachs. It was Buddha, who hadn't even raced.

Brice saw that I was occupied, trying to keep my guts from coming out of my mouth, so he announced the finals. I leaned against a telephone pole to watch. Everyone cheered as the four racers took off. A few minutes later they rounded the last corner and headed back towards the screaming crowd. The winner was, of course, John on his fancy Specialized racer. It was a triumph that would scandalize delivery circles for months. All of the macho dudes who'd told me just how the race "Has to be", most of whom hadn't even shown up, would all come up to me later saying, "Don't you think that's bullshit?" No, I didn't. True, had John ridden a cruiser, Mitchell probably would've won. But I didn't care. Mitchell didn't seem to care, either. I plopped the crown onto John's head and raised his arm up. Crusties cheered. Shyman's cheerleaders defected and also cheered.

Fuck no, I didn't care. What I cared about was that, even though the temperature was still steadily dropping, we were all out on the street, away from work, away from the bars, screaming and laughing and puking and having a good time, on bikes. Since the automobile took over as top of the transportation food chain, bikes have been forced into the slot of a children's toy, a plaything. In the world of delivery bikes are a tool used to get a paycheck. That night, though, down on Press and Burgundy Streets, we were all reminded that they can be both. Yeah, it sucks having to knock yourself out getting some yuppie's pizza to him, and your ass gets sore on those seats, and delivery bikes need constant maintenance, but despite all of that, damn...bikes are fun.

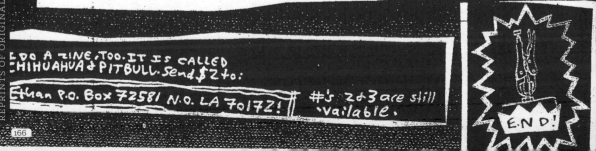

END!

i recently read this story in andalusia's zine called elitical mass (po box 71357 pgh pa 15213 - it is great!). the story blew my mind: mary wrote of so many things that i have experienced being a female mechanic in a shop. it was just amazing. i kept thinking "i must know this person," or "how could that possibly have happened to her too!" i admired her honesty about her frustrations and anger. so i wrote her and told her that and asked if i could re-print the story. she said yes and encouraged me to write about my experiences too... so here are both stories, both so similar and both so different, in so many ways... lady mechanics - write me!

The Girl at The Bike Shop: A Tale of Biceps Bitterness and Grease

by Mary Christmas

In the mid-late nineties, I was getting fed up. I had been, for years, one of a few active women in a apolitical, alcoholic, offensive indie rock scene in the Midwest. The Neo No Wave art philosophy (really not a philosophy at all but a common undercurrent that seemed to connect all of these individualist wierdos) was bent on destruction of norms such as Pop sound and even "norm" punk aesthetic, but too often I found it to also be bent on destroying sensitivity of any kind, the kind I needed to survive. In other words, the art I was making with male friends had a certain necessary emptiness, but in the chaos of all the experimentation around us I would run smack into hatred, misogyny, racism, and stupidity. It was a "Vice magazine" kind of crowd. It was where I was at the time... I even posed naked for the local male-run indie politics magazine, thinking "what's the big deal?" But even then, before my brain popped on and I began to see through feminist-colored glasses, it felt lonely and at times a little scary.

That time in my life is like a binge in my memory. The kind of symptomatic mess where you can only take in so much of other people's anti-values before you grow lumps of cancerous behavior or you explode with craziness. After a few years of drug and drink, and playing in bands with men who were essentially feelingless robots too happy to use my ideas and not credit me for them, after years of being scoffed at, asked if "the guys" wrote the songs, being told "oh great, another girl in a band" as if it was really that common at all, having no space to talk about the reality I lived which was different, as a young woman, than these guys, I eventually snapped. The last thing I remember before quitting the whole music scene was hitting this guy over the head with a guitar at my house with "no provocation." I mean, out of nowhere I just swung the fucking thing at him. But now, looking back, I see how much it was deserved among all of them, how I was reflexively acting out with the tool that had come to symbolize the trap I was entrenched in. What a bunch of assholes.

Right after that period, I decided to empower myself. What that meant, I wasn't sure. I knew that I wanted to deal with my childhood rape, and change my body to have more strength and muscles, and have more women friends. I wanted to be tough, to learn more about feminism and what

...going to figure out a way to survive emotionally and be fulfilled instead of just taking what I could get. I had been hooking up sexually with other girls here and there, and wanted to bring it out as more of my identity. All of these related desires are what drove me, strangely enough, to the bike shop.

It was the "cool" bike shop, the kind of place that has a bunch of shoddy welded art hanging from the storefront in lieu of a sign, and an ad in that same lefty indie rocker magazine mentioned earlier. I used to go there because it was in the neighborhood, next to Quimby's Queer Store where everyone went for comix. They had a woman at the front register, and as I became a regular customer I noticed they even had a female mechanic (granted, one out of several guys). One day, I worked up the nerve to march in and pitch my dream to the owners: I offered to work for free as an apprentice for a while if, in exchange, they would mentor me as a mechanic and teach me how to fix bikes. Surprisingly, they agreed. I would be monitored for a bit, and if I was any good, they might be able to keep me for The Season, the busy spring-summer rush, and pay me minimum wage.

I worked about five days a week. At the time, I either had money saved up or was dancing at a peep show to make rent. I can't remember. The shop owners started me on building new bikes out of the box so I could get familiar with the parts. Working on bikes was frustrating, hard, filthy, exhausting, yet in some deep way very satisfying. Even if I was just taking out the trash, I felt good because I was lifting something heavy and getting my hands dirty. And every time I did something right, like adjust the brakes so that they were no longer aimed at the tire and now rested appropriately on the spoke hub, I felt so good. The muscles were growing in my arms, and I even discovered muscles I didn't know I had, like this one in the forearm that comes from repetitive twisting, cranking motions. Fuck yeah! I fell into a rhythm, getting up at dawn every day to make my lunch and bounce off to the shop just in time to help take down the gates and face the desperate, pre-work crowd and their broken chain disasters. As I became a part of the shop, my routine of dragging bike boxes up from the basement and assembling the new rides became peppered with ringing up gel seat purchases and fixing flats by replacing the blown-out tubes. As I learned the language of bike repair, I learned the luxuries of the shop. We never patched a tube; we just replaced it and charged for the new one, which was always guaranteed to last longer. I never had to try and make a screwdriver function as a vice grip, or some other impossible task- all the tools of my wildest dreams were in my sweaty, greasy, black hands. No more squeezing an upside-down 3-speed in between my thighs while leaning precariously over to put a wheel back on. I had a stand that adjusted every which way. The owners had introduced me to bike repair manuals I never could have afforded to buy on my own, and there was always someone around to do whatever repair was not in my basic skills repertoire. All in all, I was lucky and learning very fast. My bosses seemed genuinely shocked that I was picking it up, and they offered me a job, starting at minimum wage.

Enter the "dark side." Sure, the muscle tone and pride in being a newbie mechanic was a major boost to my 22-year old, lacking-in-feminist-empowerment self. But it was not too long before I began to experience the drawbacks of being a powerful, butch young lady in a two-wheeled

One day we were putting up the window gates after closing and my male co-worker had to run inside for a second, leaving me out on the street in still-sunny early evening with a bunch of six-foot metal cheese grater thingies. I continued sliding them into the window frame (this is to prevent people from breaking the glass and stealing everything), when suddenly a man appeared out of nowhere and began to *do what I was doing*. It took me a minute to figure out, and then I spoke to him: "Who are you and what are you doing?" He explained that I shouldn't be trying this alone, that the gates were too heavy for me (!), that he "will do this now." I got in his way and blocked the window, saying "Sir, I work here. This is my job and you have your hands on our property, and I think it would be best if you let go and continued on your way." When I put it that way, all official sounding, he put down the gate and sort of backed off, saying "oh, okay, okay, sorry" and then standing there watching me for a minute as if to make sure I wasn't going to drop anything. Eventually, he shuffled off in silence, and I had to explain the whole frustrating incident to my co-worker.

More than half of the time, a male customer whose bicycle I was going to do some work on would insist on carrying the bike back into the shop and putting it into the stand "for me." When I actually did repairs as opposed to just building new Treks, it was almost always under the suspicious scrutiny of the customer. They would stand right next to the island I'd be working at, with a pained look on their faces, often contributing a ridiculous amount of suggestions. "You should probably use a 16 wrench on that," they'd comment, as if I didn't already know. More than a few times we had to ask guys to leave the shop area so that I could work in peace.

It's true that I was no master mechanic. I was just learning. Which is precisely why these men were overreacting, because the only repairs I was ever given to do were so minute and simple it begs the question: "if you're such a goddamn expert, why aren't YOU fixing this?" My job was generally to assemble brand-new parts, with the occasional flat fix, brake adjustment, or wheel truing. Whatever I had shown ability to do, I did. But if the boss didn't trust me with it, I wasn't given the job, period. Still, I had male customers butting in on jobs that didn't even involve them or their bikes! Like the time a man followed me into the basement when I was dragging an assembly box back down because there was no stand to work on- he wanted to follow me to make sure I "had it!" Again, I had to tell him that he didn't work there and could not walk into our basement. Sigh.

I wish the annoyances would have stopped with the offensive customers, but they didn't. One of the shop mechanics was a pain in the ass, too. He was a strange, kind of sad character, the kind of guy you want to make fun of at first but then can't. Like the comic book store owner from *The Simpsons*, this man was roly-poly, balding (but with long hair), sweaty, wore heavy metal t-shirts, mumbled passive aggressive commentary, and had been on Methadone for about ten years. He was a total asshole to everyone, but he was small and always looked on the verge of tears, so people were generally nice to him. I could not afford such clarity, however, in light of the constant death rays he shot at me from his blurry eyes. Whenever I needed a tool from his station, not only did I have to endure the urine stench, but often his grumbling and sighs and eventual "oh, okaaaay, I guess." One day he wouldn't let up with the "I detest you" vibe, and I was probably ignoring him too much for his liking, because suddenly he burst out with a magnificent roll call of insults aimed at me loud enough for the whole store: "why don't they hire a REAL mechanic, stupid girl, bla bla bla!" I remember having a moment of "I can't take this anymore," and leaving to go cool off for awhile. I complained to the boss, who took the stance that I should be more *understanding* to Comic Book Man, because he was… you know… *sad*. I kept it in mind, but I don't think my boss fully grasped the amount of pressure that had led up to this being my first "last straw."

The boss was another issue altogether. Generally nice and encouraging, he showed a personal side that I couldn't deal with on what would be one of my last days working there. In a random discussion about one of his buddies, my boss mentioned that the friend, a man in his early thirties, was dating a thirteen year old girl. I was grossed out, and expressed such. A thirteen year old girl? That's not *dating*, that's child molestation, I told him. The boss responded sincerely that his friend and the girl were in love and that I was being silly. We argued to a fairly heated level and I left early for the day. Thoughts ran through my head: my boss had a young child, my best friend at thirteen was being molested by her stepdad, one of my mom's friends wanted her to set me up with him when I was fifteen, I was raped when I was seven. The intersection in my mind of all these memories and facts helped me to conclude that it was important to take a stand against older men fucking around with pubescent girls. I had thought I was working at the progressive bike shop. What kind of people was I working for?

Bike shops operate in seasonal cycles and this one was no different. During the winter months, when there was little to no money coming through the store, I found work elsewhere. Then in the summer, I began to hang around and ask if I could get some hours. In warm weather, I was basically at the shop every day. I lived down the street, and besides, it was my life. At the time, when I wasn't working on bikes, I was training for triathlons, doing karate at Thousand Waves, playing drums in the Slits tribute band, and hanging with my gymnastics instructor girlfriend. It was all so butch! So lesbian! So Olympian! My lifestyle had reached a rare kind of completeness, wherein I discovered an ability to focus on one kind of expression, that being muscular. And it would have stayed that way, had I not made a shocking discovery that hurt my feelings and blew my bike shop days into the past.

It is a typical day. Let's say it's early June. Smooth, warm Chicago spring winds barely rattle the clunky bike-part sculpture outside. The backdoor is open, bringing a sweet, grassy scent in to the shop area to mingle with the usual grease and rubber. The startling whoosh of compressed air pops out every minute or so, the clang of metal against metal rings through the air, and the occasional "motherfucker" can be heard pleasantly muttered under the breath of any given mechanic. Ah, a day at the shop. I'm working on truing some wheels -even though I'm much more skilled now and could be fixing flats or something, I find wheel truing very Zen- and wondering how I'd care to strike up a conversation with the new guy working next to me. He's a preppy-scruffy kind of guy, college age like me, and generally real quiet.

Memory doesn't serve me well, but I think it all happened like this: I had knowledge of the exact amount of the new guy's paycheck -perhaps I had seen it amongst my own- and I knew that he was being paid more than me. Naturally, as the lowest-paid mechanic in a shop tier based on skill, I figured that he was getting more money because he had more experience. But today, given the chance to have a little friendly work chat with him, I found out the opposite was true. Just making conversation, I asked where he had worked before. His reply was that he had *never* worked on bikes in his life, that, in fact, he felt quite lucky to have this job, since he had told the owners up front about having zero experience and "just wanting to learn." How nice of them to take in this completely unskilled young man and not only give him a chance to learn, but pay him quite well for it!

I was fuming. I felt sick. So that's the way it was, huh? I work for two weeks straight without pay, somehow live off of minimum wage for a couple months, and now in my second year working, a guy waltzes in off the street and not only doesn't have to go through the trial-by-starvation period, but gets paid a bigger hourly than I *ever* have? What the fuck! Whatever happened to all the surprise at how good of a mechanic I turned out to be? What about all the praise I received? Hell, what about all the bullshit I went through? Didn't I deserve more than some unskilled skater dude? I expected so much more from a family owned, ethical neighborhood business. I mean, they even participated in Critical Mass: we had the posters in our window every month!

I left the bike shop that day, never to return. I never explained what it was that made me say goodbye to the biz. I never demanded back pay, threatened to sue for discrimination, or even yelled at my boss. I did nothing at all. Now, at 27, having been through various levels of workplace sexism- from sexual harassment to glass ceilings- I understand that it is not unusual and that it's always important to take a stand in order to try to change unfair dynamics. But back then, I was just really, really hurt. It was hard for me to

truly know my worth as a tradesperson, when there was so much telling me that I couldn't or shouldn't do it, and I took the final blow very personally. But, in retrospect, I was a fucking great bicycle mechanic, and my bosses just took advantage of a cloudy situation. Let this be a lesson to all women working: to never let anyone suggest that we are somehow unworthy of respect, a equal wage, and a chain whip of our own.

Cut this Out

for your own mini-zine

OUR tale begins with ME & two co-workers going to the westbank to try & hit the DMV.

As we cross the bridge I commented on the fact that we were on "E". She assured me it was fine (my story short we took the wrong exit & wound up in the toll line heading back to the city.....

On our second attempt into the dreaded W.B. we get off where we're supposed to this time. I think I know how to get there this time. Typically I wouldn't get involved with cars or instructions but you know the ole' sayin' "when on the westbank"...

I NEVER TAKE FOR GRANTED the love I HAVE FOR MY bike!!!

ANYWAY they listened & next thing I know we're passin' above the DMV. in this MYSTERY LANE. #2 All this confusion it's Also Raining & the detour won't work. All to quickly we realize we're in the police lane that RUNS between the main lanes. They panicked. I laughed. THIS WAS the beginning OF MY day...

I get dropped off at home with just enough time to grab my bike & get off to work in the RAIN. HALFWAY their Ridin As FAST As possible to beat traffic my back hub explodes & bike guts spew everywhere. leaving me stuck on foot on a work day. THIS is my story.....

a heartbreaking tale of lost love in the city of new orleans.

"WHEN YOUR LOVES AWAY" by the one & only Pee Jay

Feel TRAPPED without MY BIKE. THIS IS HOW it'll be when I'm old except MY PARTS ARE NOT REPLACABLE...

My bike is MY FAVORITE thing on earth. MY CRIME PARTNER. iT. beTTer THERAPIST. THAN girls. Knows All MY SECRETS. IT'S ONLY BEEN 1 DAY.

Fucks MY entire schedule. ONLY HAVE 60 MINS. to get FROM Frenchmen to Jackson. THIS MEANS A CAR RIDE WORSE THAN THAT iT MEANS A CAR RIDE I HAVE to PAY FOR. DRATS

At nite I dream of ROLLIN THROUGH A NEVERENDING CITY.

MY BIKE THAT ON THE RARE OCASSION iT BREAK I'M LOST... NAVIGATING THROUGH THE QUARTER ON FOOT IS TERRIBLE, CHEST DEEP IN TOURISTS 3 MONSTERS...

WORK THE DAY AWAY WHILE MY BIKE IS GONE

173

New Orleans Bike Terminology

See if you can match the way people say it in N.O. with the "proper" terms!

① SEAT PIPE
② STUNT SCREWS
③ GRIP PLIERS
④ WIND BACK
⑤ WOPPED
⑥ BUTTERFLIES/WINGS
⑦ KICK BRAKE
⑧ TRUCK BIKE
⑨ PRESSURE LOCKS
⑩ BALL BERRIES
⑪ GEAR BOX
⑫ SAFETY HAT

— coaster brake
— freewheel
— rear derailleur
— helmet
— seat post
— bearings
— vice grips
— sidepull brakes
— out of true/bent
— pegs
— bar ends
— beach cruiser

the sleeplessness is persistent,

weakness of the heart

ANSWERS

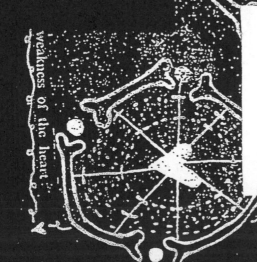

OHNO! LIL' TIMMY THE TWO-WHEELER NEEDS A TUNE-UP AND HE'S LOST HIS WAY! HELP TIMMY FIND HIS BIKE MECHANIC FRIENDS AT THE BIKE PROJECT!

PLAN "B", THE NEW ORLEANS COMMUNITY BIKE PROJECT IS A NON-PROFIT, DO-IT-YOURSELF BIKE SHOP THAT OFFERS FREE USE OF TOOLS, HELP FIX-ING YR BIKE + CHEAP USED PARTS + BIKES! COME VISIT US!!!

511 MARIGNY

PLAN "B"

... are you the mechanic ???

(another girl at the bike shop)

by shelley

i started working at french quarter bicycles about four years ago. the winter of 1999, when the boss came up to me in a decatur street bar and said, "hey, so do you still want a job?". i hardly remembered complaining that i wished he would give me a job last time i had been in his shop - complaining to my house mate about my current job at the whole foods market. i worked there stocking shelves, a job that required so little skill and so little challenge that my mind would travel to its deepest depths during each 8 hour shift. until there was nothing that i hadn't remembered, re-lived, re-processed, re-created and wallowed in from the moment of my birth to that present time. i went home so depressed every day that making it to my next shift was getting increasingly more impossible.

so, i took the job from billy at french quarter bicycles.

french quarter bicycles is a tiny shop. tiny. there is just enough room for one mechanic, one person sitting lazily at the computer, and the masses of bikes to be repaired, built and sold. there is really no room for all the parts, pieces, and garbage that lay about, but somehow it is still there, on the floor, in piles, in every little nook in the shop there is stuff lying around taking up precious space. billy always says he likes to hire women because they make better mechanics, but i think it is really because we clean up after him, keeping the counters clean and the floor occasionally swept. one summer, when i was away travelling and sherry came back from a trip herself, she came back to find the narrowest pathway between these swollen piles of things, just wide enough to get a bike to the stand in the back or to make it to the restroom. the boys had wrecked the shop while we were away, but had a great summer together. sherry of course had the shop together again in a couple of days, i am sure.

it is a funny place to hang out. being located in the french quarter, things happen there that i am positive rarely, if ever happen in any other bike shop, anywhere in this country. the world maybe. from people coming in so drunk that they can't figure out why they can't get any air into their tires (with the caps still on the valves of course, blowing air all over the damn place), to people coming in with drinks in hand, smoking, yelling, being beligerent and often still awake from the night before. the best of new orleans musicians come in regularly to have their bikes repaired. little freddie king stops by every sunday for a little air and to tip me five bucks for putting it in for him and chatting a little. lee the jackson square drummer comes in and

calls me sweetie and tells me stories about growing up in new orleans in the 70's, playing music, fixing his bmx bikes, and fighting with his daddy who apparently was a pimp and is now an aging 90 year old who lee cares for. his stories are so colorful, so steeped in the culture and history of this city that i can listen to him for hours while i am fixing bikes

we have had all types come into the shop. actors, artists, delivery
people. even some big time folks have come in for repairs or to
rent bikes. sarah fixed bob dylan's bike during the jazz festival. john cusak rented some during his movie filming. even fran-
cis ford copola and the guy from the red hot chili peppers have
come in. i have been cursed out by unhappy customers, called a
fucking cunt and been called baby and darling. i have been tipped money, beer, art, and even had attempts at tipping me coc-
ain and weed. i have fixed bikes , trikes, tall bikes, clown
bikes, tandems, pumped up tires for little kids, and even just
yesterday repaired holes in a 7 foot tall blow up penis for a
local photographer who uses it as a prop for an all star calen-
dar. i've dealt with the sweetest and most appreciative people and
i have dealt with total assholes. had men say, "ya, i don't mind
if a chick works on my bike. " ("its a good thing" i say), and
others say, "i only come when you are working now 'cause i trust
you."

the job is a constant battle in the sexism department. so many
guys only want to talk to the boss, or walk into the shop and instantly begin asking questions to the male friend i am sitting and
chatting with, never for a second considering that the girl (me)
sitting holding tools and covered in bike grease is actually the
mechanic. but, if someone crosses the line and really disres-
pects me, the boss reserves me the right to 86 them. like the
guy whose lover called me a fucking cunt. that guy came back to
apologize, gave me 25 bucks for lunch and billy 86ed him anyways.
remarkably the guy understood. and apologized again. and i still
fix his lover's bike.

FRENCH
QUARTER
BICYCLES
522 Dumaine Street
New Orleans, LA 70116
50█ ███ ████
www.fqbi█

PATCH
For Bicycle Tu█

the atmosphere of the shop i think surprises first timers. it
is small, as i said, dark, and the walls are either made of wood
or are painted black. the "repairs" sign is hand painted by a
local artist and depicts a naked lady (from the neck down) riding a bicycle. there are posters of ladies in bikinis on the wall and
billy's leftover beer bottles lying about. the boss is always
smoking a cigar and doesn't look like some bike racer type for sure.
we are always playing some loud music, whether it is mitchells
(another former co-worker) band- ye old buttfucks , or rebirth
brass band, or old john prine on the record player. it is like the
dingy bar of bike shops. sometimes i even begin to have doubts
about the place, like, how can this place keep functioning like
this? but then i remember, we are small and therefor cheap, and we
get work done fast. we might not look like it but we actually care.
the boss keeps the prices super low, and purposely keeps the
place simple and un-intimidating so that biking can remain accessible to all kinds of people. people come in every day and say,
" man, i am so glad ya'll are here, that other guy would have
charged me double for this." we fix anything, and we do it cheap.
we never make anyone feel bad for riding a crappy bike.

the shop has changed a bit over the years. well, the SHOP has
stayed the same, some of the same crap is in the same corners,
same fancy rims hanging up that we will probably never sell.
but the workers have changed.   when i first started it was
just billy and julie. julie was an amazing mechanic, confident
without being a show off. she loved showing me little tricks she
knew and i was really happy when billy put me on shifts working
with her. it was so nice. we got to be friends and there were
never any weird feeling between us. she showed me that a female
mechanic is best when she doesn't have to make the point that she
is a FEMALE mechanic, that strength is found in confidence..
nobody ever second guessed her work or her knowledge. both were
as solid as her personality.

there have always been difficult sides of the job as well. like
coming back from a long vacation and getting re-hired, only to
later find out all of my co-workers, mostly male, were getting
paid way more than me, though i had worked there longer and
was just as good a mechanic. there have been times when i felt
underappreciated. times when i had some heavy competition going on
with a female co-worker, who, despite her strength would get into
blaming me for things i hadn't fucked up, causing more than one
fight between me and the boss. i often felt i had to defend my
work and my place in the shop. it took me three years to be trust-
ed to run the shop alone, thoughbilly handed the keys to the shop
to other co-workers without a second thought. somehow it has
always been a bit of a struggle there to feel appreciated. mostly due to billys and my love-hate relationship for each other more
than any kind of gender dynamics. situations just get created
where the workers get pitted against each other, like any other
job. and i can get pretty possessive about that job, and the
place in general. because i love it so much, feel proud of the
shop and my work and because honestly, if it were not for that
place i don't know what i would have done for all of these years.
billy is the only shop owner who would hire a woman mechanic in
this town seems. if it weren't for that i might have left here a
long time ago.

all in all the job has taught me so much, and not just mechanical
skill (which has gotten so much better over these years - i could-
n't even change a tube before!), but also i have learned people
skills, how to assert myself, how to help people, not just with
their bikes but with their LIVES. i have even learned to feel ok
about selling things (billy always said i wasn't enough of a capitalist to sell bikes, but now i feel good helping someone get
something that will improve their life so much), AND i have learned to overlook the temporary downsides of my workplace to see how
i can grow by sticking with something until it becomes part of me
instead of something i feel like i am fighting against. the place
may be weird, but it is beautiful too. I LOVE FQB!!!

make your own Bucket Paniers!

by joe biel of microcosm!

When i first became a commuter cyclist, i hit the continual roadblock of how to transport things to and from my house. Trips to the grocery store and the post office became a big ordeal, limited to what i could carry on my back. Over time i picked up a bike rack, but it still limited me to transporting primarily boxes or else the cargo would be prone to falling off my bike. In 2001 i got sick of the rigamarole and set out to build my own panier buckets. These were quite a bit more adaptable -- allowing me to fill the buckets with whatever i wanted and easily remove and add things at my leisure. Also, the biggest advantage that keeps me using the buckets to this day is that mine sit flush (at the top) with my rack, allowing me to attach boxes across the top with a bungee cord, which i can then deliver and continue biking around town without the added weight of the box. the buckets are also waterproof and have lids so people cannot see inside of them. In almost three years i have never had anyone steal anything out of my buckets even when i have left them on my bike outside for hours. i have however had people leave their garbage in my buckets when i don't have the lids on them.

SO! without further ado , let's build some bike buckets!

first you'll need to aquire some four gallon buckets. these can be found in the garbage of many restaurants and brewpubs as many commercial grade food and grocery items come packaged in them. as do things like detergent and kitty litter. if you don't have any luck finding them you can also ask some kind employees of such places for empty ones they no longer have a use for. you will need at least two of them, one for each side of your rack. only one bucket will leave your bike unbalanced, causing it to lean heavily to one side, which will warp your wheel in the rear pretty badly over time.

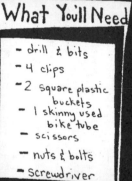

← Clip

← 2 for each bucket

Next you will need four clips to attach the top of the buckets to the top of the rack. there is a commercial product for this (found in most bike parts catalogs which any shop can order from) but it will run you about a buck fifty per clip, and diy is supposed to be cheap, right? They should look like these---------

Make sure they are sturdy and will not bend. hardware stores generally have something simi-lar, and they shouldn't cost you more than 20-50 cents each. what a deal!

You'll also need a drill and some nuts and bolts (about 8 for each pair of paniers). the size doesn't matter too much as long as the bolts aren't too big or too small for the holes in the clips.

The bottom of the buckets can be best attached with some old used inner tube. skinny ones work best, the tubes like on a road bike.

First, take your buckets and measure them against your rack. Align the top of the rack with the top of the bucket, and put a clip on each end of the bucket, about 1 inch from the edge. Mark where it goes on the bucket, and mark where the holes go for the bolts

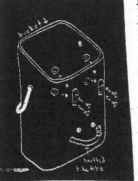

Drill two holes for each clip and bolt the clips on to each bucket. Put the buckets on the rack and see how they line up. Do you see any potential trouble with the buckets hitting your derailleur, feet, or other parts? If the buckets don't sit or line up properly, try again. if you have mangled one side of the bucket with too many holes you can always turn it around and work on the other side.

Once your buckets line up properly you'll want to work on attaching the bottoms of the buckets. Put two larger holes (in one line) about four to six inches from the bottom of the rack (depending of the height of your rack). Put the holes about two inches above this (***) part of your rack centered on the bucket and horozontally in line. the two holes should be about two inches apart, each about one inch from the center. cut a 6-8" length of inner tube and make a knot in one end. run it through one of the holes from the inside out and then into the other hole. tie a knot in the other end (which will be inside the bucket). This tube wraps around this (***) part of the rack. →

Now, put the bucket on the rack. Does it sit level? does it want to fall off? If it feels solid you are pretty much good to to go. If not, try putting it on the other side of the rack. If it still doesn't sit properly there you will have to examine your clips to be sure they are on evenly from the top of the bucket. If they are even and your bucket still doesn't sit right, your holes on the bottom probably are not centered. It took me a few tries to make beautiful, functional buckets. Keep trying! I left the handles on to have something to carry them with, and kept the lids to protect from the rain and from prying eyes.

Good luck! and please send me your questions and experiences. I'd love to hear how they have worked for you, or how you have used them for your own applications...

write to: joebiel@ureach.com or po box 1four332 portland, or 97293

"MISTER JOHN"

THAT'S WHAT THE KIDS KNOW ME AS AT SCHOOL, MR. JOHN. WELL, I CERTAINLY WASN'T GOING TO GO AROUND BEING CALLED "MR. GERKEN", YOU KNOW?

I HELP TEACH A BICYCLE REPAIR CLASS AT CHARTER MIDDLE SCHOOL HERE IN NEW ORLEANS. AT THIS SCHOOL, THE TWO PERIODS AFTER LUNCH ARE ALL ELECTIVE CLASSES, TAUGHT BY ALL KINDS OF PEOPLE IN TOWN. CLASSES INCLUDE SOCCER AND FOOTBALL (FOR GIRLS AS WELL AS FOR BOYS), PAINTING, DRAMA, AFRICAN DANCE, CAPOEIRA, RHYTHMS OF BRASIL, MARDI GRAS INDIANS, GARDENING, AEROBICS, CHOIR, COMIC BOOK DESIGN, AND OUR BIKE CLASS. IT'S REALLY AN AMAZING PLACE, ESPECIALLY CONSIDERING IT'S AN INNER-CITY PUBLIC SCHOOL. MOST OTHER SCHOOLS IN TOWN SEEM LIKE LITTLE JAILS.

I'VE LIVED IN NEW ORLEANS FOR CLOSE TO TWO YEARS NOW, AND MOST OF THAT TIME I'VE BEEN INVOLVED WITH PLAN B, THE NEW ORLEANS COMMUNITY BIKE PROJECT. IT'S WHERE I'VE LEARNED MOST OF WHAT I KNOW ABOUT BIKES, AND IT'S WHERE I FIRST DEALT WITH KIDS IN A LEARNING ENVIRONMENT. THAT'S GOT A LOT TO DO WITH ME HAVING THIS JOB (AND BECAUSE OF SARAH D. PASSING ALONG WORD OF THE OPPORTUNITY - THANKS!). THIS JOB, WHICH IS A JOB I FIND MEANINGFUL AND FULFILLING - A RARITY IN MY EMPLOYED LIFE. OUR SCRAPPY AND GLORIOUS DIY BIKE SHOP, AND THIS SCRAPPY AND BEAUTIFUL SCHOOL. BETWEEN THE TWO, I FEEL LIKE I'M REALLY GROWING ROOTS HERE, INVOLVED IN GOOD THINGS.

REALLY, I HAVE JUST AS MUCH TO LEARN FROM THE KIDS IN MY CLASS AS THEY DO FROM ME. IT SOUNDS CLICHÉ, BUT IT IS TRUE. SURE, THEY MIGHT LEARN SOME BIKE STUFF, OR AT LEAST HOW TO PATCH A TUBE. HOPEFULLY USING TOOLS CAN TRANSLATE INTO A BROADER CONFIDENCE WITH HOW THINGS FIT TOGETHER AND WORK,

THE BASIC PRINCIPLES OF SIMPLE MACHINES. RIGHTY TIGHTY, LEFTY LOOSEY. THE KIND OF STUFF I NEVER KNEW AS A KID, WHICH IS WHY IT'S IMPORTANT TO ME TO BE TRYING TO NURTURE AN INCLUSIVE LEARNING ENVIRONMENT. THE KIND OF PLACE WHERE PEOPLE FEEL CONFIDENT TO ASK QUESTIONS AND TRY THINGS, EVEN IF THEY'VE BEEN TOLD THEY WON'T BE GOOD AT IT BECAUSE THEY'RE CLUMSY, OR A GIRL, OR ANY OF THE OTHER WAYS THAT TOOLS AND MECHANICS IS MADE INTIMIDATING. IT'S THAT WAY WITH ANY SPECIALIZED KNOWLEDGE, REALLY. BUT NOBODY JUST PICKS UP A WRENCH AND FIXES THINGS. WE ALL HAVE TO LEARN TO USE THE WRENCH IN THE FIRST PLACE.

~~BICYCLES ARE SUCH OPEN POSSIBILITIES~~

BICYCLES ARE ALREADY SUCH OPEN WINDOWS OF POSSIBILITY, IMAGINATION AND DESIRE LAID BARE. YOU CAN JUST GET ON THEM AND GO (ONCE YOU'VE LEARNED HOW TO RIDE). YOU CAN LEARN TO FIX IT ALL YOURSELF. YOU CAN MAKE IT WHATEVER YOU WANT. PEOPLE HAVE TALL BIKES AND BIKES DECORATED LIKE TRASHPICKING SEA CREATURES. PEOPLE CARRY ALL SORTS OF THINGS ON THEIR BIKES. CARRIE MADE A SIDECAR SO HER DOG COULD RIDE ALONGSIDE HER!

AND WORKING ON BIKES WITH KIDS, I'M EXPOSED TO THESE IMAGINATIVE UNDERSTANDINGS OF THE WORLD. SO OPEN. IT'S WHY WE SEEK TO BE EXPOSED TO OTHER CULTURES IF WE HAVE THE CHANCE, I GUESS, OR WHY WE LEARN OTHER LANGUAGES. TO BE SHOWN OTHER UNDERSTANDINGS, NEW UNDERSTANDINGS OF THE THINGS WE TAKE FOR GRANTED.

dealing with Carpel Tunnel Syndrome

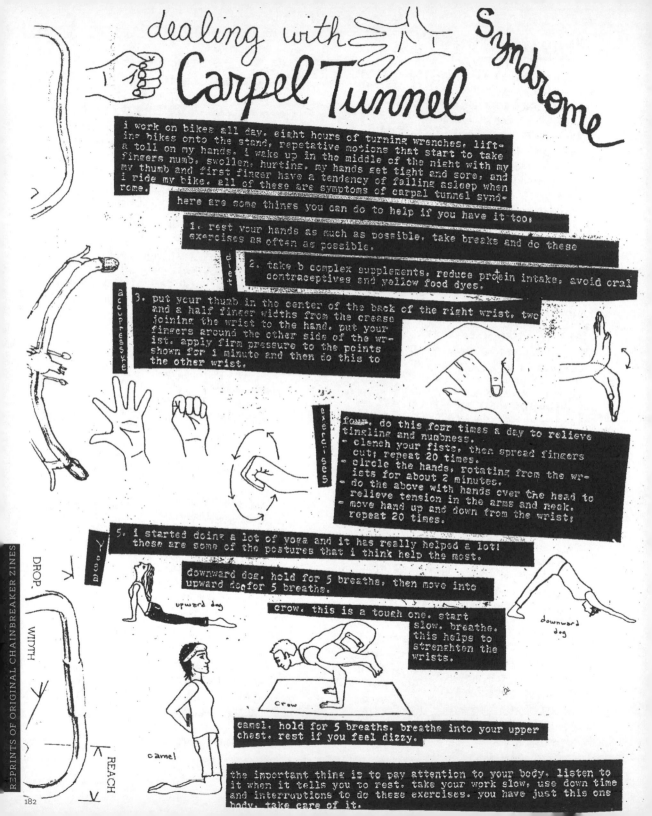

i work on bikes all day. eight hours of turning wrenches, lifting bikes onto the stand, rapetative motions that start to take a toll on my hands. i wake up in the middle of the night with my fingers numb, swollen, hurting. my hands get tight and sore, and my thumb and first finger have a tendency of falling asleep when i ride my bike. all of these are symptoms of carpal tunnel syndrome.

here are some things you can do to help if you have it too:

1. rest your hands as much as possible. take breaks and do these exercises as often as possible.

diet

2. take b complex supplements, reduce protein intake, avoid oral contraceptives and yellow food dyes.

accupressure

3. put your thumb in the center of the back of the right wrist, two and a half finger widths from the crease joining the wrist to the hand. put your fingers around the other side of the wrist. apply firm pressure to the points shown for 1 minute and then do this to the other wrist.

exercises

four. do this four times a day to relieve tingling and numbness.
- clench your fists, then spread fingers out; repeat 20 times.
- circle the hands, rotating from the wrists for about 2 minutes.
- do the above with hands over the head to relieve tension in the arms and neck.
- move hand up and down from the wrist; repeat 20 times.

yoga

5. i started doing a lot of yoga and it has really helped a lot! these are some of the postures that i think help the most.

downward dog. hold for 5 breaths, then move into upward dog for 5 breaths.

upward dog

crow. this is a tough one. start slow. breathe. this helps to strenghten the wrists.

crow

downward dog

camel. hold for 5 breaths. breathe into your upper chest. rest if you feel dizzy.

camel

the important thing is to pay attention to your body. listen to it when it tells you to rest. take your work slow, use down time and interruptions to do these exercises. you have just this one body. take care of it.

DROP. WIITH REACH

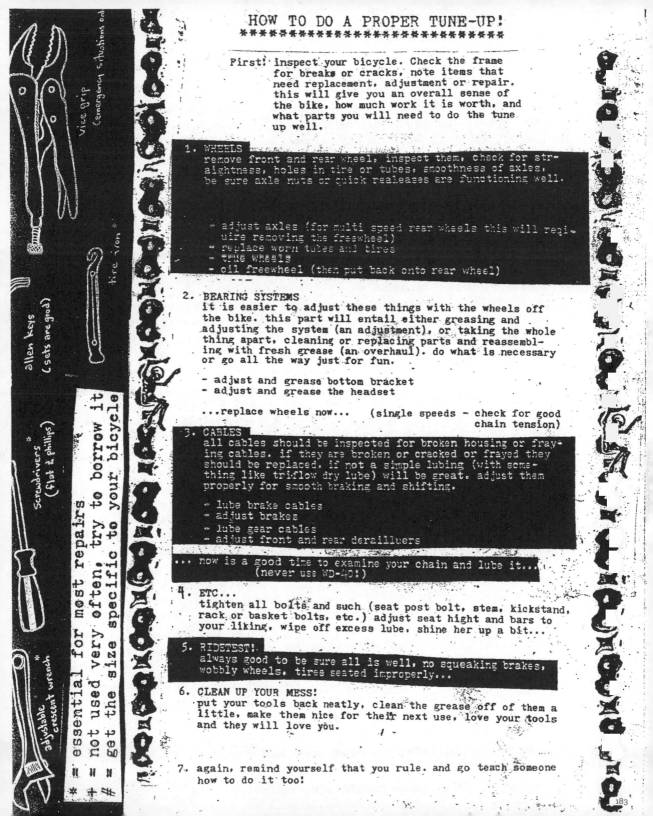

HOW TO DO A PROPER TUNE-UP!
★★★★★★★★★★★★★★★★★★★★★★★★★

First! inspect your bicycle. Check the frame
for breaks or cracks, note items that
need replacement, adjustment or repair.
this will give you an overall sense of
the bike, how much work it is worth, and
what parts you will need to do the tune
up well.

1. WHEELS
remove front and rear wheel, inspect them, check for straightness, holes in tire or tubes, smoothness of axles.
be sure axle nuts or quick realeases are functioning well.

- adjust axles (for multi speed rear wheels this will requ-
  uire removing the freewheel)
- replace worn tubes and tires
- true wheels
- oil freewheel (then put back onto rear wheel)

2. BEARING SYSTEMS
it is easier to adjust these things with the wheels off
the bike. this part will entail either greasing and
adjusting the system (an adjustment), or taking the whole
thing apart, cleaning or replacing parts and reassembling with fresh grease (an overhaul). do what is necessary
or go all the way just for fun.

- adjust and grease bottom bracket
- adjust and grease the headset

...replace wheels now...   (single speeds - check for good
                             chain tension)

3. CABLES
all cables should be inspected for broken housing or fraying cables. if they are broken or cracked or frayed they
should be replaced. if not a simple lubing (with something like triflow dry lube) will be great. adjust them
properly for smooth braking and shifting.

- lube brake cables
- adjust brakes
- lube gear cables
- adjust front and rear derailluers

... now is a good time to examine your chain and lube it...
           (never use WD-40!)

4. ETC...
tighten all bolts and such (seat post bolt, stem, kickstand,
rack or basket bolts, etc.) adjust seat hight and bars to
your liking, wipe off excess lube, shine her up a bit...

5. RIDETEST!
always good to be sure all is well, no squeaking brakes,
wobbly wheels, tires seated improperly...

6. CLEAN UP YOUR MESS!
put your tools back neatly, clean the grease off of them a
little, make them nice for their next use, love your tools
and they will love you.

7.
again, remind yourself that you rule. and go teach someone
how to do it too!

vice grip (emergency situations only)

tire iron

allen keys (sets are good)

Screwdrivers (flat & phillips)

adjustable crescent wrench

* essential for most repairs
\# not used very often, try to borrow it
\# get the size specific to your bicycle

How A Bicycle saved my Life   by hope

it wasn't the bicycle that xxalmost killed me., it was the
car le aning a little to the right which led me to the emerengcy
room with two broken bones, a concussion, and no memories of details such
as the color of the car, but a sharp knowledge of the feeling of impact.

a nurse in the eme rgency room heard that i'd been to the hospital
before when a car door was opened int o my bicycle's back t ire, toldme:

" MAYBE YOU NEED TO START DRIVING. "

and t he reactionary and ble eding head that was me wanted to say:

" FUCK YOU! Maybe you need to start looking where you're going. "

people ask, if i'm afraid to bike now but it wasn't my bike
that hur t me. my bike responded as i e xpe c ted. i rode it down the
busy st ree t wit h the speedy cars and confusing intersection. my bike
moved forward when i pedale d, stopped when i squeezed t he brake
le vels and flew to the side of the road without me whe n i was hitt
from behind while biking down the right side of the street.

my bicycle would never leave me strande d in a sea of strip malls
and and highways. my bike would find the secre t path to the oce an.
so when i took a trip to visit a friend and ended up in seaside
california. i wished for wheels. i was visiting a high school friend
who i had knot seen in se ve n ye ar s. we'd been writ ing let ters for
the past year and x he told me about the beautiful place   where
he live d. the re should be a warning labe l attched to punk kids

DO NOT LEAVE ALONE IN SUBURBS
without a viable means of escape.

at le ast give us a map t o the library. j. picked me up at t he bus
station, took me to a burrito shop, then dropped me off at his house
saying he 'd be back fr om work in a few hours and oh, don't hang outt x
too long in the park at the end xof the st treet. no e xplaination. the
door close d and he drove awayleaving me in his stuffy x living room wit h
an indiffere nt cat, a few overflowing ashtrays, and a pile of books next
to the fireplace which i later learnedhad bee n foundin the garage and xxx
would be xxx burned for the sake of fire . there was a sink full of dirty
dishes and no vege ta bles but celery in the re fridge rat or, so i rolle d
up my sleve s and thought about an escape as i cleaned pots and pans.

the worst part about the accide nt was not the broke n bones, really,
but that it shook up my ideas of se cur it y. i had a prett y unst able year
but was begining to enjoy t the regular pace of my job, volunte ering at
plan b, and hot summer life in new orleans. but i couldn't work for 2
months, had no money, decided to move home and now felt like i regressed
at least six months in te rms of self- assurance. i t hought this one
month travel to visit friends would give me persp ctive and support but

my first stop, so far, was awkward conversation, some fxsx realizations
about how comfortable i am woth my life styde and my fr ie nds, and how
infre quently i step out of that. while m j. liked his ne w home for the
view of the ocean, the maze of houses and plazas be tween us and t he xx
water made me dizzy.

when the dishes were clean, i found a way through the parking lots
and residential stre ets to a grocery store i so i could cook dinner.
j.'s roommate came home first and asked me what my plans were
for my visit to monterrey. i had been x sche e ming to build abike
or a tabogge n to get down the hill. the re was a bus that we nt t o
monterrey which had a coffee shop, a bookstore and a free museum. and
a beach. maybe i'd just hang out in town and write all those lett e rs
i'd been meaning to send.

"you can borrow my bike."   she said.

she drew me a map to the bike path that she x saidfollowed to coastt
along the pe nninsula for a bit . she gave me the lock and key and
said ki sh ould come by her office if i was bored.
j. and i staye d up late talking, drinking bee r, and playing part s
of songs on his five xstring guttar. but there were so many things
we didn't talk aeut. we talk about how things ar e ge tting bett er
but not exact ly whefe they we re . i don't te ll him that i felt
vulnerable aft er i got hit by a car but it had not hing to do with my
bike . i felt mortal, older and su bject to the effects of time.
the next morning i woke to the sunny califnia sky , made a sandw
and put t he map in my pocket. the map left out an important turn and i
ende d up on the highway for a mile or two so when i passed the visitor's
center, i inve sted a dollar in a be tt er map that included a detail of a
road around the penninsula and also t he highway to big sur.
there is a road for tourist s with cars called the seventee n mile
drive. half of that is bike friendly and the re st , well, tr affic is slow
and aware so i followed it all the way to carmel with huge houses and
famous golf courses on my left and the ocean on my right. like meditation,
a long bike ride gives perspective, the repetion of rightleg up left leg up,
the monotony of tire s against road. my ankle bone, recently declared heal-
e d by the doctor, didn't complain a bit. i walke d along the sandy whi te
beach, a dirty kid on a borrowe d bike on rich people's land ignori ng
the ir housse s and sun porches just looking towards the wate r and the lightt.
so what if my friend in oakland was going to europe and not coming back
for a few years--that was good for him. sure , my friends will always live
in diffe rent cities as long as i keep traveling and making new frie nds.
and maybe my high school fr iends are not the ones who really know me , not
all of them at least . i wasn't going to write letters that day, i was going t
to write all the stories i'd been keeping to myself. tthe stor y of a once

broken ankle bone that made it twenty-five miles in one day. about
the collar bone connected to the arm writing this. about the bike
tire that he ld toge ther u ntil i got back int o town and then wentt
flat. about the nicest bikeshop non-dude who lent me the tools to
fix my flat, e ven when it took me an hour, and to adjust my brakes,
without trying to tell me what to do. i need to write about a girl
who j. said was crazy, who left me money in an envelope for fixing her
bike that she had lent to me, i wouldn't return it with a flat tire,
and she wrote me a note thanking me for my help and My pre sence
in the house. she didn't eve n realize she had given me the key to
the ocean, a way past the obstacles directly to where i ne e ded t o go.
i rode as far as i could until my head cle ared and i pr ove d t he
strength of broken bones heale d. and she thought she was just
le nding me he r bike.

SPIT ON

RUN DOWN

CUT OFF

CHASED

HONKED AT

SCREAMED AT

LAUGHED AT

CURSED AT
DISRESPECTED
GIVEN THE FINGER
HARRASSED
PUNCHED
PULLED
FRIGHTENED
HIT
KILLED.

all just for riding my bicycle.

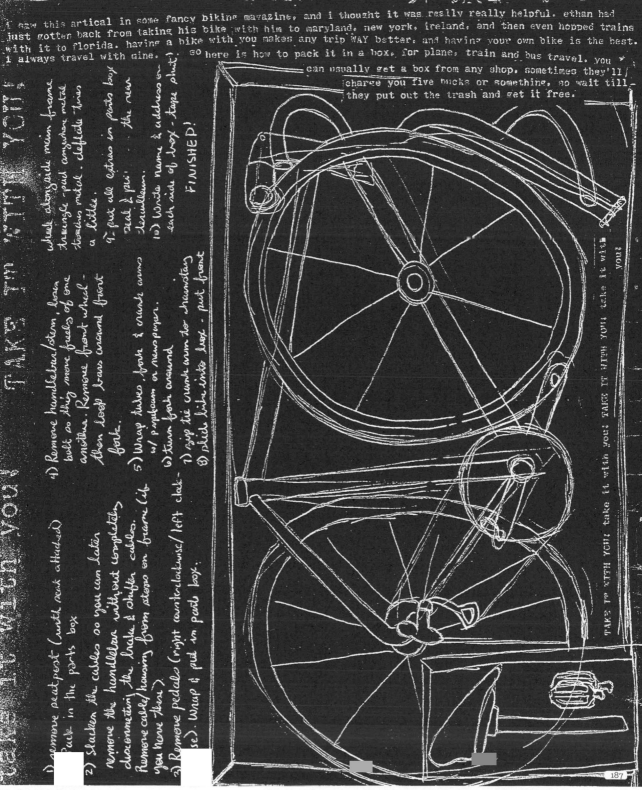

i saw this artical in some fancy biking magazine, and i thought it was really really helpful. ethan had just gotten back from taking his bike with him to maryland, new york, ireland, and then even hopped trains with it to florida. having a bike with you makes any trip WAY better. and having your own bike is the best. i always travel with mine. so here is how to pack it in a box, for plane, train and bus travel. you can usually get a box from any shop. sometimes they'll charge you five bucks or something, so wait till they put out the trash and get it free.

1) Remove seatpost (with seat attached) pack in the parts box

2) Slacken the cables so you can later remove the handlebar without completely disconnecting the brake & shifter cables. Remove cable/housing from stops on frame (if you have these)

3) Remove pedals (right counterclockwise/left clockwise). Wrap & put in parts box.

4) Remove handlebar/stem from bolt so they move freely of one another. Remove front wheel - then loop straw around front fork.

5) Wrap tubes, fork & crank arms w/ papfoam or newspaper.
6) turn fork around
7) zip tie crank arm to chainstay
8) slide bike into box - put front wheel alongside main frame triangle - pad anyhow metal touches metal. deflate tires a little.
9) put all extras in parts box - seal & put the rem handlebar.
10) Write name & address on each side of box - tape shut.

FINISHED!

CHAINBREAKER

hello! it is another fall here in new orleans, waiting for halloween madness to roll around, and the city-wide scramble for all of us to finish our zines in time for the new orleans annual bookfaire! it seems all the more challenging for me this year, with tons of other projects and priorities on my plate. and a terrible addiction to the news. i am uncontrollably distracted by the latest news and talk of presidential debates, election talk, protest updates, and waking up every morning to the body count and tales of bloodshed in iraq. while disturbing, it makes the writing of this zine all the more important and relevant.

this issue is dedicated to the city.

why the city, and why is it relevant?

the city, because i am finding myself in the 9th year in this city of new orleans, being blown away every day at how much i love this place. i feel about this city the way one dreams of feeling about the perfect love affair. i feel connected, forgiving, in full admiration and acceptance for its beauty and its shortcomings. i never thought i could feel this way about a place.

so i started thinking about this city's structure, and about how much it is what i love most about the place. i thought about the freeway being high up above the streets and how innocuous it makes the thing seem, about the narrow, often one way city streets, about the hundred year old architecture all over the place. it struck me that the things that i love about this city are things i may not have noticed or appreciated enough if it weren't for my mode of transportation, my lovely bicycle.

where i grew up in southern california, traffic was a huge part of daily life. everyone had a car by the time they made 16, and we all drove everywhere we went. and many of the places we went required use of a massive freeway system, with traffic lights at the entrances to all of the freeway ramps to control the massive flow. a fifteen minute drive to the beach on a weekday would be a two hour drive to the shorter distance to downtown during peak traffic times, and the much shorter distance to the shopping mall area would become an hour long drive on the week ends due to the consumer drive of most southern californians. it became such a negaitve impact on my life that i swore i would never live in a city with a main highway again.

oh?

189

but here in new orleans, because the city is so old, and so physically maxed out (and often protected by "historical distinct" building codes) we don't have malls, lots of billbo ards, fast food places in long strip malls, or even a huge downtown structure. and

most of those things are outside of the city, in met-airie, a place i never ever go. if i can't get it within the seven mile radius of new orleans proper, i simply must not need it badly enough. because of this i do very little freeway driving, and i have yet to experiece the morning and evening traffic of the sub-urbanites coming into the city for their day jobs. the only traffic i fight is the blurry eyed out-of-towners drunkenly making their way through the french quarter during mardi gras. not being part of the traffic struggle has been a major contributor to a massive improvement in my life.

and why is the topic of the city so relevant right now? well, during this election time we are being bombarded with the greater vision of what america is (or at least is trying to portray) about. and how we expect that vision to impact the world. capitalism is one of the biggest parts of that vision, whether we are talking about health care, war, or the environment. any work we do for those things always boils down to profit. privitization, oil consumption, and land use are all key players in those things. we talk (or we hear the candidates talk) of democracy, and spreading the freedom of a democracy to other nations, and what they are really talking about is spreading capitalism, compition, and the possibility for america to profit off of another nations successes. they are talking about money, and the almighty dollar's value being more valuable that a human's vote in a democratic government. we are talking about re-building nations, not street by street to make the people of those nations more happy individuals, but rebuilding those nations to make whole new societies living packaged lives that we can sell those pack-ages to - packaged food, packaged media and tele-vision shows and packaged ideologies. expanding the capitalist system to the whole world. the goal of our prospective leaders, be them democrats or republi-cans. but do they ever look at how we americans, the supposed success story of capitalism, feel?

how do we feel? we are depressed, overmedicated, un-der exercized, under educated. we are gun crazy, para-noid and road raged. we are greedy, self serving and basically unhappy imperialists. freedom is something that one buys, and it is making all of us sick.

so what the heck does all of this have to do with bikes? isn't this a bike zine?

it has everything to do with bikes! this whole zine i is here to show that! from how capitalism moulded the way our cities were built in their beginnings, to how to av oid getting sold out into the consumer trappings of our culture and ruining the beauty and simplicity of bikes and biking. many people wrote in stories about their daily rides. their use of cycling in daily life - for commuting. for work. for escape, and all of them discussed the freedom (in its true sense) one feels with their bicycle, while never forgetting the war we must wage every time we get on our bikes, against the car driving capitalist machine that fights us at every turn, challenling our nonconformity, while we chose a differnt mode of transportation and of life, demanding our space and respect, despite the common rule of"bigger is better".

it is also relevant because with outsourcing our jobs to other countries, cities in america are getting desperate to sell themselves to companies for their tax dollars and to touristsfor the money they bring to small and big businesses alike. this is one time when capitalism is on our side, because parts of those selling tools have become better modes of transportaion (like streetcars, light rail, bike lanes), due to terrible highway traffic into downtown areas. innercities are being rebuilt and resold (at exorbitant prices) due to this as well, and cities are beccoming denser. dense cites mean parking structures (for the skyscrapers) and huge parking lots (for the "landscrapers" - like walmarts) and both mean traffic woes to us all.

Country	Private car ownership per 1000 population		
	1980	1990	Increase (%)
USA	548	648	18
Denmark	271	312	15
France	357	417	17
Great Britian	278	376	35
Italy	310	433	40
Portugal	114	242	112
Sweden	347	421	21
Switzerland	356	443	24

this is our opportunity as bikers to open the discussions on city planning to wiser transportation plans, and it is time for us to organize to do this while we can. npr just reported that bicycle use is decreasing in china with the expansion of the middle class. they are going through now what we went through in america 75 years ago. so wouldn't it be better for us to forge ahead now, and show how to build our cities right, showing other "developing" countries how to avoid the massive mistakes we have already made?

(this is also reason for us to love and admire our fellow cyclists who have created bike paths and routes through the city of their own - like j.'s zine (reviewed later) on his routes through minneapolis which avoid massive vehicle thoroughfares, and like icky who showed me around portland , moving from neighborhood to neighborhood thru small residential streets with virtually no traffic. j., icky, and all cyclists have until now blazed our own trails and bike paths through our cities, based on safety , space and the excitement of finding lost treaures of our lost cities.)

so here it is, a compilation of stories and information, ideas and inspirations, to excite you about the city around you. i hope it can make you look at your place with new eyes, and see the possibilities of making your place what you want it to be. we can make our cities like a little country oasis - like farmer john, like long, middle-of-nowhere bike paths-like j., or places for learning, teaching and growth - like the kids at plan b. whatever you want it to be, realize the possibilities of making them just that, with pure intention and with the strentgth and patience it takes to fight against the powers which hopefully, will not always be.

thanks for reading, and thanks to all of you who contributed!

♡... shelley.

please write! send comlaints, contributions, ideas, art!, & whatever. issues 1, 2 &3 are still available through me at 621 north rendon, new orleans la 70119, or through microcosm at 5307 n. minnesota, pdx, or 97217. two bucks each, stamps are appreciated, and i love to do music (long live mix tapes!) or art trades! thanks!!!

"do another zine!" to kristen, the best lady friend ever, who said, "do another zine!" to kristen, the best lady friend b. french plan b. french to everyone who contributed!, adee sean aaron especially!!! to ethan, adee sean aaron especially!!! extra special thanks to everyone quarter bikes and especially NEW ORLEANS!!!

bike art wall! thanks for sending stuff ya'll!

REPRINTS OF ORIGINAL CHAINBREAKER ZINES

Ride me Like You Ride That Bike, Girl.

me riding hard sweaty

ONE SHOE IN THE ROAD:
Struck Riders and Their Stories
an audio documentary

The moment the metal meets your skin, and you feel all that weight and velocity and power, you know everything from that point on has changed forever. You might realize it when you're sitting up in the road in a pool of your own blood, or when you first wake up on the gurney in the hospital. That night i rode down the sidewalk ramp into the street, out of the shadow of the semi truck parked idling at the corner and into the path of all that accelerating mass, i was lost in my thoughts, completely taken by surprise. The bumper's impact on my left leg sent me up in an arc and down hard onto my arm and face into the pavement.

One bike fork-like titanium rod in my left leg, one six inch plate in my left arm, and seven weeks of recovery later, i got the call that nobody wants to get. Orion Satuchek, Caroline Buchalter, and their friend i hadn't met named Angela had been struck from behind by a drunk driver on a blissful late night group ride down Mt. Tabor in Portland, Oregon. Orion and Angela were killed. This dear inspiring friend, endlessly creative musician, instrument builder and fixer, gardener, was stolen from us by all that momentum and murderous negligence.

I knew instantly that i needed to do something beyond mourning and ranting to my friends, and with the dynamics of interactions that happen during critical mass rides leaving me frustrated, i wanted to move from being locked outside those thick car doors with my mouth moving silently, obscured by all that

glass and steel and climate control. I wanted to penetrate that shell, with big, scary,
beautifully designed billboards that would
really capture a driver's imagination, like
a giant multi-color woodcut rider with the
caption: "My body is my vehicle." Or what
about...the radio?! Fancy billboards and
slick p.s.a's on corporate radio take big
money, but what about public radio? With
visions of a feature about struck riders on
This American Life ringing through the sound
systems of suburban vehicles all across the
land, i called up erin in portland, an experienced audio documenter and friend, and
she was excited to help.

Nine long interviews and many hours of editing later, the project's almost finished. A
sixty minute interview/story, the anatomy of
an accident, as told by the survivors, with
original music by many of those interviewed.
Excerpts of anti-cyclist hatred from morning
commuter radio shows. A 45 minute version,
edited for public radio. Sinister stories
with ghosts dancing around the edges, but
there's also some bizzare funny moments,
people talking about how they overcame their
awkward injuries, the exhilirating and empowering feelings of biking.

We are making CD's to send out to radio
stations, as well as CD's and tapes to sell,
with the money going to help start a struck
cyclist memorial program in new orleans, and
to promote and distribute the radio program.
So- if you know someone involved in public or
college radio that might air this story, get
them in contact with us! They will be ready
to send out by February 2005. Contact:

Don Godwin ipcp@juno.com 504.949.2920
  Trd W/D po box 52096 new orleans LA 70152
Erin Yanke eriny_@hotmail.com
  Life During Wartime po box 1113 PDX, OR 97207

hey diddle diddle

hey diddle, diddle
the bicycle riddle -
the strangest part of the deal.
just keep your accounts
and add the amounts
the sundries cost more than the wheel.

      - old cycling song

since the early 1900's people have been going crazy for bikes, and for bike accessories. in 1896 the public spent 200,000,000 dollars on bicycle accessories and only 300,000,000 on the actual bikes! bicycle clothing, gear, accessories , the "look" has been as important to cycling as the bike itself since the beginning. but does it really have to be that way? i mean, having nice stuff IS, well, nice. but a lot of it isn't stuff one needs. and there is no need of course, to get it just to fit in, to look the part, or to get all the punk points on can... you know, timbuk 2 bag, check, fancy clipless shoes, check, multi-tool on the belt, check, track bike, triple check, cute little mini krypto lock (now useless) to fit in the back pocket, check. come on! i have been to portland, or philly, or chicago... it is all the same. it is un-necessary! it is buying into consumer culture! being sold out! isn't that what we, as cyclists are avoiding? if not fighting against? well maybe not. not all of our idea-ologies have to match up, nor should they, but isn't it worth discussing? investigating? if at the very least, to make bike culture more accessible to the people, to newcomers?

i'll give you a few examples...

one...

i recently came across a bicycle catalog by a company called rivendale. a lot of you big bike enthusiasts out there may have heard of them before, but for me, it was the first time. now, mind you, i am not trying to promote their company, or their bicycles, but their ideology. their catalog is different from most in that it is small, first of all, and in that there are lots of words in it. words of advice about what kind of bike to look for, how to care for your parts, and most importantly, when to spend money and when not to. they are great about finding the best product for the cheapest price, and being honest about when you shouldn't waste the money on some fancy thing you just might not need. but also, when you should spend the extra dough on something quality that could save you some bucks in the long run.

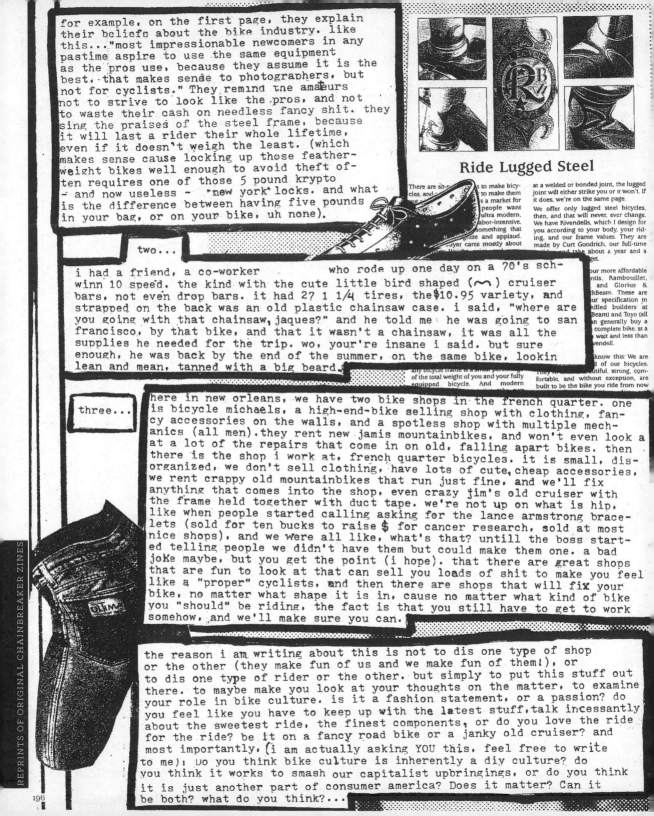

for example, on the first page, they explain their beliefs about the bike industry. like this..."most impressionable newcomers in any pastime aspire to use the same equipment as the pros use, because they assume it is the best. that makes sense to photographers, but not for cyclists." They remind the amateurs not to strive to look like the pros, and not to waste their cash on needless fancy shit. they sing the praises of the steel frame, because it will last a rider their whole lifetime, even if it doesn't weigh the least. (which makes sense cause locking up those feather-weight bikes well enough to avoid theft often requires one of those 5 pound krypto - and now useless - "new york" locks. and what is the difference between having five pounds in your bag, or on your bike, uh none).

Ride Lugged Steel

There are so... to make bicycles, and... to make them
... a market for
... people want
... ultra modern.
... labor-intensive.
... something that
... prize and applaud.
... uyer cares mostly about

at a welded or bonded joint, the lugged joint will either strike you or it won't. If it does, we're on the same page.

We offer only lugged steel bicycles, then, and that will never, ever change. We have Rivendells, which I design for you according to your body, your riding, and our frame values. They are made by Curt Goodrich, our full-time ... and take about a year and a ... get.

two...

i had a friend, a co-worker who rode up one day on a 70's sch-winn 10 speed. the kind with the cute little bird shaped (⌒) cruiser bars, not even drop bars. it had 27 1 1/4 tires, the $10.95 variety, and strapped on the back was an old plastic chainsaw case. i said, "where are you going with that chainsaw, jaques?" and he told me he was going to san francisco, by that bike, and that it wasn't a chainsaw, it was all the supplies he needed for the trip. wo, your're insane i said. but sure enough, he was back by the end of the summer, on the same bike, lookin lean and mean, tanned with a big beard.

ur more affordable
...ntis, Rambouillet,
... and Glorius &
...ckBeam. These are
... ur specification in
... killed builders at
...Beam) and Toyo (all
... n generally buy a
... complete bike, at a
... wait and less than
...vendell.

...know this: We are
... d of our bicycles.
They... ...utiful, strong, comfortable, and without exception, are
built to be the bike you ride from now

three...

here in new orleans, we have two bike shops in the french quarter. one is bicycle michaels, a high-end-bike selling shop with clothing, fancy accessories on the walls, and a spotless shop with multiple mechanics (all men). they rent new jamis mountainbikes, and won't even look a at a lot of the repairs that come in on old, falling apart bikes. then there is the shop i work at, french quarter bicycles. it is small, dis-organized, we don't sell clothing, have lots of cute, cheap accessories, we rent crappy old mountainbikes that run just fine, and we'll fix anything that comes into the shop, even crazy jim's old cruiser with the frame held together with duct tape. we're not up on what is hip, like when people started calling asking for the lance armstrong brace-lets (sold for ten bucks to raise $ for cancer research, sold at most nice shops), and we were all like, what's that? untill the boss start-ed telling people we didn't have them but could make them one. a bad joke maybe, but you get the point (i hope). that there are great shops that are fun to look at that can sell you loads of shit to make you feel like a "proper" cyclists, and then there are shops that will fix your bike, no matter what shape it is in, cause no matter what kind of bike you "should" be riding, the fact is that you still have to get to work somehow, and we'll make sure you can.

the reason i am writing about this is not to dis one type of shop or the other (they make fun of us and we make fun of them!), or to dis one type of rider or the other. but simply to put this stuff out there. to maybe make you look at your thoughts on the matter, to examine your role in bike culture. is it a fashion statement, or a passion? do you feel like you have to keep up with the latest stuff, talk incessantly about the sweetest ride, the finest components, or do you love the ride for the ride? be it on a fancy road bike or a janky old cruiser? and most importantly, (i am actually asking YOU this, feel free to write to me): Do you think bike culture is inherently a diy culture? do you think it works to smash our capitalist upbringings, or do you think it is just another part of consumer america? Does it matter? Can it be both? what do you think?...

BIKE NATION

by moose

I'm sitting here, licking my broken teeth that I got from being nailed by a minivan on my bike, thinking about the cyclist that got killed in the French Quarter last night, and the guysthat tried to murder my buddy in their truck a few nights ago, driving up one way streets,and onto sidewalks in an effort to mow him down while he was on his bike delivery job. I'm thinking about my dad and brothers and uncles and cousins, who have lost decades of health and happiness slaving in Detroit auto factories, the fights we've had with Ford Motor Company for humane conditions, fair wages, compensationffor work induced illness and injury. I'm thinking about the vast fucking wasteland of this country, the strip malls, the suburbs, the communities of disassociated drones; forced to put most of their wages back into their cars, or paying for roads or being controlled and regulated and ripped off by insurance companies and the department of motor vehicles. I'm thinking about cop cars, the sinking feeling you get whenever one skulks by you, or when you pass one on the highways. I'm thinking aboutthis beleagured planet, constantly being raped for nothing, to maintain a bloated industry through corrupt legislature and wars and monopolies and by hiding options for safe and sustainable technologies. All because some assholes stand to make a shitload of morally bereft and ultimately, worthless money.

BROTHERS AND SISTERS! The automobile is the death of this land! It's got a chokehold on us, it encourages violence and hatred, destroys our health and safety, it keeps us all seperated, all while holding us hostage because we think we need it t survive in this society. but, ther are a few of us w

Earlier this year Plan B (the New Orleans Bicycle Project) hosted the Bike! Bike! Conference, a gathering of radical community bike projects from all around the country, to talk about these issues and more. We held workshops for each other, discussing issues that arise because of reasons like the fact that we are mostly a bunch of dirty white kids in poor black communities (common, but not across the board), or because of the fucked gender associations that come with (yes, even bike) mechanics, about class and privelege, about creating community, about struggling to find egalatarian and effective means for organizing ourselves, and about working with kids.

It would be impossible to recount everything here that we learned during the conference. For one, we didn't take very good notes, and the afterthought of a zine to document it all never did materialize. (note to self: next time work some note taking vehicle into the structure of the workshops.) Secondly, the various bikeshops have a variety of prime motivations, challenges, levels of proficiency and professionalism, budjets, and communities served. No group or topic really dominated the discussions. However, two topics did emerge as being problematic:

We didn't really set up a workshop on "dealing with kids" but it rapidly became apparent that many groups found this aspect of their mission particularly challenging. We acknowledged that we wanted to offer kids the respect they rarely get at home or at school, but that we are also not social workers and don't have all the skills needed to handle some behaviors. We talked about theft by kids, partnering with schools, better teaching techniques, language, etc. There is still a lot more to discuss for nex next year.

Our discussions on class and gender issues were long and difficult. I personally didn't sit in on it due to organizational fatigue. (ed. note - it was unanimously decided that such a heavy discussion shouldn't be saved for the VERY END) I was told that the group used a discussion tactic where one gender group sat in a circle to to share their feelings, while the other sat behind listening, then the positions were switched. The people i spoke to about it said that it was an emotional discussion, and that though some bridges were crossed, many were left to be built.

Stuff like this is usually hard to do, often seems like a futile attempt at being grown-ups, leaves me feeling frustrated or overwhelmed with the amount of work left to do. But, Bike! Bike was a smash success. We learned so much from one another, we strengthened each other, and were inspiried by the achievements of people like us with little resources. We got to drool at all the nice old roadbikes, beloved and worn and huddled together; a happy tribe.

I thought of my Shawnee relatives who would refer to a race of animals as a nation, like the bear nation or the horse nation. This was a bike nation. Or as one friend said to me while watching a mass of (slightly tipsy) bikers leaving the bar, "what would you call that? a 'swerve of bike'?"

So this year I am happy. Happy to see myself and friends taking bigger steps toward autonomy. Building stable means of survival that doesn't rely on petro-domination. I see human power as a basic tool for winning back some of our freedoms. I am happy to be building relationships and building bikes. Taking the tools for fixin' some shit in my own hands, and actually developing some proficiency with them.

We still have a long road ahead though. I hope you'll join us ne

yes!!! moose is right, Bike! Bike! was a smash success!
i had just gotten back to new orleans after being four months in india, just about a week before the conference happened.
i was so impressed at all the work plan b-ers had done to get
it together, and when arriving to the get-to-know-one-another
party, still a little culture shocked, to find the pool at our
own crazy country club filled with friends and strangers naked
or fully clothed, drinking and socializing, dancing, i thought
- ah! HOME! i was so happy! there were people there from pittsburgh, portland, philly, detroit, denver, austin, tuscon, ithica, all over the place! having arrived by bike, by train, plane, all sweaty in the new orleans heat. the best part of it all
was simply meeting all of the people who do what we do in other
parts of the country, to know we aren't alone, and that we share
so many struggles. the workshops were great, the bike rides,
food, getting to geek out about bikes to people who understood
totally. meeting people i had only heard of, whose shops i had
been to and admired. it was great. SO! for all of you all who
didn't get to come, or who might want to go next time, tuscon's
BICAS (bicycle inter-community arts and salvage) has offered to
host it next year, in the spring. contact them at 44 w. 6th st.
tuscon, az 85705, or call 520-628-7950. for more info about the
new orleans bike! bike! event contact plan b 511 marigny new orleans la 70117, or look us up on the computer, under plan b or
bike! bike! let's all see each other next year!!!

                                          love, shelley

① PLAN "B": THE NEW ORLEANS COMMUNITY BIKE PROJECT
511 MARIGNY ST. (DECATUR ST. DOOR) (504)-944-0366
YOUR HOSTS FOR THE AFFAIR!! PLAN "B" IS
A 501-C3 NON-PROFIT, VOLUNTEER-RUN, D.I.Y.
BIKE SHOPPE THAT OFFERS USE OF TOOLS, RE-
CYCLED BIKES & PARTS, LOANER BIKES & HELP
REPAIRING YOUR OWN BIKE.
  WE WILL HAVE SOME BIKE! BIKE! WORKSHOPS
HERE, AND OUR REGULAR HOURS IS:
    MON & SAT. 4-8PM, THURS. 2-6PM,
   TUES. WOMEN ONLY 5-8PM.
IN THE SAME BUILDING IS THE IRON RAIL
BOOK COLLECTIVE, A POLITICAL BOOKSTORE &
LENDING LIBRARY. THEY'RE OPEN MON-SAT. 1-7PM

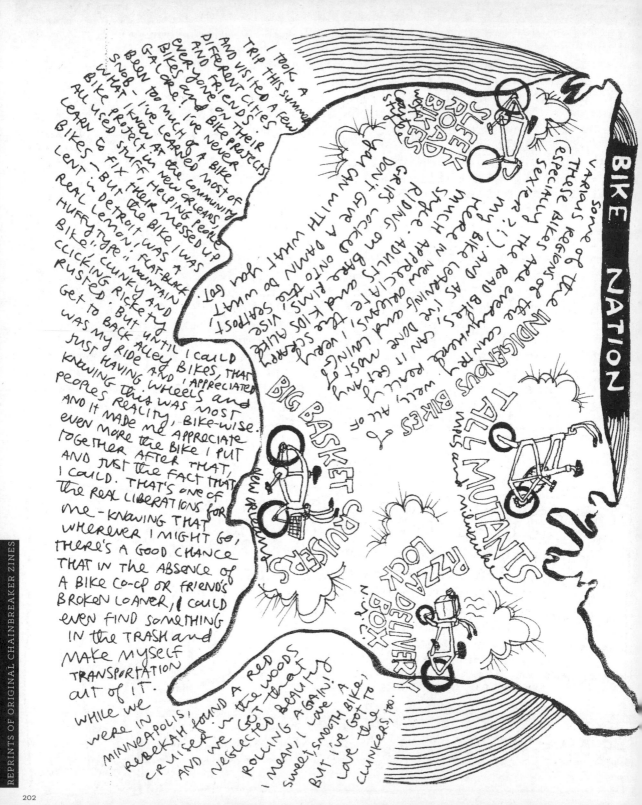

I took a trip this summer and visited a few different cities and friends. Everyone on their bikes and bike projects galore! I've never been too much of a bike snob - I've learned most of what I know at the community bike project in New Orleans, helping people learn to fix their messed up bikes. But the bike I was lent in Detroit was a real lemon! Flat-black Huffy "type" mountain bike. Clunky and rusted rickety clicking. But until I could get to back alley bikes, that was my ride and I appreciated just having wheels and knowing this was most peoples reality, bike-wise. And it made me appreciate even more the bike I put together after that, and just the fact that I could. That's one of the real liberations for me — knowing that wherever I might go, there's a good chance that in the absence of a bike co-op or friend's broken loaner, I could even find something in the trash and make myself transportation out of it.

While we were in Minneapolis, Rebekah found a red cruiser in the woods and we got that neglected beauty rolling again! I mean, I love a sweet, smooth bike, but I've got to love the clunkers, too.

Some of the various regions of these bikers! (especially the indigenous sexier?) Well, all of the everywhere, really

DON'T GIVE A DAMN DO WHAT YOU GOT

RIDING ON BARE RIMS ADULTS AND KIDS ALIKE APPRECIATE THE SCRAPPY SHAPE MUCH IN NEW ORLEANS, AS I'VE DONE

SLEEK BLOCK BIKE DORK SANTA CRUZ STYLES

GRIPS AND LOCKED ONTO THE SEATPOST

INDIGENOUS BIKES

TALL MUTANTS wheels and miniature

BIG BASKET CRUISERS NEW ORLEANS

PIZZA LOCK DELIVERY BOX N.Y.C.

ETHAN GOES TO NEW YORK. BY Ethan

LIKE A MILLION TONS OF ELEPHANT POOP, THE REPUBLICAN NATIONAL CONVENTION PLOPPED DOWN ON MANHATTAN LAST WEEK. I WAS THERE, WANDERING AROUND AMONGST THE HORDES OF PROTESTORS, CLUTCHING THEIR CARDBOARD-TUBE PICKET SIGNS LIKE SHOVELS. THE PROTEST WAS EXPECTED TO DRAW AS MANY PEOPLE AS THE DONNA SUMMER CONCERT, BUT ENDED UP EXCEEDING EVEN ART GARFUNKEL'S TURNOUT. UNLIKE THOSE EVENTS, HOWEVER, THE PROTEST WAS NOT BEING ALLOWED TO TAKE PLACE IN CENTRAL PARK. IT WOULD DESTROY THE GRASS, THEY SAID. APPARENTLY ACTIVISTS' FEET ARE MORE DESTRUCTIVE THAN THOSE OF DONNA SUMMER AND ART GARFUNKEL FANS. THE LACK OF PERMITS TO USE THE PARK DID LITTLE TO DISSUADE PROTESTS

I DIDN'T HAVE ANY CARDBOARD TUBE PICKET SIGN. NOR DID I HAVE AN AFFINITY GROUP OR ONE OF THOSE "PEACEFUL PROTESTER" BUTTONS THAT GOT YOU DISCOUNTS AT APPLEBEE'S. WHAT I HAD WAS A BIKE. ACTUALLY, TWO BIKES, ONE WELDED ON TOP OF THE OTHER INTO A SINGLE, BRAKELESS, SIX-FOOT TALL BEAST. I'D SPENT MY FIRST TWO DAYS IN NEW YORK PIECING THE THING TOGETHER WITH MY FRIENDS JOHNNY AND (NEW FRIEND) CONRAD IN THE SECRET HEADQUARTERS OF THE BLACK LABEL BIKE CLUB, A.K.A. CONRAD'S GARAGE.

THE FRIDAY BEFORE THE CONVENTION, I MADE MY WAY TO UNION SQUARE FOR WHAT WOULD TURN OUT TO BE THE LARGEST CRITICAL MASS BIKE RIDE EVER IN NEW YORK EVER. I STOOD ON THE BASE OF A LIGHTPOST, LEANING ON MY SWEET NEW RIDE, WATCHING AS THE CROWD SWELLED AND PICKING OUT FAMILIAR FACES.

I WAS STAYING WITH JOHNNY, FAE AND MEREDITH, IN THEIR CRAMPED CHINATOWN APARTMENT. THE APARTMENT WAS SERVING AS THE BASE OF OPERATIONS FOR "MANY," MEDICAL ACTIVISTS OF NEW YORK. MANY IS A COLLECTIVE THAT PROVIDES MEDICAL TRAINING AND DIRECT ACTION STREET CARE DURING PROTESTS. THE APARTMENT WAS LIKE GRAND CENTRAL STATION. MEREDITH FIELDED CALLS ON THE MANY HOTLINE. VARIOUS MEDICS DROPPED INTO PICK UP FANNY PACKS FULL OF SUPPLIES, WHILE

FAMOUS, TRULY THE QUEEN OF HER DOMAIN, MOVED ABOUT IN THE BEDLAM, ORGANIZING PILES OF GAS MASKS, TINCTURE BOTTLES, SWABS, BAGGIES AND ACCUPUNCTURE SUPPLIES, AND SINGIN'S ALONG WITH LORETTA LYNN. JOHNNY, WATCHING ALL THIS, LAMENTED THAT HE WOULDN'T BE INVOLVED IN THE MEDICAL ACTIONS THIS TIME. INSTEAD, HE WAS GOING TO BE COURIERING. JOHNNY AND A HANDFULL OF OTHER BLACK LABEL BIKE CLUB MEMBERS HAD PUT TOGETHER AN AD-HOC COURIER TEAM TO RIDE FOR THE INDY-MEDIA CENTER. THEIR

JOB WOULD BE TO SWOOP INTO THE MARCHES OR DIRECT ACTIONS OR WHATEVER AND GET FOOTAGE AND FILM FROM IMC JOURNALISTS, THEN DELIVER THE STUFF TO SAFETY.

OUT AT B.L.HQ. (CONRAD'S GARAGE) (WHILE I PATCHED TOGETHER BITS OF CHAIN FOR MY TALL BIKE, THE BLACK LABEL CREW STRUGGLED TO MAKE THEIR STRIPPED DOWN TRACK BIKES CONFORM TO SOME OBSCURE N.Y. CYCLING LAWS THAT THEY'D DUG UP. CONRAD CRAMMED HIS HANDLEBARS WITH THE NECESSARY ACCOUTREMENTS: A NOISEMAKER THAT CAN BE HEARD 50 FEET AWAY (IN MANHATTAN!;), A BRAKE THAT CAN "SKID ON DRY PAVEMENT," A REFLECTOR, A LIGHT. CONRAD AND THE OTHERS REMINDED ME OF KIDS BEING FORCED TO DRESS UP FOR CHURCH. "MANY "CONRAD MUTTERED AS HE FLIPPED THE CRAPPY MOUNTAIN BIKE LEVER HE'D JUST INSTALLED, "LOOK AT THIS STUPID SHIT."

I WAS SURPRISED AT BLACK LABEL'S POLITICAL INVOLVEMENT. I'D KNOWN SOME OF THEIR MINNEAPOLIS COLLEAGUES AND THOUGHT THAT THEY NORMALLY STEERED CLEAR OF SUCH THINGS, INSTEAD FOCUSING ON CHAOTIC PARTIES, TALL-BIKE JOUSTING & BIKE RODEOS,

ONE MY MEMBER, BEN, PUT IT LIKE THIS: "I'M NORMALLY APOLITICAL, BUT BUSH IS JUST SUCH A SYMBOL OF EVIL TO ME." THE PROTESTS DIDN'T OFFICIALLY START UNTIL THE WEEKEND, BUT THE MEDICS AND OTHER GROUPS (INCLUDING, WE'D FIND OUT LATER, THE COPS) WERE LOOKING AT FRIDAY'S BIKE RIDE AS A KIND OF WARM-UP. THE COPS HAD SAID THAT THEY'D BE "CRACKING DOWN" ON CY-CLISTS DURING THE RIDE, BUT NO ONE PAID THE THREAT MUCH MIND, BECAUSE ON PAST RIDES THE COPS HAD ACTED AS ESCORTS. ONCE, I'M TOLD, MOTORCYCLE COPS HELPED C.M. RIDERS GET ONTO THE HIGH-WAY.

AROUND 7:30, SOMETHING LIKE 5000 CYCLISTS PULLED OUT OF UNION SQUARE. SPOTTING CONRAD IN THE CROWD, PUSHING HIS OWN TALL BIKE, I FELL INTO BESIDE HIM. WE WALKED ALONG FOR A LONG TIME. THERE WASN'T ENOUGH ROOM TO MOUNT A REGULAR BIKE, NEVERMIND THE TALL ONES. CONRAD GOT A CALL (CALL OF THE B.L GUYS HAD TO GET CEL. PHONES FOR THEIR COURIER WORK. JOHNNY WAS SO UNUSED TO HIS THAT EVERY TIME IT'S "MISSION IMPOSSIBLE" THEME "RINGER RANG, HE JUMPED) FROM SOMEONE AT THE FRONT OF THE "RIDE." 14 BLOCKS AWAY, AS WE FLOODED ALONG, LIST-ENING TO THE HEARTFELT BUT GRAMMATICALLY DEPLORABLE CHANT. "MORE BIKES, LESS CARS," A THOUGHT IT ACCURRED TO ME. "HEY CONRAD!" I YELLED. "IS THIS WHAT IT WOULD BE LIKE IF EVERY-ONE STARTED RIDING BIKES ALL THE TIME?" "SHIT, I DON'T KNOW!" HE YELLED BACK, "THIS SUCKS!" BUT THEN WE GOT THROUGH THE BOTTLENECK OF CAPS, COP CARS AND COP PHOTOGRAPHERS, AND SADDLED UP. I WAS PRETTY SHAKY AT FIRST, AND NERVOUS. SOON, THOUGH, AS WE PASSED THRONGS OF PEDESTRIANS SCREAMING THINGS BOTH SUPPORTIVE & DERISIVE, AND HIT TIMES SQUARE, MY INHIBITIONS FELL AWAY (ALONG WITH A FEW NUTS + BOLTS FROM THE RICKETY TALL BIKE). WHEN SOMEONE SCREAMED, "WHOS STREETS?!!" I LOOKED OUT AT THAT SEA OF CYCLISTS, AND THE ROARING RESPONSE CAME BACK, "OUR STREETS!!", AND IT WAS TRUE.

FOUR HOURS LATER, THE NEARLY 300 OF THE RIDERS WERE LOAD-ED INTO MAKESHIFT CELLS IN A PIER ON THE HUDSON. I WASN'T IN THE LAST BUSLOAD OF ARRESTS. AS THEY SHUT THE FINAL CELL DOOR ON US, SOMEONE SCREAMED "WHO'S CELL?!!" AND EVERY-ONE ELSE JUST GROANED.

AFTER A COUPLE HOURS OF RIDING, THEY'D HEMMED US IN ABOVE THE LINCOLN TUNNEL. AS SOON AS I SAW THE ROWS OF SCOOTER COPS IN FRONT OF AND BEHIND US, THE THIRTY FOOT DROP BESIDE US, I REALIZED WE WERE SCREWED. THEN OUT CAME THE FLEXI-CUFFS AND POLAROID CAMERAS. I RAN INTO MY FRIEND ANDY CASO ON A TALL BIKE! YEAH!) AND WE CAUGHT UP AS WE WERE ARRESTED TO-GETHER. THE ARRESTS WERE SLOW. ALL THE COPS, ROOKIES WHO'D BEEN BROUGHT IN FROM OTHER BOROUGHS, WERE VAGUE ON BOTH THE "WHY?" AND "HOW?" ASPECTS OF THIS MASS ARREST.

THE SOLDIERS FROM WIZARD OF OZ OR SOME OTHER CARTOONISH ARMY OF MIN-IONS. AS THE ROOKIES TWISTED OUR CUFFS AND SET THE FLASH OFF IN EACH OTHER'S EYES, THE STARCHY, WHITE-SHIRTED SEARGENTS WOULD OCCASIONALLY SWOOP IN AND SCREAM, "YOU'RE MESSING IT ALL UP!" I EXPECTED SOME 3-STOOGES-ESQUE HEAD-BONKINGS, BUT WAS DIS-APPOINTED.

THEY'D COMANDEERED CITY BUSES TO TAKE US TO THE PIER, PIER 57. ON THE RIDE, WE WERE SUBJECTED TO THE COMIC-STYLINGS OF A GUM-SMACKING WISE-ACRE COP WHO JOKED ABOUT US BEING TERRORISTS AND KEPT TELLING US THAT WE'D BE OUT IN TIME TO GO TO SOME BAR IN YONKERS, WHERE HE WOULD BUY US ALL DRINKS. AFTER THE THIRD MENTION OF THIS, ANDY, WHO'S EYES LOOKED READY TO EXPLODE FROM THE PRESSURE OF HIS SWOLLEN BLADDER, YELLED OUT, "QUIT TALK-ING ABOUT DRINKING!"

LEGAL HOTLINE
8018.013.718

TEMPORARY TATTOO HANDED OUT BY LAWYER'S GUILD!!

AFTER A WHILE, THOUGH, A KIND OF CAMERADERIE DEVELOPED IN THE GROUP. WE POOLED QUARTERS TO CALL THE LAWYER'S GUILD, WHO KNEW EVERY ARRESTEE'S NAME AND WERE TRYING TO GET US OUT. IT WAS ILLEGAL FOR THEM TO HOLD US LONGER THAN 24 HOURS, AND WE WERE QUICKLY APPROACHING THAT MARK. EACH PHONE CALL BROUGHT HOPE, THEN THE COPS WOULD COME LIE TO US TO BRING US DOWN. SOMEONE HAD SMUGGLED IN A "CLAMOR" MAGAZINE, WHICH ME AND ANOTHER GUY READ OUT LOUD FROM. THEN, AROUND HOUR 26, THE LAWYER'S GUILD SUCCEEDED. WE WERE RELEASED FIVE AT A TIME. THEY KEPT THE COURTS OPEN ALL NIGHT WHICH HASN'T BEEN DONE SINCE ED KOCH'S REIGN. EVERY NAME THAT WAS CALLED FOR RELEASE, EVERYONE CHEERED AND YELLED, "GO TEAM!! GOOFY? YEAH, BUT ENDEARING.

BY DAWN ANDY + I WERE IN A VAN WITH FRIENDS, HEADED OVER THE WILLY-B BRIDGE.

I PRETTY MUCH STAYED OUT OF THE MADNESS FOR THE REST OF THE CONVENTION. MY LAST NIGHT IN TOWN, THOUGH, JOHNNY AND I VISITED FAMOUS AT THE CLINIC IN ST. MARKS CHURCH. THERE, I WATCHED A GIRL COOKING AT THE HUGE OUTDOOR KITCHEN, CHOPPING A PILE OF ONIONS WHILE WEARING A GAS MASK. I STARTED TO GET A LITTLE CHOKED UP WATCHING HER, AND MY MIND DRIFTED TO A CONVERSATION THAT I'D HAD WITH MY BROTHER A FEW NIGHTS EARLIER. HE'S A WALL STREET ACCOUNTANT WHO LIVES JUST A FEW BLOCKS FROM THE CHURCH.

I'D BEEN ATTEMPTING TO EXPLAIN TO HIM ABOUT MANY, ABOUT FOOD NOT BOMBS, KISS-INS, BLACK LABEL AND ~~CRITICAL~~ CRITICAL MASS. I WAS TRYING TO EXPLAIN ALL OF THESE THINGS HAPPENING IN A CITY THAT WE COULD'VE LOOKED OUT OVER HAD MY BROTHER'S BIG SCREEN T.V. NOT BEEN BLOCKING THE WIND. I TRIED TO EXPLAIN... AND IT WASN'T WORKING. FINALLY HE LOOKED UP AT ME FROM HIS BIG LEATHER COUCH TO SAY, "IS SOMEONE PAYING THESE PEOPLE?"

I WANTED TO SCREAM, TO GRAB HIM BY THE ARM, DRAG HIM SIX FLIGHTS DOWN AND SHOW HIM THAT NO, THESE PEOPLE COOKING AND SNEAKING THROUGH BARRICADES AND TREATING PEPPER SPRAY VICTIMS AND FIGHTING SO HARD, THEY'RE NOT GETTING FUCKIN' PAID. BECAUSE THE MONEY IS ALL ON THE OTHER SIDE OF THOSE BARRICADES, THE SIDE WITH THE DELEGATES, THE JUDGES, THE JAILS AND PIERS, THE GUNS AND BOMBS AND TEAR GAS AND HORDES OF COPS...

INTO CELLS, WHERE WE STAYED 'TILL MORNING. THERE WEREN'T ENOUGH BENCHES, SO MOST OF US STRUGGLED TO SLEEP ON THE OILY FLOOR. EVERYONE WAS BUMMED AND WORN OUT. PLUS, WHEN THE, "SO WHAT DID YOU DO?" CHANNEL OF CONVERSATION IS TAKEN OUT OF YOUR JAIL EXPERIENCE, THERE'S NOT THAT MUCH TO TALK ABOUT. SO EVERYONE WAS PRETTY QUIET. WHEN THE SUN PEEKED THROUGH THE FEW WINDOWS AND WE REALIZED WE'D MISSED OUR DRINK DATE IN YONKERS, EVERY ONE GOT QUIETER.

AROUND 10 A.M. WE WERE LOADED ONTO A REGULAR PRISON BUS. WE COULD SEE THE SUN REFLECTING OFF OF THE HUDSON, DIRECTLY IN FRONT OF THE BUS. "MAYBE THEY'LL JUST DROWN US." ANDY THEORIZED. NO SUCH LUCK THOUGH. WE WERE LOADED ONTO THE BUS AND DRIVEN OVER TO CENTRAL LOCK-UP, THE TOMBS.

WE WERE PROCESSED AND PUT IN YET MORE CELLS. BY THIS POINT, THOUGH, TENSIONS WERE RUNNING HIGH. EVERYONE HAD SLEPT A LITTLE AND THEY WERE GETTING WORKED UP. THE PHRASE, "HUMAN RIGHTS VIOLATION" WAS BEING BOUNCED AROUND. I CHATTED WITH A GUY NAMED SAM, WHO, IT TURNED OUT, HAD LET ME SLEEP ON HIS COUCH IN PHILLY A COUPLE OF YEARS AGO. "ALMOST AS BAD AS BEING IN THIS CELL," SAM SAID, "IS LISTENING TO THESE DUDES WHINE ABOUT IT." SOME HAD ACTUAL COMPLAINTS. ANDY GOT WEIRD BURNS FROM THE SPILLAGE ALL OVER THE PIER FLOOR. HE'D STUFFED HIS ARMS IN HIS TANK TOP TO STAY WARM AND RUBBED THE SHIT ON HIS CHEST. HE DIDN'T COMPLAIN, EXCEPT TO A GUARD, WHO GAVE HIM SOME ALCOHOL RUBS. "GREAT," HE MUTTERED, DROPPING THE LITTLE PACKETS ON THE FLOOR.
AND WE SAT. WE SAT AND SAT AND SAT. PEOPLE STARTED TO PANIC.

WE LEARNED WHAT AN INCREDIBLY ANNOYING NOISE IS MADE BY CYCLING CLEATS PACING ON A CEMENT FLOOR. WE GOT TO HEAR ⚡ THE PHRASE, "I CAN'T BELIEVE THIS IS HAPPENING TO ME" SO MANY TIMES THAT I WANTED TO SCREAM "IT'S YOUR FUCKING FOURTEEN! BELIEVE IT!!" BUT I BIT MY TONGUE.
THESE GUYS, MOST OF THEM, WEREN'T PROTESTORS. THEY HADN'T EXPECTED THIS. THEY WERE CYCLING ENTHUSIASTS. MOST OF THEM DIDN'T EQUATE THE RNC WITH CRITICAL MASS IN ANY WAY. YOU'D THINK THEY WOULD'VE WONDERED WHY THERE WERE SUDDENLY THOUSANDS MORE IN THE RIDE THAN USUAL, BUT HEY.

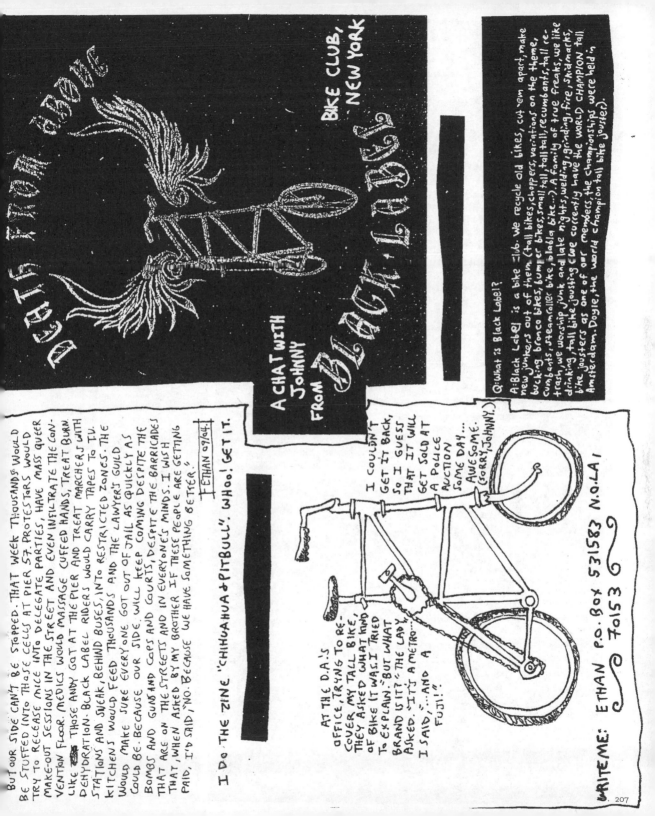

DEATH FROM ABOVE

A CHAT WITH JOHNNY FROM BLACK LABEL BIKE CLUB, NEW YORK

Q: What is Black Label?

A: Black Label is a bike club. We recycle old bikes. We take junkers out of them (tall bikes, choppers, vacations on the theme, bucking bronco bikes, bumper bikes, small tall, recumbants, tall re-cumbants, streamroller bike, blabla bike...). A family of true freaks, we like trash, we worship junk and late nights, welding, grinding, fire, skidmarks, drinking, tall bike jousting. Clee currently have the WORLD CHAMPION tall bike jousters as one of our members. the championships were held in Amsterdam. Doyle, the world champion tall bike jouster).

But our side can't be stopped. That week thousands would be stuffed into those cells at Pier 57. Protestors would try to release mice into delegate parties, have mass queer make-out sessions in the street and even infiltrate the convention floor. Medics would massage cuffed hands, treat burn like those and got at the Pier and treat marchers with dehydration. Black Label riders would carry tapes to T.V. stations and sneak, behind buses, into restricted zones. The kitchens would feed thousands and the lawyers guild would make sure everyone got out of jail as quickly as could be. Because our side will keep coming despite the bombs and guns and cops and courts, despite the barricades that are on the streets and in everyone's minds. I wish that, when asked by my brother if these people are getting paid, I'd said, "No, because we have something better."

—Ethan 09/04.

I DO THE ZINE "CHIHUAHUA & PITBULL". WHOO! GET IT.

At the D.A.'s office, trying to re-cover my tall bike, they asked what kind of bike it was. I tried to explain. But what brand was it? the lady asked. "It's a metro—" I said,...and a Fuji!"

I couldn't get it back, so I guess that it will get sold at a police auction some day... Awesome. (SORRY, JOHNNY.)

WRITE ME: ETHAN P.O. BOX 531583 N.O.LA 70153

REPRINTS OF ORIGINAL CHAINBREAKER ZINES
AT THE PIER, WE WERE FINALLY BECOMING...

AFTER A WHILE, ...

208

Q: What's the M/F ratio. Is gender an issue?

A: B.L. is surprisingly balanced, gender & race. Not perfectly, more White kids.

Q: Is there a president? How do you make decisions?

A: There is a president, Leo. The president is a traditional figure, who acts as more of a point person than a decision maker. Up until recently everything was decided by concensus. As time went on B.L. was challenged with more and more ethical questions. Sometimes we split, many heated meetings, screaming, fighting, blood. We decided to adopt a vote system, but only when we need it, so really we use both. Voting and concensus.

Q: Is some sort of social change trying to be made w/the club? Is there a mission statement?

A: In the activist world there has always been a split between people who do things directly to affect change, and people who live a certain way to affect change. I've always liked the idea that for a split second, you can get people to believe anything, even if it's just for a split second. Then you have changed things, just a little. A mission statement? Well no, but we get thousands of people, to have faith in the ridiculous for seconds at a time, faith that we're all not so fragile.

Q: What's been the strangest B.L. event ever?

A: The "Run for Your Life" Art Show, 3 day event, film fest. Art in a real gallery. The art was a bunch of cool shit we all made, and then we decided to put all our bikes in the gallery, too, so we could rip the art off the walls and ride it away.   Except, during the show everybody got real wasted and we decided to ride the bikes inside the gallery, for like 6 hours straight. That would've all been just fine with me, except one of our bikes was a steamroller bike, this 350 pound steamroller wheel attached to two bicycles. We made a real mess, people went nuts, they just kept gettin' on all the crazy bikes and ridin' around in a circle. Like, it became a raceway all of a sudden, we kept puttin' bigger and bigger stuff on the track so the steamroller bike would smash it, so finally we just a bike on the track. SMASHO!

All the events were pretty wild, people get all excited. All the trash became ammo for the audience/riders. Only one person got hurt that time. Minor, too.

Q: How many chapters are there?

A: Austin, Reno, Minneapolis, Nowhere, NY, Vegas?, Montana, Next, Worldwide.

Q: How do the different chapters differ? How are they similar?

A: It seems like different people give them different flavors, along with their cities. Like N.Y. for example. All these galleries, co-operations, artists, filmdorks, videographers, blablabla's kept buggin' us and following us around, filmin' us, trying to capture what it was that we were doing. The reality is that this is New York, we're plagued with mass media, if you're just doing your thing, you're bound to end up on a billboard if you're not careful. How are we different? Compare NY with Reno. How are we similar? We run with a sense of family, clan, tribe. If you're in the club, you're taken care of. If we got it and you need it, no problem, you're in the club.

Q: What are typical B.L. activities? meetings, rides, etc.?

A: Yes, meetings, rides etc. Sunday brunch at somebody's house, meeting then a ride. Anywhere we want. The beach, Coney Island, the abandoned insane asylum, the east river, the Puerto Rican Schwinn clubhouse.

Q: What do you have to do/done to you to join?

A: I think you're s'posed to ride naked over the Willy-B Bridge, but the whole club gets naked. Or is it the Brooklyn Bridge? I'm not sure, when I joined we didn't have the tradition, so I never did it. I'm hoping nobody noticed.

Q: How many members are there?

A: 37. That's right, thirteee seven.

Q: How the hell do you get away with things like drunken tall bike jousting in the street, in the West Village, in the middle of the night?

A: Cops show up and you can tell they're tryin' to figure out if it's illegal or not. I'm not really sure either. Sometimes you just pick up yer shit and split, other times you just keep on your business like you couldn't give a shit what they did.

Q: How do people react to B.L. events?

A: Some people think it's stupid, some think it's funny, other people get really into it. Sometimes you get some freak that really wants some fuckin' blood. I try and chill those people out a little, cause shit, that's no about/asshole.

A: I wanted more of a cult than it really is, but hopefully we'll keep doing what we are, it's ours, nobody gets to have it but us/ no selling out, no M.T. Dew commercials, capitalism doesn't get us, see. It has no claim. We're free.

Q: What's the future of Black Label look like?

I am a bike mechanic, a wrench.
I am a girl.
These 2 phrases, despite popular belief, Are not in contradiction.

I've been working at my grandmas little bike shop since I was 14. Yes, we are related, yes, that is why I got the job, but that does not mean I have not picked up a thing or 2 in 5 years, and it does not mean you can call me cute.

At first I told myslef they never thought I could do it b/c I was so small. Or b/c I was so young. Now I am a college sophomore and Im pretty sure I could take down half of my offenders. Not to mention (but Im going to, of course), it has just become glaringly obvious that customers dont trust me b/c I have breasts.

Camera pans across rows of bikes to father/son standing facing sales girl. Her arms are black nearly to the elbows w/ grease. "Look, son, a giiirrll who knows more about bikes than you!" laughter from father. xSon, who appears to be 10 to 12 turns deep redand hangs head in humiliation.

The worst one of all time was just a few weeks ago.

Camera catches 2 older men on either side of a counter & cash register. The one on the right, presumably the owner & founder, rings up the other mans's repair tag while explaining the work done on the customer's bike. From the background, a young woman in a mechanic x t-shirt walks the bicycle to the front. As she rights it and lowers the kickstand:

CUSTOMER: This your granddaughter Wally?39.
WALLY: Yup.
CUSTOMER: She's a cute one.

Camera cuts to young woman, face flushed w/ anger, glaring at customer in vain attempt to pierce his flesh w/ her violent disapproval -- not anywhere fatal of course, a flesh wound is all she asks.

First of all, the tone in his voice was kind of inappropriate, but that he made

SHE'S A CUTE ONE.

hey.

SHIT!

WEST NILE.

Protecting Customer Information Refer

a <u>great</u> logo for a lady owned bike shop run by sarah in kansas city mo! they do repair sales custom frames and repair frames. contact the them at acme

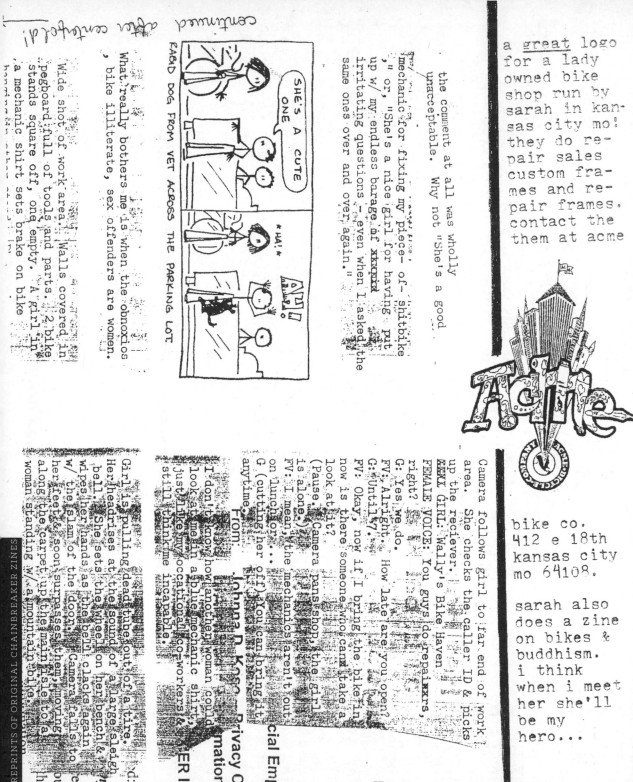

bike co. 412 e 18th kansas city mo 64108.

sarah also does a zine on bikes & buddhism. i think when i meet her she'll be my hero...

the comment at all was wholly unacceptable. Why not "She's a good ..."

"mechanic for fixing my piece- of- shitbike", or, "She's a nice girl for having put up w/ my- endless barage of irritating questions - even when I asked the same ones over and over again."

SHE'S A CUTE ONE

HA!

AH ARMO!

RABID DOG FROM VET ACROSS THE PARKING LOT.

What really bothers me is when the obnoxios bike illiterate, sex offenders are women.

Wide shot of work area. Walls covered in pegboard full of tools and parts. 2 bike stands square off, one empty. A girl in a mechanic shirt sets brake on bike ...

after centerfold!

Camera follows girl to far end of work area. She checks the caller ID & picks up the reciever.

FEMALE VOICE: You guys do repairs, right?
G: Yes, we do.
FV: Alright. How late are you open?
G: Until 7.
FV: Okay, now if I bring the bike in now is there someone who cant take a look at it?
(Pause. Camera pans shop, the girl is alone.)
FV: I mean, the mechanic is he ... on lunch or ...
G (cutting her off) You can bring it in anytime.

From: Johnna D Koss

Girl is pulling dead tube out of a tire. Her head rises at the sound of a large sleigh bell. She sets the wheel on her bench & wipes her hands as the bell clacks again w/ the slam of the door. Camera fails to reg her feet & soon surpasses them, moving along the carpet up the main isle to a woman standing w/ a mountain bike ...

I don't know how another woman could look at me in a blue mechanic shirt, just like my occupational co-workers & still think me incapable.

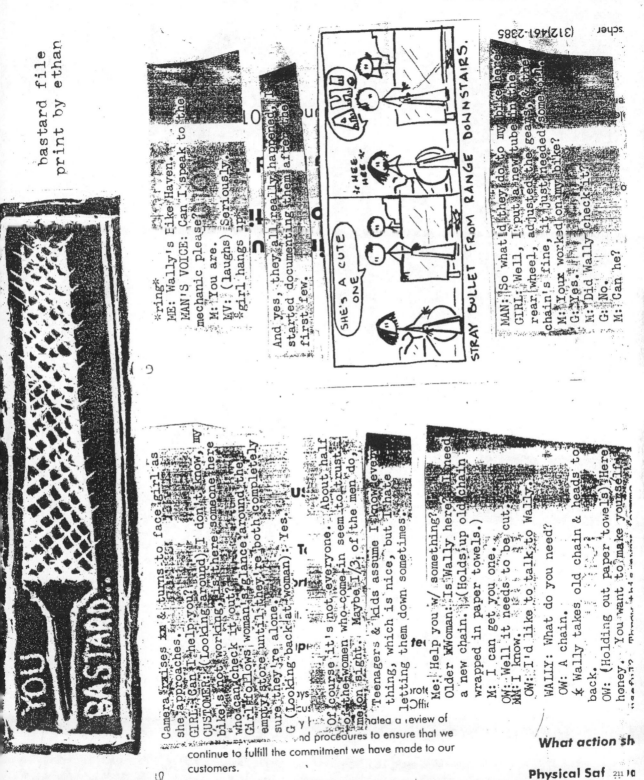

YOU BASTARD...

ring
ME: Wally's Bike Haven.
MAN'S VOICE: Can I speak to the mechanic please?
M: You are.
MV: (laughs) Seriously.
girl hangs up

And yes, they all really happened. I started documenting them after the first few.

MAN: So what'd they do to my bike here?
GIRL: Well, I put a new tube in the rear wheel, adjusted the gears, & the chain's fine, it just needed some oil.
M: Your worked on my bike?
G: Yes.
M: Did Wally check it?
G: No.
M: Can he?

SHE'S A CUTE ONE

AH!

HEE HEE

STRAY BULLET FROM RANGE DOWNSTAIRS.

scher.   (312)461-2385

Camera raises & turns to face girl as she approaches.
GIRL: Can I help you?
CUSTOMER: (Looking around) I don't know, my bike's not working, is there someone here who can check it out?
Girl follows woman's glance around the empty store until they're both completely sure they're alone.
G (Looking back at woman): Yes.

Of course it's not everyone. About half of the women who come in seem to trust me on sight. Maybe 1/3 of the men do. Teenagers & kids assume I know everything, which is nice, but I hate letting them down sometimes.

Me: Help you w/ something?
Older Woman: Is Wally here? I need a new chain. (Holds up old chain wrapped in paper towels.)
M: I can get you one.
OW: Well it needs to be cut.
M: I know.
OW: I'd like to talk to Wally.

WALLY: What do you need?
OW: A chain.
& Wally takes old chain & heads to back.
OW: (Holding out paper towels) Here honey. You want to make yourself useful?

hated a review of procedures to ensure that we continue to fulfill the commitment we have made to our customers.

What action sh

a rough guide to bicycle maintenance.

WHAT IS YOUR FAVORITE REPAIR???
write it or draw it out and send it to me, i'll put it in the repair manual i am compiling! this is an ongoing project i hope to add to for a long time to come. the format is 8 1/2 x 11 folded and artwork is greatly appreciated. send it to me, shelley at 621 north rendon new orleans, la 70119. and if you want one, send me a dollar and i'll send you one. postage paid of course. thank you!::

My only comfort is to think that they leave & their bikes are perfect, maybe -- just maybe -- they start to thank for the briefest of moments that they shouldn't've assumed.....

I'm to the point now where I don't leave the work area unless it is absolutely necessary. "Seeing is believing anyway, right?

SHARK

Advertisement

Restrict data access to a your supervisor or mana suspicious attempts to g current policies and pro customer must be verifie about that customer's a ...osing to a c ...ustomer ...d u

...address protection st...

Logical Safeguards

BOOKS
TAPES
T-SHIRTS
RECORDS
STICKERS
ZINES

Microcosm Publishing
PO Box 14332
Portland, OR 97293-0332
joebel@reach.com
alexywrek@hotmail.com
503-285-7038
www.microcosmpublishing.com

...address prot...n
...cop...scume...or
...rma...

alexis does an awesome zine called blank pages write her at alexis freed po box 1431 mchenry IL 60051

Breaking Away   J. Gerlach

Despite promises that this would be the summer I made it back over to Europe to ride my bike, I spent another season here, in this city, doing most of my riding to and from. Instead of coasting through the French countryside, anonymous and foreign, I find myself sitting at one of those familiar red lights, breathing in exhaust, looking at the twisted faces of the car drivers, waiting.

Sometimes I long to ride in open spaces, where the scenery is inspiring instead of imposing. Somewhere, where one wrong move doesn't mean the end; where the only sound is the wind rushing past my ears.

Yeah, I know I could drive a couple hours out of town to find some lightly-trafficked roads that climb over rolling hills, passing farms and flowers and into quaint little villages. But one of the main reasons I love the bicycle so much is that you don't need a car to use it. I like the rides that begin and end at my back gate. The rides that take me through old familiar neighborhoods, winding crazy loops that criss-cross the city and eventually, bring me back home again. Some days I leave the house with an empty bike bag and return with it stuffed to overflow. Other days I'm towing my daughter on the trail-a-bike, running late for school on the other side of town. It's empowering to use a bicycle to go anywhere, trying out alleys and sidewalks, bike lanes and dirt trails, discovering how the pieces all fit together. But there are days that I'd like to forget my city and my place in it. If I can't go riding along French rivers, or past Cuban sugar cane fields, then at least I want to ride somewhere where the rush of air is the only sound I hear.

There is a trail that begins not too far from my house. It follows an old train line out to the far suburbs and then back in to town again. I like to ride it in the morning, to stretch out my legs and to put my head in the right place for the day ahead. This is my yoga and my meditation, a way to find the day's rhythm without any interruption, alongside the wildflowers and the train tracks, headed out of town.

I take my fast bike out, later in the morning, after most of the workers have parked their cars and taken their seats in all those tall office buildings; after I have had my coffee and before the day has taken its toll. Shifting gears, warming up legs, I cross the river and skirt the arty edge of downtown. Architects and web designers pose on loading docks with their sleek, silver coffee mugs. Across the street, waitresses in panty hose try to smooth out tablecloths for the impending lunch crowd. I avoid the scowling faces of the car drivers, entice the pedestrians with a smile and try to hang on to that half-asleep feeling. When I reach the beginning of the trail, at the end of all those parking garages and exit ramps, I let out a deep breath and descend.

ride any bike

Some days it's hard for me to get out on the trail, to make the commitment when I'm pretty comfortable on my porch, reading and drinking coffee. But there are precious few mornings like this around these parts – warm sun on bare skin. And it's these days, begun and ended on the bicycle, that I'll miss most when the snow is piled high and the wind is howling. These are the longest days of the year. I'll need all this energy I get from beginning the day on my bike, warm sun on bare skin. It keeps me going through work shifts, errands and unexpected encounters, until I head home fifteen hours later, from the café down the street or the rock bar in St. Paul. Out here I can compose songs and stories, hatch plans and remember people I need to find, before they find me.

Part of the trail passes through newer condo complexes that make me wince with what could be. Cul- de-sac beigeness; automatic garage doors stuck half open, contractor trucks always updating something. The sun seems to glare out here and I notice more signs telling you what you can't do. There are real basketball nets on all the hoops and well-groomed ball fields that sit empty this time of day. Shiny cars and perfect settings. These are the places that I imagine I could go crazy, once and for all.

And that's another reason I like riding out this way. It's an excuse to check in on all kinds of scenes, in parts of town that I wouldn't otherwise visit; to catch a glimpse of existences that I try not to think about. I travel along a corridor that is neither city, nor country. It's not really even suburban. It's a bit of all those places without ever having to be stuck there. The backdrop and mood changes frequently, taking me through quiet, shady stretches along bubbling creeks before spitting me out at a busy intersection to dodge the trucks and super woofers and fast food debris. But then, just as I am growing sour in the condos, I see a bunch of schoolkids, walking the trail up ahead. I slow down as I approach the kids, who are scurrying to get off the trail and up onto the grass. As if on cue, they all smile and wave and sing out, "hi!" at me as I pass. They're so excited - the kids, the teachers, everybody - jumping up and down, waving and screaming, so happy to be witnessing this exact moment. And the excitement rubs off. I feel like an explorer, a wonder from far away, smiling silly and rolling through these kids' world for a second on my way to further adventures. I wave and shout, hoping to soak in that thrill, wanting to participate in this moment too.

The end of the trail winds through all my old neighborhoods, back to where we started, from a different approach. Every break in the trail branches off into another era of my life; each crossing leading to old friend's houses and promises buried long ago. When I take one of those turns, I am almost always prodded by a surprise memory, as I inadvertently pass by the little bridge I once used as my meeting spot, or the beach of midnight swims. First kisses and bloody noses lurk around every corner. Each park or lake the site of naïve moments. Whether it's keg party awkwardness or grand revelations, it's all part of the past - my past - that comes back to haunt me, however it wants to. I laugh, as today's memory plays out in my head, because some things never change. I still feel awkward at parties and I still go out late at night, hoping for the taste of blood or a big, wet kiss. These memories aren't just some silly, throwaway moments from impetuous youth, they are the foundation of who I am now. The details might be embarrassing, like early graffiti or the first song ever recorded, but I don't want them erased. It's nice to see that time passes and realize that the present isn't so important. It's nice to feel the wind rushing past me as I head towards home, ready to make new memories out of the old ones; blacktop over rutted paths. Sure, I can ride faster and farther now, and maybe I have come a long way from those old days and old neighborhoods, expanded my horizons, so to speak. But as I exit the trail, returning to the city, headed towards my back gate, I realize that I'm still just riding in one big circle.

The first high of the day feels like the best ever. I embrace the adrenaline rush that comes from a brand new summer day laid out in front of me, the body fresh and familiar, the mind uncontaminated. I might even be able to hold onto this optimism - me and my bike, ready to take on whatever lay ahead. I propel myself forward into the first curve, unafraid and excited.

The city falls farther and farther behind and the wildflowers stretch out in wide fields that fall into lakes and climb to the tracks. To the right, huge mounds of dirt rise four stories to the sky. Signs that say, 'clean fill only,' and, 'gravel' stick out of each one. Oversized piles of used and broken concrete lounge in a far corner. Pipes, springs and porta potties lay scattered about.

Huge dumptrucks pull in and out at a steady pace, lurching and huffing towards some pre-destined pile; adding or subtracting, all part of some grand plan. This is where the city puts all that extra stuff, the dirty leftovers from building and demolishing; the decaying remnants of old city vehicles.

Apparently, it's also a nice location for some beach volleyball.

To the left is the freeway, somehow still backed up with morning traffic, and beyond, the nicest homes, built on the highest land. I am not in any of those places. I am riding below the immediacy of it all, escaping the city of 'right now', with its errands and urgency and always-another stoplight. I am riding my fast bike through fields of prairie flowers, following the old freight train lines out of town.

The trail was recently paved over with smooth blacktop, but it runs over rutted ground that I've known for years. I remember high school parties under the pedestrian bridge, learning to drink beer and how to use the magical night air until the cops showed up, forcing us all to make getaways on slow moving trains. Before that, I played soccer on that field, the one that now sits empty, on the other side of that set of tracks. A summer league during one of those super hot seasons, drenched with sweat, that we don't seem to have anymore. After I moved away from this town, and then back again, I used to come down here a lot, wandering the prairies and rutted trails along the lake, when I needed to get some distance from my neighborhood and its inhabitants. Later, I used it as my late night escape route from the downtown rock club. It's always been a secret way to move around the city, from downtown to the old neighborhoods; to picnic spots and swimming holes. Below ground and out of sight.

The sun is climbing into the late summer sky, melting away any of yesterday's lingering worries. My legs are warmed up now and pumping faster. Without realizing it, I have bent over to flip the lever on the downtube, seamlessly slipping into higher gears, keeping stride. By the time I hit the tunnel I have passed a wobbly guy on a bike two sizes too small and a shirtless man with a ponytail on a loaded mountain bike. A couple racer dudes come from the other direction, heads bent down, serious eyes bulging behind aerodynamic sunglasses. I wear a pair of cutoffs over bike shorts, some regular, old man shoes, and a sleeveless tee shirt. The cool air of the tunnel feels amazing on my arms, and I slow my pace a bit to make it last.

slows into the city. I lose myself in train hopping fantasies, admiring the graffiti show dragged along by the train. My favorite place for graffiti is on the sides of trains. The show always changes and even if the pieces seem incomplete, they seem to fit with the grit and grime and squeals of an old freight train. I've never realized that dream of hopping a freighter out of town but I've imagined it almost every time I'm out here. As I head onto the main loop of the trail, I notice a couple regulars out today; the super-fast walker that looks like John Kerry, and the skinny woman with gentle eyes who always rides the loop clockwise. For some reason, I always ride the other way. I wonder if I'm known by some other trail regular as 'that guy who wears beat-up clothes and always rides counter-clockwise.' I try to pay attention, peering at those I pass, to see if anyone else is taking notes.

But at least for today, most of my fellow trail-users seem to be uninterested in each other. I offer a smile and a nod of my head to the spandexed flyer as he passes me slowly on the left, close enough to kiss. But he can't even acknowledge me. He's in racing mode and I'm one of those guys from the movie, 'Breaking Away.' I'm just some townie on an out of date racing bike - a pesky fly. I let him get a little distance and then I kick it up a notch. I don't feel very competitive about bicycling but I still like to see if I can keep pace with the fancy riders. It seems like too much hassle to worry about heart rate monitoring or racing tactics but it is fun to ride fast. Before I know it I'll be off on an impromptu race, trying to keep up with a speedy woman's team ride or chasing some mad speed demon around the loop. But I prefer the camaraderie of cycling – the attitude that we're all in something together. I root for the solo riders and the small packs that ride across town on a moment's notice, taking on the car-driven society that is shoved down our throats; enjoying the amazing amount of freedom and energy you get from using your body to take you places. I love to see other riders when I'm out alone, late at night, or during rush hour in downtown traffic. It makes me remember that there are so many of us out there riding bikes. There's power in those numbers, a confidence that you can take with you on your solo rides, through the heart of the city or out on some quiet trail. It only seems right that we say 'hi' to each other, or ride together for a bit, even if we are all doing it for different reasons, with different gear and different heart rates.

A strong, luscious smell of chocolate and sugar takes over just on the other side of another freeway overpass. The vents at the back of the candy factory are pumping out perfect combinations of Red #6 and Yellow #3 today, making my stomach rumble, forcing me to snap out of my daze. I breath in deep smells of sweetness as industry fades into nature, inner suburbia sprawl giving up at last, ceding to green fields and community gardens. Cresting at the end of a soft S curve, the trail empties onto a huge, open field spreading out to the left, train tracks sliding in on the right, and another set of tracks passing over everything, on an old trestle bridge up ahead. I half-jokingly revive my dream of this being my final resting-place, just because it's so peaceful and quiet. After a long and fruitful life, I could end up here, in this field on the edge of the city. I dream of a slow bike procession winding along the trail, under a moonlit sky. All my friends, riding all the bicycles from my garage, out to this field to dump my ashes in the wind, scattered over the weeds and rocks and wildflowers. Then they could ride off with their new bikes, in packs of two or three, into the night.

The far side of the trail loop curves through shady stretches backing up to quaint backyards and small lakes. Often I see old-timers walking slowly, arm in arm and boys wading around in creeks, killing another summer day. Groups of dudes sit on benches, laughing and nodding or reading the newspaper. Once I even witnessed the sweetest embrace of two teenagers, with huge smiles on their faces, so innocent and blissed-out, standing there next to that glimmering pond. I slow my pace to match the setting, letting the fresh air rush over my body.

ride an

Critic
of Ever
Daley F

ver, cleaner,
oCritical

talking with
Farmer John

john is an urban farmer. he does all of his gardening and market selling by bicycle.

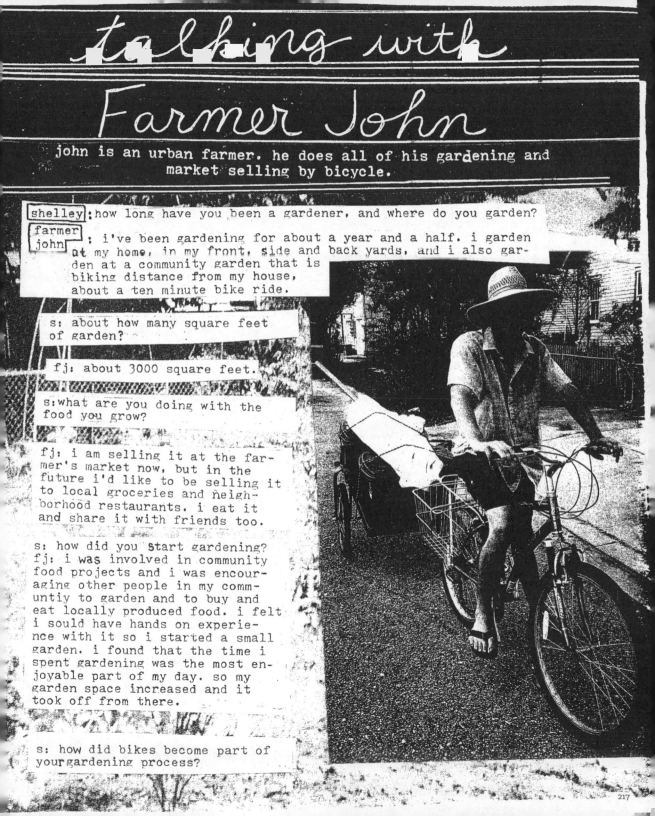

shelley: how long have you been a gardener, and where do you garden?

farmer john: i've been gardening for about a year and a half. i garden at my home, in my front, side and back yards, and i also garden at a community garden that is biking distance from my house, about a ten minute bike ride.

s: about how many square feet of garden?

fj: about 3000 square feet.

s: what are you doing with the food you grow?

fj: i am selling it at the farmer's market now, but in the future i'd like to be selling it to local groceries and neighborhood restaurants. i eat it and share it with friends too.

s: how did you start gardening?
fj: i was involved in community food projects and i was encouraging other people in my communtiy to garden and to buy and eat locally produced food. i felt i sould have hands on experience with it so i started a small garden. i found that the time i spent gardening was the most enjoyable part of my day. so my garden space increased and it took off from there.

s: how did bikes become part of your gardening process?

fj: oh! one thing is that i don't own a car. but that is important because i purposely don't use a car. i thought that i could use a vehicle for my gardening and i consciously chose not to. i consiously chose not to use tillers, which were offered to me, and cleared the space by hand. i probably could have gotten done what i did in a month in, like, three days with a tiller.

s: do you feel like gardening by bicycle has become part of like, a mission statement for you? do you like people to know about it?

fj: ya, i really like it to be known that i got there by bike, the point is, that from the whole process, from putting the seed in the ground, to a peron bring the food home and cooking it, the whole time, i am working in harmony with the planet. and, you know, a lot of my motivation for being a gardener is that. for example, if i chose to use pesticides or chemical fertilizers, those kinds of practices aren't benificaial to people or the environment. so on the same vein, it doesn't make sense to garden organically and take it to the market so people can consume locally grown food-but i am using a vehicle to take it to the market. that's like doing a lot of good and a little bit of bad. i fell really good going to market on bicycle. i wouldn't be comfortable using a car. it wouldn't make sense to me.

s: do you think that is because you have been a cyclist for... how long now?

fj: since i have been in new orleans. before that i took public transportation. like 7 years. if it weren't for that, ya, i might not have seen the possibility. like i couldn't have taken it so far. it's hard to say though. cause i have always been concerned about the environment. it's really what i like least about cars, is that they don't function in harmony with the environment.

s: so, what kind of trailer do you have and where did you get it?

fj: sarah danforth built a trailer for me out of old bed fra-mes, with some old bicycle wheels on it, and it hooks up really easily to the back of my bicycle. (sarah built it at plan b in a welding class. it is made so john's market table fits into the bo-ttom to create the base. it's great!) it's a little more work than it would be if i had a car, but obviously i think it is worth it.

s: what lessons do you think you have learned from this? is there anything you'd like to share with others?

fj: i've learned that you can haul just about anything on a bike. if i lived in the country and came into the city for market it would be - well i think bicycles are ideal for urban environments. nothing is really too far to ride a bike to. taking things to the market on my bike has really made me aware of how much ot-her people are not aware. i feel very much like i am going against the grain. like one day i was riding to the market with all my vegetables on my bike trailer and i saw this big oil tanker that was refilling the gas for the gas pumps. it all seemed so big to me. all of these cars in line, cars and trucks whizzing by, and just lit-tle me on my bike. it felt so surreal. it made me a little sad honestly.

s: do you feel like you want to stay within the city and be an urban farmer?

fj: oh, absolutely. with some creativity there is really great potential to garden and eat the food right from your own urban envi-ronment without having to rely on any motor transportation.

s: do you feel like in a perfect world, local food would be so local that everyone could bike their produce in , and bike in to buy it?

fj: ya, you know, it used to be that people grew their own food. but now everything is completely different. you know with suburbs and cit-ies. people who lived in the city worked in the city. you know. i guess there was just a day that i was at my garden, thinking, i can do this. i can bring all of this to the market on a trailer. there is no reason i can't do this.

s. any final statements?

fj: one thing that seems really really glaringly obvious is that people have this idea of what is a benificial or harmful way of doing things, and that people will take things to a certain point, but for whatever reason, not complete the whole process. and using a bicycle to take my produce to tha market, i feel it completes the whole circle. for me to use organic methods, and not use gas powered macheinery and grow food to share and sell withing my local community, to do all of this in a benificial way, and then get in a gas powered vehicle to drive four or five miles to the market, it just seems like a small piece that is missing in all of these other good things. every other vendor at my market uses vehicles, the majority of the people going to the market are using vehicles too. here is this beautiful inspiring thing, growing and selling locally grown nutritious and healthy food and people are overlooking this thing that is detrimental on so many levels. for whatever reason, maybe it is lack of awareness or consciousness or probably just out of habit, people are just not taking this extra step. maybe it is because i have been riding my bike for transportation for so long, that i am out of this car culture and i can see it. you breathe in the car exhaust when you are outside of a car, you see cars in a different way. so taking that last step, of using my bicycle feels complete to me. i mean, ya, it's kind of a pain sometimes, youknow, loading and unloading, pulling the trailer. it's be really easy to just go there in a car. the market is set up for vehicles. each vendor has a parking spot and they park their vehicles and they work out of their tailgate or the back of their truck. what i do is an oddity! all of the vendors live in the country. they are regional more than local, so it wouldn't make sense for them. i'm about as local as it gets.

s: do you think you are inspiring others?

fj: i think it is mostly that, this is what i am comfortable with, more than how i am influencing everything else, it is that this is how i operate. this is just what makes sense to me. there is no way i am gonna use a car. it doesn't work for me.

ill peejay broke his elbow and can't make pretty

tattoos to pay the rent

soooo... we're having a

ART SHOW and BAKE SALE

please bring artwork to show and sell — (or bake something!)

(all money goes to pj's rent)

monday july 26th 8 pm
at hope and moose's
1324 marigny street
(three blocks behind the hi-ho

"'cause we gotta help our peeps!"

---

pj fell on his elbow while practicing wheelies on his bicycle. man, he broke that thing and then stayed home for days, dealing with the pain afraid to go to the hospital. when he finally went, it was too late for a cast, and they sent him home with a sling; some pills, wondering if the feeling would come back to his fingers. pj is a tattoo artist, and a generous one too, most of my friends have free pj artwork on them, yoni got his official plan b (the new orleans bicycle project) tattoo from him, moose got his tag from him too. how was pj gonna pay the bills, with no hands to tattoo with?

we all discussed it and finally put together this flyer→ for a benifit for him. we passed it out and posted it up and the night of the event rolled around, and we were all a little nervous. i made a huge pot of vegan red beans and rice, some weird not-so-good cookies, and brought some art fro m me and kristen. the food sat lonely on the table, and the art lonely on the walls of hope and moose's house. but it didn't take long for it all to grow. hope's stencils went up, some cookies arrived. ally showed up with her amazing photos, heather with her ceramic tampons, kt came with cookies that looked like dollar signs, and even pj hung up like 50 hand made, left handed artwork postcards. the walls filled and the table filled up with cake and cookies, man, so many cookies! cheap beer for a dollar and we were all sure to have terrible hangovers in the morning! we set jars all over the place for donations, for food, beer and art. all the proceeds went to pj's rent, and at the end of the night, we counted it up, and i swear it was exactly four hundred and fifty dollars. the exact total of his rent! a totally fun and successful night, no stress. just hanging out and talking and being totally blown away by the art, the generosity, the people who walked in with a box of food and toilet paper, the older guy who sits in the corner at the cafe who came just to look at the art (he is always sketching the people in the room with him), people i didn't even know made art coming out with the most beautiful things!

it was all totally inspiring, easy. think of it. the damn government won't take care of us, health care sucks and all we are left with is each other. none of us really had any money, but all of us, strangers even, throwing our change in a jar for some art, some food, it all added up and came together. pj's arm healed and he's back at tattooing again.

Glossary

Bike co-op/Bike project: non-profit or not for ptofit shop that lets people work on their own bikes, use tools, and get help building and fixing bikes. See previous list.

Brazed: brazing is how all bikes used to be built. It's like welding, but the metal doesn't get melted together, it just gets heated up and stuck together with a filler material, usuallly brass or on nicer stuff. All frames used to be brazed, but lots are now TIG welded. Also all the little extra stuff on bikes like water bottle bosses (where the bottle holder screws in) are brazed and called braze-ons.

Chainbreaker: chain tool for popping out and putting in chain rivets. Also, best zine ever. (thanks Ethan!)

Chain tensioner: tool that takes up the slack in a chain, usually on a one speed or other bike with no derailleur.

Cheater bag: a long pipe slid over the handle of another tool, like a wrench or ratchet. This gives more leverage for removing a tight nut or bolt by increasing the distance one has on the turn.

Chromoly: a steel alloy used for frame tubing.

Dished: the alignment of the rim to the hub. A wheel must be properly dished to clear the frame and brakes on a bike. Dishing is done by loosening the spokes on one side of the wheel and tightening them on the other.

Droptooth: a tooth on a cog that is slightly smaller or appears broken, which helps the chain shift between cogs.

Fixed gear/track bike: bike that doesn't coast (or, traditionally, have brakes), built for racing and, apparently, riding to coffee shops in Williamsburg.

Drivetrain: the chain and cogs of your bike, everything that makes it go.

Freehub body: ratcheting, splined spindle that is attached to the hub of wheels that accepts cassettes. The cassette slides onto the freehub body and attaches with a lockring.

Freewheel: ratcheting cog on the back of a bike that allows coasting.

Geometry: the angles of your bike. Cruisers and bikes meant for comfort have 'laid-back' geometry/slacker angles of the seat and head tubs and forks. Bikes for racing and speed have tighter, steeper angles.

Janky: not in the best working condition. A little old, rusty, rattly, and wobbly. Conditions that can be fixed but most likely won't be because, somehow, it seems to fit that the object is a little "off".

Keyed Washer: washer with a little tooth that fits into a groove. Keyed washers are used between the cones and locknuts of one-pieced bottom brackets to keep the cone from moving when you tighten the locknut.

Plan B: a bike co-op in New Orleans, located at 511 Marigny Street.

Rockachaw: spiky ball that sticks to your clothes, usually on the beach. Might pop tired. The Rockachaws were also the team mascot of the boarding school that Ethan went to in ninth grade.

Spider: the part of the crank that the chainrings bolt to. These come in lots of specific sizes and you need the right chainrings to fit em'.

Splined: something that is splined has little grooves on it that fit into a corresponding component, like a freehub body or new, fancy bottom bracket spindles.

Sutherland's Manual: big-ass technical manual used by shops that breaks down all the different specs of bikes and components, like bottom bracket width and torque specs on certain bolts.

Truing (wheels): pulling bent rims back into alignment by adjusting spokes (and occasionally whacking on the sides of tables).

Wheel: the rim, spokes, and hub of your bike, not to be confused with tire.

Wonky: in good shape, new even, but needs a little T.L.C., some tightening, some attention, and then it would be good as new.

Y'heard: New Orleans slang. Short for "You heard me?" Used obsessively.

ABOUT THE AUTHORS.

Shelley Lynn Jackson is from California, but spent fifteen years happily maintaining the fleet of janky bikes that kept the po'boys delivered and musicians at their gigs in the great city of New Orleans. She learned everything she knew about turning wrenches under the guidance of Billy Moss during six perfect years at the long gone but never forgotten French Quarter Bicycles. She also worked at Plan B, the New Orleans Community Bike Project and at Gerken's Bike Shop at 2703 St. Claude Avenue (they are still there!). She now lives deep in the Ozark Mountains at a Tibetan Buddhist retreat center in rurual Arkansas, gardening, meditating, building cabins and living in a crappy but lovely old trailer with the happiest dog alive, William. You can write to her if you'd like at: hc 72 box 54b Parthenon, AR 72666.

Ethan Clark is from Mississippi but currently resides in a Toyota Tacoma somewhere in North America. A floundering writer and cartoonist, Ethan was previously a bike mechanic at three commercial shops and a volunteer at Plan B, the New Orleans Community Bike Project. He wrote *Chihuahua and Pitbull* and *Leaning With Intent to Fall* (Garrett County Press).

Thank you to everyone who helped with editing: J. Gerlach (and for being a great friend too), Tammy Martin, and Joe Biel (who suggested that this thing happen!), and everyone else at Microcosm. Thanks to Happy for her illustrations, Plan B for helping so many New Orleaneans build and repair bikes, and to everyone who encouraged us to do this. Everyone.

SUBSCRIBE TO EVERYTHING WE PUBLISH!

Do you love what Microcosm publishes?

Do you want us to publish more great stuff?

Would you like to receive each new title as it's published?

Subscribe as a BFF to our new titles and we'll mail them all to you as they are released!

$13-30/mo, pay what you can afford!

microcosmpublishing.com/bff